Fantastic Trees

Fantastic

Trees

By Edwin A. Menninger, D.Sc.

NEW YORK / The Viking Press

First published in 1967 by The Viking Press, Inc.
625 Madison Avenue, New York, N.Y. 10022

Published simultaneously in Canada by
The Macmillan Company of Canada Limited

Library of Congress catalog card number: 66-19165
Printed in U.S.A. by Halliday Lithograph Corp.

Second printing October 1968

Contents

Prologue

There is hope of a tree, if it be cut down, that it will sprout again, and that the tender branch thereof will not cease. —JOB 14:7

Dr. William C. Menninger†
The Menninger Foundation
Topeka, Kansas

Dear Brother Will:

I've written a book about trees of fantastic behavior. Perhaps I should consult a psychiatrist about them!

So many trees behave like people. Their environment affects their size, their longevity, their rate of growth, even their usefulness. Certainly it affects their behavior, their shape, the development of poisons in their systems, the growth of thorns along the trunk and branches to fight off neighbors, the creation of abnormalities in trunks, branches, roots, flowers, and fruits and, worst of all, it confuses their sexual lives.

Rather than attempt to change the distortions in people's thinking, psychiatrists devote their energies toward healing the wounds of those who have been crushed by their environment. Then there should be a way to help some of these trees that are under too much pressure or that need encouragement to get some of the kinks out of their systems. If there are countless types of aberrations in the human personality, I wonder how

† October 15, 1899–September 6, 1966

ix

many more you could find in the tree world. Among the millions of trees in the forests of the earth, and a few of the deserts, some have developed peculiar aspects. They have not been able to get along with their environment, or their neighbors, or the soil nature put them in, or some other factor, so they are confused. These are the trees which color the pages of this book with their strange conduct.

Some trees are gregarious and like to live and love with other trees all about them. Others prefer solitude and shun their own kind. Here in the United States we have solid stands of white pine, or of redwood, or of Douglas fir. But in the tropics where mahogany trees grow, one mahogany seldom lives within sight of another. We might call these trees asocial. Then what shall we say about the true hermits of the tree world, the ombú[1] in Argentina? They grow so far apart, literally miles and miles, that pollination between them is almost impossible. The ombú makes for one of the mysteries in this book: nobody has ever seen a dead one! Don't these trees die?

Some trees are contented with their lot. In the southwestern deserts the big Joshua-trees[2] never complain of loneliness or isolation. They develop a tough hide, learn to live almost without water in the boiling sun, and like it. They never think of moving to another climate or even taking a vacation at the seaside. But many other trees do migrate, invade lands where they do not belong, often crowd out native vegetation, and become pests—just like people!

In some of the extra wet places on the earth a lot of trees have developed nursery habits. They have lost control, and they have to be treated like the overgrown infants that they are.

Many trees have preferences of soil, climate, moisture, so marked that they will curl up and die if they cannot have their own way. The coffee-tree[3] from Ethiopia abhors the land of its nativity, but when turned loose on the sun-kissed hills of Brazil, it bursts with prideful efforts to give all. Has it ever struck you as queer that most of our chocolate nowadays comes from Africa, the bulk of our cashew nuts from India, and our natural rubber from Malaya, although the trees that produce these important commodities are all natives of tropical America, including Brazil? Is this some sort of a show-off by these plants? Or would you call it proof that the environment of their native lands required adjustments they were loath to make?

An effort has been made in the pages that follow to group trees by their peculiarities, but eight of them defy classification. Some unknown torques have twisted them to produce distinctions unmatched by other plants and hard to explain. Here are eight incredibles:

In central Africa grow twenty kinds of *Brachystegia* trees. Nineteen of them are tall timber monarchs, but one kind[4] refuses to compete with its fellows, so it never grows more than 6 inches high. Why?

A fruit tree[5] in central Africa, akin to the celebrated mangosteen, often suddenly sends up thousands of vertical shoots—a whole forest of upright stems on its long horizontal branches. Is this a precipitate, unrestrained yearning for motherhood?

In Southern Rhodesia grows an *Acacia*[6] that comes into full leaf during the dry season when all the other trees are dropping their foliage, but during the rains it becomes deciduous and bare as a jay bird. Can there be any excuse for such perversity? Must there always be a wrong-way Corrigan?

Some travelers in Peru and Chile[7] two hundred years ago were much impressed by the fragrant *Plumeria* trees whose flowers later became popular with Hawaiians in making leis. These travelers reported that cuttings of the trees "last two or three years without drying out after they are cut, and they take root easily if planted after one or two years." If this record is true, here is a tree that does not have sense enough to die when it is chopped down. Is the germ of life susceptible to being sealed up for years inside a stick?

On the front lawn of the Menninger Clinic building in Topeka stands a ginkgo, usually called maidenhair-tree because of the fernlike foliage. When it gets very old, stalactite-like growths may dangle, here and there, from the trunk and big branches, resembling nothing so much as a cow's teats. What are they for?[8]

Some trees are over-eager. Two[9] in Malaya produce new leaves and flowers every day in the year so long as they live. Are these over-sexed?

At the other extreme, the monkey-flower tree[10] in Guatemala, when transplanted to Florida, waits fifty years to flower; why reluctant for so long? A Brazilian tree[11] blooms only once every fifteen years; a Malayan tree[12] flowers at intervals of twenty years or more. Does such behavior reflect indifference or a sort of shyness?

Last among these forest dwellers that defy grouping because each has a peculiarity entirely foreign to all others is an evergreen in the Malayan lowlands that is commonly called tree-of-glory.[13] Its 3-foot leaves are unique, which means there is nothing like them anywhere else in the tree world. Can you imagine a human hand on which the first finger is long, the next one short, the next long, the next short, and so on? Ridiculous! Of course not! Yet such is the construction of the leaf on the tree-of-glory. It has a dozen pairs of leaflets along the midrib, the first pair short (maybe 2 inches), the next pair long (up to 6 inches), the next pair short, the next pair long, etc. This fantastic form is unlike any other leaf in the world.

You psychiatrists find your most difficult job is to pierce the façade which hides the nature and cause of a patient's turmoil. The exterior aspect is often bland and serene, although underneath the going is rough. In the forests of the world there are many trees like this, for they hide extreme disturbances under a smooth, unruffled bark.

I could burden you with more of these complex problems of the tree world, but each one needs a case history if you are going to give its peculiarities any thought. Perhaps it would be easier for you just to drift through the circus tent while I stand outside as a barker, calling to the gawkers to come see all these strange, queer, peculiar, freakish, and unusual denizens of the forest, arrayed here in all their glory.

Affectionately and arboreally,
Your brother,

EDWIN A. MENNINGER

June 1, 1966

Fantastic Trees

This palm tree (*Astrocaryum aculeatum*), in the jungle of French Guiana, erects a formidable barrier of thorns. (Photo: Francis Hallé.)

BELOW: A Joshua tree (*Yucca brevifolia*) in the California desert. (Photo: Ralph D. Cornell.)

ABOVE: After the top of this pine was broken off in a storm, it grew twin trunks, welded them together overhead, and then threaded the needle's eye! (Photo: Walter P. Marshall, American Forestry Association, Savannah, Georgia.)

Introduction

Solomon's wisdom excelled . . . and he spake of trees.
—I Kings 4:30, 33

Along the paths that lead through the forests of the world are many strange trees. Something important happened to make them very different from others of their kind. What was it?

Most trees are long-lived, like people. They cannot adapt quickly to changed environment as do insects or bacteria or other short-span creatures which produce great numbers in each generation, with a corresponding ease of mutation. Many factors, from glaciers and land upheavals to sudden desiccation or the migration of mankind with his soil-destroying methods, have served to change the conditions under which trees grow, and they are thereby left to develop within themselves a means of surviving. This adaptation may take many forms, such as redevelopment of cellular structure to facilitate the hoarding of moisture or to exclude excess water. The trees may develop physical structures that will assist in survival, or they may modify their leaves to block transpiration rather than assist it. Many trees re-allocate roots above the soil rather than under it. They may establish an alliance with animals, if doing so promotes survival.

This book is about those trees which, in their determination to stay alive, have established new patterns of existence—changed physical appearance, metamorphosed habits, modified and sometimes distorted behavior, and a different kind of usefulness.

They may be faced with incredible handicaps in connection with their

3

food supply, altered constituents in the soil, the amount of moisture available to them in a year, or the volume of respiratory gases they can get. Some trees may be burdened with too rocky or too marshy a terrain, or suffer occasional or frequent flooding, or have no room in which to grow. Their difficulties may force them to change their manner of living, their appetites, their stature, their growth habits, even their methods of reproduction.

Trees afflicted with such adverse circumstances will fight back rather than submit. Even when unmercifully fireswept or sunburned, they refuse to surrender. They make all kinds of adjustments in a desperate determination to keep on living. They are incapable of moving to a more congenial location, so they stand still and adjust to the lashings of adversity.

Some of the world's most remarkable trees stand along the banks of the Amazon and on the islands in its channel. Bound to the earth by their roots, incapable of escaping to higher ground when the flood waters come, these trees stand for six months at a time with their roots and half their trunks under water. Do they die from this inundation? They do not. They have evolved a new pattern of life. They develop waterproof hides. They store enough gases in their roots during dry seasons to carry them over when the high waters come. They produce their seeds in boatlike pods that are adapted to floating ashore and reproducing the species. They overcome the difficulties of their environment.

Part of this book is a study of the ways in which trees have solved their problems. Through its pages runs a parallelism with human behavior, for in many ways the adjustments that trees make, rekindling daily an apparent determination to stay alive, are very similar to the changes and adjustments made by people—and for the same purpose. Frequently these changes bring both trees and people into conflict with others of their kind; this seems to be the theme of existence.

One marvels at how tough human beings (and trees) can be and what an enormous capacity they have for overcoming obstacles not only in the struggle to survive but in the effort to become mature, creative adults. This book portrays these battlings in the tree world, but it cannot fail to reflect similar wrestlings in the human world—among people we know.

Part of this book deals with trees that are unique, perhaps as the result of heredity, or accident, or because encumbered by human superstition or folklore, or merely by the circumstance of being constructed differently from others. Many trees achieve fame because of exceptional size, incredible age, or an ancestry dating back to the dinosaurs. Sex plays a part in making certain trees different from their comrades. And then some trees might well be considered queer because they flap their leaves, make noises, display affection for other trees, do arithmetic, tell time, predict changes in the weather, or even produce their own rain. Environmental difficulties had nothing to do with these creatures; they enjoy being different. Their behavior highlights the heritage of our forests.

Thousands of people crowd their way daily into "jungle gardens" or similar tourist attractions. They do not come to observe beauty, because in these places pretty flowers are the exception. They come to see the queer or unique—the cannonball-tree, the strangling figs, the man-eating tree, the writhing lianas, the fireproof tree, the two-headed palm, the sausage-tree, the monkey's dinner bell whose fruits explode, and other similar, loudly advertised attractions. They spend millions of dollars annually for these sightseeing privileges. Something in the nature of trouble-ridden mankind makes spectators of us all, wanting to see the trees struggling to combat the hardships of their environment or trying to live up to a heritage. The tallest, oldest, fattest, most awkward trees are cynosures for the curious. Gawking provides vicarious enjoyment of the adversities and peculiarities (the other fellow's) that make life difficult or fascinating, depending on the point of view.

Perhaps this volume should be considered a gawker's handbook, with several hundred trees vying for attention, many of them enmeshed in myths and mysteries that are hard to believe or to understand.

PART I

Trees Whose Parts Are Peculiar

ONE

Trunks Are Not All Alike

The trees of the Lord are full of sap.   —PSALMS 104:16

A tree trunk, ordinarily, is a cylindrical log that connects the leafy crown to the ground. Long or short, fat or thin, it is usually covered with bark, and it may give rise to a few branches on the way up. However, in this museum of fantastic trees, these familiar trunk characteristics have no place. Look at these:

1. Some trees have no bark; others do their best to get rid of what they have.

2. Instead of being smoothly cylindrical, some trunks are fluted like organ pipes, while others resemble a lumber pile standing on end.

3. Some trees have a dozen trunks, all in competition with one another.

4. Some trunks grow with a hollow center and with holes as big as a human hand all through the remaining wood. For ventilation, no doubt!

5. One tree, when its bark does not fit, appears to let it flow down the trunk like pancake batter, and the bark forms at the base of the tree what looks like a huge puddle sometimes ten feet across.

6. The color of a tree's bark is usually brown, gray, or black, but the forests of the world offer interesting exceptions to the commonplace.

7. Some trees have no branches. Their leaves spring directly from the trunk. Because this trunk is generally of extraordinary girth, these trees are called pachycaulous.

Here are the strange ones.

1. The Strip-Teasers

On the West Coast of the United States, the tattered eucalyptus trees called stringybarks (most of them brought to this country from Australia) have become a familiar sight. They are always shedding strips of bark, as though their covering were uncomfortable—much like a boy getting rid of his jacket at a baseball game.

Another Australian immigrant, the punk-tree or cajeput,[1] ravels its bark to the four winds but lacks power to kick it off. Many of its family are called "paperbarks" by Australians because of this untidy habit. Related trees in the myrtle family, including the guava[2] and a few kinds of *Eugenia*, also some of the crape-myrtles[3] (not in the myrtle family) and the snake-barks,[4] as well as the common sycamore[5] and scores of other trees, shed their bark in patches which often reveal exquisite coloring. In Zambia two different trees[6] shed their bark in large transparent sheets.

All these "strip-tease" trees seem bent on disrobing themselves. If they had hoped that a new layer of bark would fail to appear, most of them have been disappointed.

Some trees are involuntary bark-shedders: the cork oak,[7] the mahoe (which provides a strong fiber),[8] and the baobab.[9] For commercial reasons, men often completely strip the trunks of the baobab, cut away the hard bark, and remove the inner bast (which yields a particularly strong and durable fiber) in sheets. "Comparatively young trees are often treated thus, but the bark seems to have some power of regeneration like that of the cork oak," according to J. M. Dalziel.[10]

There are plenty of trees which have no regular bark in the first place. A familiar example is the shavingbrush-tree,[11] common in southern Florida. True, its trunk has a green skin, but there is no bark.

2. Organ-Pipe Trees

Trees in certain families that inhabit tropical rain forests develop trunks that look like organ pipes, but nobody seems to know the reason. Reports from botanists[12] who have traversed the tropical forests in many parts of the Old World bespeak the frequency of such fluting in tree trunks. It is noteworthy that buttresses are also frequently seen on rain-forest trees. Are the flutings incipient buttresses?

The Tahiti chestnut,[13] usually called *mapé* in the South Sea islands, develops massive buttresses in New Guinea and Polynesia, but not in Malaya. Everywhere it grows the trunks are so fluted that they look like giant lianas.

LEFT: A candy-striped bark distinguishes a Chinese maple tree (*Acer davidii*). (Photo: J. E. Downward.) RIGHT: The shagbark hickory (*Carya ovata*), an American tree that struggles to shed its bark. (Photo: Arnold Arboretum.)

The cajeput or punk tree (*Melaleuca quinquenervia*) splits its paper-like bark and attempts to shed it, though with little success. This Australian immigrant has become naturalized in the Florida Everglades.

ABOVE: A ventilated pillar or "archer's window" tree (*Adina polycephala*). (Photo: K. M. Kochummen, Forest Research Institute, Kepong, Selangor, Malaya.) ABOVE RIGHT: A false paddlewood or parakusan (*Swartzia*) in British Guiana. (Photo: Forest Service, British Guiana.) RIGHT: Tahiti chestnut trees (*Inocarpus edulis*), photographed by Harrison W. Smith in his garden at Papeari, Tahiti.

RIGHT: Grotesque trunks are not confined to any one kind of tree; this one belongs to a common paper-mulberry tree (*Broussonetia papyrifera*) at Williamsburg, Virginia. BELOW: The trunk of a Lawson false cypress tree (*Chamaecyparis lawsonia*), which can be hard as nails. (Photos: Arnold Arboretum.)

ABOVE: This yew tree (*Taxus baccata* L.) keeps adding new trunks; it is said to be more than five hundred years old. (Photo: A. Walker, Guildford, Surrey.)

11

LEFT: The smooth-bark apple (*Angophora lanceolata*) of Australia is normal in most places, but here—in the Hawkesbury sandstone belt near Sydney—the bark flows toward the ground. (Photo: Harry Oakman, Canberra.) RIGHT: A cotton-wood tree (*Populus deltoides*) in Colorado, which is perhaps afflicted with a virus disease; its gouty stem has more bark that it can accommodate. (Photo: U. S. Forest Service.)

The ombú tree (*Phytolacca dioica*) in Argentina often seems to have bark that has melted and run, but actually the ground structure is part of the roots, which have developed above the ground. (Photo: Dr. T. Meyer, Tucumán.)

RIGHT: The trunk of the aky tree (*Cussonia bancoensis*) in Ivory Coast and Nigeria is a good example of prehistoric tree form. The bark is soft and spongelike. (Photo: Francis Hallé.) BELOW: A white-barked pine tree (*Pinus bungeana*), photographed by F. N. Meyer in Chu-fu, China. (Photo: U. S. Department of Agriculture.)

BELOW: Flooded gums (*Eucalyptus grandis*), so called because they often stand in stream beds and are not affected by inundation. (Photo: Dr. George H. Hewitt, Bellingen.)

In the Guianas and southern Venezuela this corrugation of the tree's exterior takes an extreme, even fantastic form in two different tree families. In that area grow some *Aspidosperma* trees (of the dogbane family) in which the trunk "is divided almost to the middle into irregular plank-like parts often only an inch thick."[14] L. S. Hohenkirk[15] says that the yaruru or paddlewood,[16] which is scattered through the forests of British Guiana, has a 50-foot trunk, deeply fluted, "as though consisting of a bundle of boards standing on end, their inner edges forming a common center. The ribs are used locally for making paddles and tool handles, the cores of large trees for mill rollers." Lindley and Moore[17] report that the trunk consists of "solid projecting radii which the Indians use for ready-made planks."

3. Tussock Trees

Why trees should not all be content with just one trunk is hard to understand; for most, one suffices to support all the greenery and crops the tree can produce. Nevertheless, a few trees produce a dozen trunks, like that of many cornstalks trying to grow out of the same hill. The Malayan forest tree *Barringtonia spicata* is a good example of this phenomenon. In central Africa the small karamba tree[18] has several trunks, all rising from a swollen base. Each has the obesity of a baobab tree.[19] Their coppery-green bark keeps peeling in papery shavings, and the branches are covered with fat, squatty spines. Fragrant, long-tubed white flowers are produced when the tree is leafless.

Old yew trees (*Taxus baccata*) in England tend to develop multiple trunks. The ages of such trees cannot be proved because of the manner in which new trunks become integrated with the old. Counting annual rings is impossible.

Ernest H. Wilson, in *China, the Mother of Gardens*, says that the beech tree (*Fagus engleriana*) in that country "always has many trunks."

4. The Ventilated Pillars

"Archery-window trees" is the best name for the *Adina* trees that grow in Malaya. Corner[20] describes them:

> Big forest trees with the trunk more or less slotted or scalloped and becoming pierced with oblong holes or slits so as to appear like a basket-work or the trunk of a strangling fig.
>
> We mention these forest trees, which are nowhere very abundant, because of their peculiar trunks. . . . How they develop is not fully understood. The

trunk of a sapling soon becomes pitted vertically with oblong slots because along these places it does not thicken. As it swells, the slots deepen. When as in old trees, the core of wood disappears and the trunk becomes hollow, it appears like a narrow wooden tower, or cylindrical shell, fitted with archers' windows. Ridley[21] [described] a curious tree of large size at Tapah with a hollow cylinder of lattice-work about 80 feet tall and large enough to contain more than one person. The perforations were only large enough to admit the hand.

The meraga[22] is a flat-topped hundred-foot tree scattered through the lowlands of Malaya. F. W. Foxworthy[23] says "the very peculiar stem formation shows a large number of openings, giving a lattice-like effect." Ridley[24] adds: "1½ to 2 feet through, remarkable for being irregularly perforated for some depth. Heartwood yellow; a hard and heavy wood excellent for building, but the irregular depressions in the trunk make it difficult to get good beams. If good, it is said to last 20 or 30 years in the ground."

Such perforated trunks have counterparts in the Guianas and northern Brazil. "Mosquito-tree" is a translation of the native name "carapanauba," given to a small tree[25] of the deep swamps of the Amazon valley "because the humid recesses of the bole harbor mosquitoes."[26] Two other species, *Aspidosperma nitidum* and *A. kuhlmannii*, have the same perforated construction of the trunk, and the latter is also called "mosquito-tree."

5. Bark That Seems to Flow

The smooth-bark apple-tree[27] of Australia is not an apple at all and does not bear edible fruit, but it is so smooth that it is slippery. It even seems to have a hard time holding itself in place. Most Australian reference books make no mention at all of the tree's peculiarity, but Harry Oakman[28] presents the facts: "The base of the tree will at times flatten out and spread over rocks, giving a most unusual effect, as though the tree trunk had at some time softened and sagged."

In correspondence Mr. Oakman adds, "These trees grow principally around Sydney in the Hawkesbury sandstone belt where some hundreds of trees with a flattened base may be seen . . . generally in bush and rocky country. . . . The *Angophora lanceolata* incidentally is a magnificent tree and is regarded as one of Sydney's most picturesque Gums with its immense columnar trunk reaching to some 40 feet before branching, and as a rule the branches are gnarled or contorted to give a most picturesque effect. An odd specimen will occasionally flower very profusely, the whole top of the tree in that case being covered with creamy flowers."

Other trees that occasionally present similar phenomena are the ombú[29] in Argentina, which appears to have a poured concrete foundation, and the Colorado cottonwood,[30] which looks as though it has the gout.

The trunk of another North American tree, the Lawson false cypress,[31] occasionally in age develops bark that looks like flowing granite that has frozen.

6. Barks of Strange Hues

Most of us think of the bark of a tree as brown, gray, or black, with a few modifications. The beautiful white birch,[32] with its chalky bark, grows naturally over much of the northern United States; hence it is not too surprising to find that other trees have white bark.

In Australia highly conspicuous examples are offered by the flooded gums,[33] so called because they frequently stand in river beds and are not bothered by inundation. The trunks are a beautiful pure white which stands out sharply against a green background.

A most unusual sight is the white-barked pine[34] in China. In Chu-fu the plant explorer F. N. Meyer photographed "the most noble specimen of it" he ever saw. The tree measured 16 feet in circumference 6 feet above the ground, and Meyer estimated its age at fifteen or sixteen centuries, although the Chinese told him it was much older than that. "For noble, serene impressiveness, I have not seen a tree yet that can be compared with this white barked pine," Meyer wrote in 1907. Another common name for this tree is lacebark pine. Normally it is multibranched from the base and develops a round head. A twenty-five-year-old specimen grows in the United States National Arboretum at Washington.

Other colors of bark might well be expected. A. H. Unwin[35] says that the bark of the dwarf ironwood[36] of Africa is naturally a bright orange color, but that it quickly darkens to brown when sunlight reaches it. The same author reports that *Cordia millennii* in Nigeria has a light-colored bark, which "when it is scaly, often gives the impression that the tree is luminous at night."

Acacia seyal of central Africa has a thin green bark covered with a cream-yellow or rust-red powder, and this sheds annually in rectangular patches. The rust-red variety, growing in southern Florida, is very conspicuous.

7. The Pachycaulous Trunks

In the evolutionary history of flowering plants, tropical trees came first. For a temperate-zone-dweller who has never been in the tropics and knows

16

nothing of tree life there, this may be difficult to accept. Yet Corner[37] has produced abundant evidence tracing the development of today's plant forms back to the pachycaulous (thick-stemmed) stage where the original tree was small of stature, massive of stem, sappy, soft-wooded or spongy, not branched (or only sparingly branched), therefore possessing no nodes from which sideways development might arise, and possibly of monocarpic habit (flowering and fruiting once, then dying). The modern world has many relics pointing back millions of years toward that original tree—the cycad or sago palm, the tree fern (*Cyathea* and others), and so on.

One conspicuous example of this pachycaulous curiosity today in the forests of the Ivory Coast and Nigeria is the aky tree, also called the forest papaw.[38] Despite its enormous size—up to 100 feet high and 10 feet in girth—this tree's trunk is soft, porous, and spongelike, and it is generally unbranched. It is a living relic of an ancient age.

TWO

Unique Branching

I have made him fair by the multitude of his branches: so that all the trees of Eden, that were in the Garden of God, envied him.

—Ezekiel 31:9

Although the branching habit of many trees appears to be sporadic and haphazard, a few kinds come into the world with a prefabricated design at which even engineers might marvel. These are not freaks, but they differ so radically from all others, and are so enormously outnumbered by the desultory types, that they are included here for an exposition of their amazing construction.

Two phenomena are presented. The first involves what are called pagoda trees because of the outline their branching presents against the sky. The Norfolk Island pine,[1] common as a pot plant in the North and as a yard specimen in California or Florida, is a familiar example.

The branches of such trees are in horizontal layers. In each layer the branches are the same length and equidistant from one another. Each layer has the same number of radiating branches (though the number is not the same in all pagoda trees; it varies from five to eight). The tree trunk, between branches, may have a few leaves on it but no odd branches. These four peculiarities separate pagoda trees from all others. They are not characteristic of any particular tree family, as witness these other examples:

White pine (*Pinus strobus*), pine family (*Pinaceae*)
Scholar-tree (*Alstonia scholaris*), dogbane family (*Apocynaceae*)

LEFT: The tiered branches of the tropical-almond (*Terminalia catappa*), which give rise to the term "terminalia branching." (Photo: Paul Root.)

RIGHT: These Norfolk Island pines (*Araucaria excelsa*) are a good example of the pagoda style of growth with tiered branches. (Photo: Douglas Elliott.)

LEFT: This Philippine tree (*Terminalia calamansana*) combines terminalia branching, the pagoda style, and the "weeping" habit.

19

Tropical-almond (*Terminalia catappa*), combretum family (*Combretaceae*)

Sterculia (two hundred kinds in the tropics), chocolate family (*Sterculiaceae*)

Macaranga (some kinds but not all), spurge family (*Euphorbiaceae*)

Kapok (*Ceiba pentandra*), bombax or kapok family (*Bombacaceae*)

Sapodilla (*Achras zapota*), sapodilla or sapote family (*Sapotaceae*)

Oil-fruit (*Elaeocarpus*, but not all kinds), elaeocarpus family (*Elaeocarpaceae*)

Wild nutmeg (*Pycnanthus kombo*), nutmeg family (*Myristicaceae*)

The second phenomenon occurs in some pagoda trees, but not all. This is a specialized system of branch growth called, for convenience, Terminalia branching, in reference to the tropical-almond tree that is cultivated in Florida and other warm places throughout the world. Corner[2] describes the oddity thus:

> Many trees have Terminalia branching . . . but relatively few have evolved the pagoda shape. . . . The branching affects the twigs. Each twig which grows from the leader shoot of the tree does so rapidly and at a wide angle from it; then, as its growth slackens, it turns up at the end and from its lower side, just at the bend, a branch arises to grow out as another twig which will follow the same course by turning up at the end and branching in its turn. Thus a limb of the tree comes to be built up of a succession of bent twigs. . . .
>
> When such a limb is growing out from the trunk of the tree, it diverges from its neighbors and begins to branch sideways: this it does by producing every now and again not one twig but a pair of twigs, or even three, which grow out from each other at a wide angle; and thus the limb develops into a fan-shaped leafy spray.

The fiddleleaf fig (*Ficus lyrata*) is a good example of the Terminalia habit, with twigs upturned at their tips, each crowned with a rosette of leaves.

In South America the genus *Colletia* has spiny flattened branches set sideways in pairs, like a ship's anchor. Other trees are branched like candelabra. For some of these see the thorn trees in Chapter Seven.

THREE

Roots That Go Wild

*The remnant that is escaped. . . . shall again take root downward,
and bear fruit upward.*   —ISAIAH 37:31

A casual observer might assume that the roots of all trees originate some-
where at the bottom of the trunk and plunge downward into the soil. Both
postulate and conclusion are wrecked among the queer trees, for some roots
grow straight up, whereas others grow around the limbs and trunk of the
tree, not down into the ground. In fact, they can start anywhere and
proceed in almost any direction. It is known from temple carvings in India
that the Hindu religion at one time developed a cult which for ornament
drew and carved trees of *Ficus religiosa* and *F. benghalensis* upside down![1]
    Aerial roots (which grow into the air, not the ground) occur in a variety
of plants. Many epiphytic orchids have attachment roots which grow along
the branches, and also more or less erect roots which grow into the humus
of fallen leaves which collects among the leaves of the orchid. Epiphytic
ferns may do the same. These establish a precedent for trees to go astray.
In many palms, the short feeding roots grow up from the soil into the
humus about the plant, even into the air. J. C. Willis[2] says that in the
raffia palm (*Raphia ruffia*) roots develop between the dead leaf bases.
"They curve upward and are said to act as respiratory organs." (For other
breathing roots see Section 7 of this chapter.)
    Ordinary roots grow down under the influence of gravity and through
the action of a growth hormone, auxin. Stems, in contrast, grow upward,
also in response to gravity and apparently through the activity of the same

hormone. Root and stem act in opposite ways to the same stimulus, much as two unequal weights attached to a rope which passes over a pulley move in opposite directions, both responding simultaneously to gravity.

But any such generalization brings forth pronouncements on exceptions. There are examples among palms (the so-called stemless palms of Brazil), in which the stem grows down, and thus acts like a root. As the stem descends, the bud curves up, but the palm stem itself is upside down. The breathing roots of black mangrove trees[3] grow up through the mud into the air, behaving as if they were stems.

Roots are supposed to be the part of the tree you never see, reaching here and there for nourishment and incidentally keeping the tree from toppling over. Of course, they collect water containing mineral nutrients for the superstructure above, and help pump it against gravity to the leaves, but they escape many housekeeping chores. Ordinarily they do not have any responsibility in connection with reproduction of the species, and they suffer few attacks from man, beast, or electric-power companies.

Nobody can explain roots satisfactorily; a book such as this can only record what happens, because tree roots may go berserk in at least eight directions—each discussed in a section of this chapter.

1. Bottom-Side-Up Trees

The roots of a gigantic New Zealand tree[4] have their own rules. *Metrosideros* is the tree's scientific name; the Down-Unders call it their Christmas tree because it blooms spectacularly at Yuletide—which is springtime in New Zealand.

A lot of these Christmas trees—called "pahutakawa" by the Maoris—are perfectly normal, except that when they grow on the oceanside they often extend their roots out into the pounding surf. But the really astonishing thing about them is that an occasional tree will develop a mass of fibrous roots that hang down from the branches. These roots never reach the ground; they surround the trunk like a hula skirt. Why? Nobody knows. One New Zealand authority[5] says: "When growing on level ground, great bunches of red fibrous roots may occasionally be seen. . . . Their function is unknown."

Two possibilities are suggested. The tree may be preparing in some way for its old age, for these trees become very tall and very old. These roots might be needed later. Or perhaps, if the tree's roots in the ground get waterlogged with ocean brine, the aerial feeder roots can extract moisture from the atmosphere.

Other *Metrosideros* trees are famous for roots. In the Pukeiti rhododendron reserve in New Zealand, there once was a very old conifer called rimus.[6] A bird perched on a branch, wiped its bill on the bark, and thereby deposited a seed of a rata vine,[7] which is also a *Metrosideros*. The seed germinated and began to grow. It dropped its roots to the ground, and in the course of years they became so gigantic that they merged to form a "trunk," which squeezed the host tree to death (see photograph, page 26). Today this rata, now a tree, is 150 feet high and 14 feet in diameter at the base. Recently fourteen schoolboys packed themselves into the cave left in the base by the rotting of the rimus that used to support it.[8]

2. Banyan Trees

A banyan is a fig tree that has developed auxiliary trunks to help support the superstructure. The word banyan signifies a manner of growth, not a kind of tree. These extra trunks may be few or they may number in the hundreds. In the Calcutta Botanic Garden is a banyan tree so enormous and with so many trunks that it takes ten minutes to walk around it. Many kinds of fig trees develop the banyan habit in time, although the Indian species[9] is commonest and most famous.

These multiple trunks originate, not on the ground where most trunks begin, but as aerial roots which develop on the branches. Usually, aerial roots keep growing downward until they reach earth, sometimes forming great festoons under the big tree. They remain fine and slender until they reach the ground and then one of them thickens into a stout limb, like a trunk supporting the branch. This is called a pillar root. All trees with this habit are called banyans, after the Indian tree. By dropping more and more pillar roots they continue to grow outward rather than up, and thus the crowns of banyans are extended far beyond the limits of ordinary trees, and those of old trees cover vast areas. In India the banyan is sacred; the dangling young roots are provided with bamboo sleeves to protect them, and the ground below is prepared to receive them.[10]

The India rubber-plant,[11] which is a pot specimen in many Temperate Zone homes, develops pillar roots in the wild and becomes an enormous banyan.

Many banyans begin in a normal way, but some start life as epiphytes, as described in the next section.

3. Epiphytic Roots and Stranglers

In the tropics many trees begin life high in the branches of other trees. This peculiarity is common among the fig trees (*Ficus*), but *Clusia rosea* and other kinds of trees often develop the same way. Birds, squirrels, or monkeys, devouring fruits of the forest as they sit on a high limb, drop a seed on the branch—perhaps as much as a hundred feet from the ground. If the seed lands in a crotch, or any other place where rain and wind do not dislodge it, it is likely to germinate.

This seed grows into an epiphytic bush—an air plant—that clings to its location by encircling the branch with strong roots. From there the roots spread down the trunk of the supporting tree to the ground, where they grow vigorously. Note that this root follows down the trunk. It does not ordinarily drop free to the ground, as do aerial roots from banyan trees. Side roots encircle the trunk of the host tree, joining other side roots where they touch and merging into a single unit. Botanists call this process anastomosing. The invading plant then starts developing aerial roots all up and down its original link to the soil, and these start dropping down and growing around the tree like interlacing basketry.

These roots thicken most on the side which is least illuminated; they grow away from the light. Thus as they grow around the host tree's trunk they crush the bark and eventually kill the tree.

Meanwhile, nourished by the principal root that has dropped from above, the bush has grown bigger and become a tree itself.

Sometimes the epiphytic bush, up on the branch, is too awkwardly placed for its wandering roots to follow the trunk downward. It may then quickly send an aerial root straight to the ground. From this root, which is like a perpendicular cable, side roots grow toward the trunk, as though they were able to see it, encircling it and ramifying over it. A long struggle ensues between parasite and host, but if the fig plant is vigorous it kills its support and finally stands in its place on a massive basket of roots. This "radical trunk" may be a hundred feet high.

The initial cables that descend from the young epiphyte are commonly mistaken for the stems of climbers that have grown up from below. The dead trunk of the supporting tree rots away over many years within the basket of fig roots. How long it takes to strangle a big forest tree we do not know, but the time span from the sprouting of the seed to the independence of the fig tree can scarcely be less than a hundred years.

All trees that go through this procedure of strangling the host tree that gave them life—kicking down the ladder by which they climbed, so to speak—are called stranglers. Many kinds of fig tree become stranglers if the opportunity offers. But sometimes the same little seeds germinate on the ground instead of high up in another tree. When this happens, the young fig tree never gets very big; it has lost the power of forming a tall trunk by itself. Such a seedling develops long limbs and long roots, but it

LEFT: The top of the rata "tree" shown below. BELOW: This is not a trunk but a cluster of huge rata vines (*Metrosideros robusta*) which started high above on another tree, dropped to earth, and fused together, killing the host tree within. (Photos: Douglas Elliott.)

BELOW: The New Zealand Christmas tree (*Metrosideros excelsa*), which occasionally develops fibrous red roots hanging from the branches; they do not reach the ground, and their purpose seems uncertain. (Photo: Douglas Elliott.)

Florida's strangling fig (*Ficus aurea*) starts life as a seed in a crevice of another tree, and eventually envelopes and kills it. Here the host tree is a silk-oak (*Grevillea robusta*). (Photo: Ricou.)

BELOW: Just four pillar roots under one of the branches of the banyan tree on the Thomas A. Edison estate at Fort Myers, Florida. (Photo: Robert E. Halgrim.)

Pandanus trees (*Pandanus tectorius*) in Hawaii, which stand on stilts to escape overflows in lowlands. (Photo: Ray J. Baker.)

A walking pandanus at McKee Jungle Garden, Vero Beach, Florida.

Two *Rhizophora mangle* trees, with water-accustomed stilt roots, readjust themselves to dry land after the mangrove swamp has been dyked and filled in.

27

TOP, LEFT: Moreton Bay fig (*Ficus macrophylla*) on the Thomas A. Edison estate at Fort Myers, Florida. CENTER, LEFT: Buttresses and snaky roots of a kapok tree (*Ceiba pentandra*) in Palm Beach, Florida. (Photo: University of Florida.) BOTTOM, LEFT: *Sterculia alata*, an Indo-Malayan tree, on the Thomas A. Edison estate—an example of buttresses that change direction. BELOW: The marara tree (*Pseudoweinmannia lachnocarpa*) in Queensland, Australia, heavily buttressed. (Photo: Francis, *Australian Rain Forest Trees*.)

RIGHT: Old bald-cypress (*Taxodium distichum*) in the Florida Everglades, with flared skirt to help absorb oxygen from the water, and "knees" which may have once acted as breather roots. (Photo: Paul Root.)

ABOVE: A Florida mangrove (*Rhizophora mangle*), forming dense and difficult tangles with its many aerial roots. (Photo: Ernest F. Lyons.)

Breathing roots of the wild nutmeg tree (*Myristica elliptica*) in the swamp forest of Johore, Malaya. (Photo: E. J. H. Corner.)

cannot grow a tall leader—the trunk. In Florida, the native strangling fig,[12] when growing in the ground, forms only a short main trunk. But let some bird plant the seed high in a host tree, and the Florida strangler can take over the canopy of the forest.

4. Parasitic Roots

Several tropical trees belong in the mistletoe family and, like their more famous relative, live off their neighbors. They steal nourishment by attaching their roots to those of nearby plants. Some of the victims do not appear to mind supporting this extra load.

Among these mistletoe trees are the West Australian Christmas tree,[13] several South American species of *Gaiadendron*,[14] three kinds of *Loranthus*[15] in India and Africa, and a tree called *Atkinsonia*[16] in New South Wales. Authorities disagree on whether or to what extent these trees are parasites, in spite of copious evidence that they really are spongers.

The controversy over the West Australian Christmas tree is typical. Dr. John S. Beard[17] summarizes the confusion thus:

> This tree has no obvious parasitic habit at all and, in fact, whether its parasitism is obligatory throughout its life is open to question. It does not stand in any obvious relation to any host plant and there are many cases where, during clearing land for agriculture, farmers have left the Christmas trees because of their beauty and they remain as the only few scattered trees in fields of wheat of huge extent.
>
> On the other hand the Forests Department found to their cost when leaving live *Nuytsia* trees in pine forests that the taproots of the pines were getting strangled by the *Nuytsia*.
>
> At the present time the principal function of the sucking organs is a mystery. The local university has been working on it without result. As far as anyone knows it is possible for the tree to grow successfully without these parasitic organs but nonetheless they are found to attach themselves freely to practically any plant, from grass to trees, occurring in the vicinity. According to the only published work on the subject, the sucking organs attach themselves only to the *phloem* tissue of the root and are thus presumably absorbing elaborated food products rather than water containing simple minerals that has been absorbed by the roots.
>
> An interesting corollary to this is that recently the U.S. Government's space-tracking station at Muchea near Perth has had trouble with buried electric cables which were plastic covered. When dug up to trace the faults these were found to have been encircled by the sucking organs of the *Nuytsia* which had succeeded in dissolving the plastic covering and causing shorts in the wires inside. It is not known what caused the *Nuytsia* to mistake these cables for roots. It does show that the enzyme which they must use for penetrating the tissues of a host plant is an extremely powerful one.

Australian Plants,[18] in its December 1962 issue, featured the Christmas tree and gave the experiences of two growers who are succeeding with this difficult subject. One found that no host plant was needed in starting the trees from seed. The other tried planting the seed with host plants and without them and found one way as successful as the other.

Anyone who needs to be convinced that this tree is a parasite should read D. A. Herbert.[19]

5. Stilt Roots

Many kinds of unrelated tropical trees develop what are called stilt roots, which means roots that spring out of the sides of the trunk *aboveground* and, in arching outward and downward into the soil, give the tree the appearance of standing on stilts. Botanists call such roots adventitious, which simply means that they are out of place.

Stilt roots appear to be formed in four different ways, although the types are related and merge to the extent that separating them is often difficult.

The Walker Type

The screw-pines[20] comprise 180 kinds of tropical trees with grasslike or lilylike foliage. The young plant throws out a downward-reaching branch, possibly for extra support. As the tree grows, particularly if it is bent by wind or circumstance, it throws out additional downward props. Each of these in turn develops downward-growing branches (roots) in such a manner that screw-pines often seem to be walking.

The Tent Type

The tent type of stilt roots is best illustrated by palms of the genus *Socratea*[21] (also known as *Iriartea*) in Brazil. Examination of a mature tree would indicate to the uninitiated that it never had a trunk at ground level, because the trunk seems to begin at a point six or eight feet from the ground, and to be supported there by a tentlike arrangement of small poles. H. W. Bates[22] wrote of this phenomenon of the Brazilian forest:

> One kind of palm, the Pashiaba (*Iriartea exorhiza*) . . . [has] roots above ground, radiating from the trunk many feet above the surface. . . . A person can, in old trees, stand upright amongst the roots with the perpendicular stem wholly above his head. . . . These roots are studded with stout thorns, whilst the trunk of the tree is quite smooth. The purpose of this curious arrangement is perhaps . . . to recompense the tree by root-growth above

the soil for its inability, in consequence of the competition of neighboring roots, to extend it underground.

The corkwood or umbrella (or parasol) tree[23] of west tropical Africa is similarly constructed, but with an added feature—wherever one of these outreaching stilts hits the ground, another tree gets started. J. M. Dalziel[24] wrote:

> It is of very rapid growth and quickly appears in forest clearings, where the leaves form a heavy layer of humus serving as a good nurse for seedlings. It soon becomes gregarious, reproduction occurring by layering from the stilt roots, an original tree becoming later the centre of a stand, the members of which are produced vegetatively. The stilt roots arise from the lower part of the stem up to a height of ten feet. They may project at a right angle and then bend to the soil, where they send up a new shoot. A broken adventitious root may fork, or alternatively may produce both an aerial shoot growing upwards and a root proceeding downwards.

The Tapering-Trunk Type

In this group the sapling tree thickens little in its lower part, so that as the tree grows the trunk tapers downward to the soil. From this tapered part many stilt roots arch to the ground. This is so similar to the process by which buttress roots are formed (see next section) that no sharp line can be drawn between these two classes of roots. The habit occurs in the stilted simpoh (*Dillenia*),[25] a lofty tree, reaching 100 feet or more. Corner[26] wrote of it:

> In the swampy forest that surrounds the rivers where they flow across the alluvial flats from the foothills to the coastal mangrove, many kinds of trees of diverse families develop stilt-roots. . . . These . . . are connected with the periodical submergence of the bole of the tree when the river rises in flood. To such a class belongs this [*Dillenia reticulata*] and the species *D. grandifolia* but both are remarkable because they grow also on the hillsides, away from streams, and yet in these places they are also stilted.

The phenomenon of stilt roots is explained by some authorities as a provision against inundation, because many stilt-rooted trees do grow in swampy places. Corner says that the only tree of his acquaintance in Malaya, other than *Dillenia*, that develops stilts on dry land as well as wet is a *Xylopia*.[27] This is a smaller tree, sometimes to 80 feet, with few to many stilt roots issuing from the trunk up to three feet from the ground.

De la Rüe[28] was impressed in Africa by the fact that the sugar-plum tree[29] grows only in dry forests, whereas other species of the same genus thrive on swamplands. All have stilt roots. The sugar-plum tree is a popular fruit tree in west tropical Africa. Often rising to 90 feet with a 6-foot girth, it produces in February quantities of one-inch bright-red plumlike fruits with three to four seeds embedded in the sweetish pulp. The fruits are sold as food in the markets of Ghana and Liberia, but the bark and flowers of the tree sometimes provide an ingredient of arrow poisons prepared by the residents of northern Nigeria.[30]

One striking African monarch in which the lower part of the trunk disappears entirely is *Desbordesia*,[31] which Walker and Sillans[32] described as "a very high, strong tree with heavy buttresses at the base. When the tree reaches a certain age, the trunk's lower part completely disappears, so that the tree rests on its buttresses, as if on pillars."

The Non-Tapering-Trunk Type

The fourth type of stilt-rooted trees is exemplified by *Blumeodendron tokbrai*, a Malayan timber tree, and another Malayan tree commonly called the stilted oil-fruit tree.[33] This grows along tidal rivers and creeks in the fresh-water zone. It is generally buttressed and provided with stilt roots. In addition it has a third soil anchor in its breather roots (see Section 7 of this chapter).

Corner[34] explains that in this type of stilt-root formation the sapling thickens normally and develops a cylindrical trunk from the ground up; later it throws out the stilt roots to support the trunk. He continues:

> In both cases (tapered and non-tapered trunk), but particularly the second, there is an undoubted connection between the production of support-roots and the flooding of the tree trunk. Stilt-rooted trees are characteristic of swampy forests, apt to be flooded. I have often observed that the height of the uppermost stilt-roots, where they issue from the trunk, corresponds with the height of maximal, normal flooding of the forest: it may be as much as 30 feet high (as I have seen in Johore, Malaya).

Corner emphasizes three main points:

> First, these roots certainly support the tree; some are flattened vertically and serve mainly as stays or tension-arches; others are cylindrical and serve as props or buttresses. Second, by no means all kinds of tree in swampy forest do this; only certain kinds have the faculty, which they develop under the appropriate conditions of flooding. Third, very few kinds of tree habitually produce stilt-roots even when not flooded.

Other trees which have conspicuous stilt roots, but which are not described here, include the following in the eleven families listed at the left:

Guttiferae	*Tovomita*	South America
	Symphonia globulifera	Tropical America
Moraceae	*Cecropia*	Tropical America
	Ficus	Pan-tropic
Sapotaceae	*Palaquium xanthochymum*	Malaya
Bombacaceae	*Pachira aquatica*	Tropical America
Acanthaceae	*Bravaisia integerrima*	Tropical America
Chloranthaceae	*Hedyosmum mexicanum*	Central America
Euphorbiaceae	*Bridelia micrantha*	Africa
Burseraceae	*Santiriopsis trimera*	Africa
Casuarinaceae	*Casuarina sumatrana*	Malaya
Symplocaceae	*Hopea mengarawan*	Malaya
Myristicaceae	*Myristica elliptica*	Africa

6. Buttresses and Snaky Roots

Many tropical trees in areas of abundant rainfall and restricted sunlight develop enormous buttresses around the base, or send snaky lateral roots over the surface of the ground as far as two hundred feet. Some of these snaky roots, where they join the tree, enlarge vertically into modified buttresses. The word "modified" is used here because trees that develop real buttresses rarely extend them far horizontally; the tendency in buttresses is to have more height than the surface dimension.

In any event, these snaky roots or buttresses separate two principal kinds of trees: (1) those that develop main taproots but few lateral roots (these seldom have buttresses or aerial roots) and (2) those that develop big lateral roots but no taproot. These commonly develop buttresses, snaky roots, aerial roots, or all three.

As always in nature, a few trees are indeterminate between these types. Generally speaking, snaky roots represent shallow, horizontal root growth. They support the tree like tension ropes, and they forage in the shallow humus and topsoil of the forest.

De la Rüe[35] wrote:

The unusual appearance near the foot of a great many trees comes as a surprise to anyone walking for the first time under the shade of a tropical rain forest. None of them is more than shallowly rooted and, far from being hidden, their great roots often creep over the surface of the ground. Many of them, belonging to such very different families as *Leguminosae*, *Bombacaceae*, *Sapotaceae*, *Meliaceae* and others, have the foot reinforced with powerful flying buttresses. These often start several yards above the ground and are prolonged to a great distance by high narrow buttress roots which are very sinuous, the whole forming a picturesque pattern of draperies around the foot of the tree.

These buttresses are sometimes so developed that the natives have no trouble in cutting planks out of them, a much easier process than cutting up enormous trunks. This is why these graceful buttresses are so often mutilated and transformed into hideous stumps.

Some authorities say that buttresses form because prevailing winds pull the tree this way or that, or that the crown gets too heavy and forces the trunk to provide additional support. More than one scientist has shown both these assumptions to be untrue, and T. Petch[36] of Ceylon cites instances of buttresses developing in small seedling specimens of *Delonix regia* and other trees that in wet forest are prone to this manner of growth.

W. D. Francis[37] speaks of many buttressed trees in the Australian rain forest. He says:

It is evident that this peculiar structural feature is not confined to any particular family of plants. . . . Buttresses are often noticeably developed in comparatively young trees. . . . This observation does not support the hypothesis which attributes the origin of buttresses to the direct effects of strain or tension induced by forces acting on the upper aerial parts of the trees. The young trees already mentioned as possessing evident buttresses were sheltered in the forest and were much below the size at which they normally develop large crowns or become exposed to the strain-producing force of winds.

Buttresses and snaky roots rarely go deeply into the soil, and when they are well developed, the tree's taproot usually rots away. C. J. Taylor[38] discusses the disappearing taproot as observed in west tropical Africa:

The rooting system of the High Forest trees is typically a shallow one, and is confined to lateral roots. Although a taproot is usually developed in the seedling, it is no longer evident once the tree reaches the pole stage.

Many of the bigger trees develop buttresses. These are due to an inherent genetical character, and the type produced is true of the species. They appear to be a peculiarity of trees in a tropical climate with an abundant rainfall. Locality factors do not seem to influence the development of buttresses, except the age when they are formed, and in causing a greater development in one particular direction to answer a physical condition. . . . *Tarrietia utilis* shows a strange formation, for as the buttresses develop so does the central rooting system disappear. At first sight the phenomenon appears like some lifting process. The result is similar to deep and narrow stilt roots. This condition is hastened where the soil conditions are wetter. [H. N.] Thompson [*Report of Forests, Gold Coast,* 1910] observed [that] buttresses of *T. utilis* represent an intermediate stage between the cylindrical aerial "prop-roots" and the typical plank buttresses.

Petch[39] wrote of the disappearing taproots:

Several similar cases of buttressed trees which lack taproots have been observed. The trees of the well-known row of *Ficus elastica* on the front of the Botanic Gardens, Peradeniya, Ceylon, began to decay about the year 1907 and one of them was blown over in that year. There was, however, no sign of a tap root. The remaining trees of the row were subsequently felled, and in all cases it was found that the stem was hollow in the center and no tap root was present. . . .

Large old trees of *Canarium zeylanicum* in the Henaratgoda Botanic Garden, which is in the low country but has about the same rainfall as Peradeniya, had buttresses extending to a height of 12 feet. One of these was blown over, and was found to have no tap root.

A parallel condition has been noted by Francis in buttressed trees in Queensland [see reference note 37]. He states: "In all instances of prominently buttressed mature trees, which have been examined by the writer, a decided diminution was observed in the size of the stem or axis of the trees from just above the buttresses towards its point of contact with the soil. The extent of this diminution was measured in a large stump of *Echinocarpus woollsii*. The stem above the buttresses measured 2 feet in diameter, whilst its diameter at the surface of the soil . . . was only 9 inches, or three-eighths of its diameter above the buttresses."

The writer would put forward as a working hypothesis, (1) that the presence of buttress roots is associated with a deficient tap root, and (2) that the formation of buttress roots is due to the restriction of food and water currents to limited narrow regions of the stem continuous with the lateral roots.

Taylor[40] calls attention to the misuse of the word buttress:

Although the term "buttress" is in general use, it would appear to be an incorrect general description of the development or modification of the root. Observations show that the function of these buttresses is usually a pull against the stem and crown, and therefore they function not as buttresses but as guys or stays. A leaning tree has its greatest development of buttresses on the side away from the direction of the slant. Similarly, a tree growing on a hillside has larger buttresses on the upper side of the slope. In such cases it is obvious that they are subjected to a tension and not a compression force.

The close relationship between surface roots on the ground and aerial roots high in the tree, is discussed by Francis:

It would appear that in those cases where buttresses have been evolved, the upper part of the principal surface roots has acquired an aerial character and is subject to some of the conditions of growth operating in stems. The perpendicular elongation of stems is a very prominent characteristic of the trees and erect shrubs of rain forests in which buttresses abound, and it is attributed to the attractive agency of light (phototropism), acting in conjunction with the normal upward growth in opposition to gravity (negative geotropism). The upper part of the principal surface roots in buttressed species may be affected by negative geotropism and phototropism either directly or indirectly through the stem; and in this manner the perpendicular extension, which constitutes buttresses, may arise.

36

Roots are most commonly subterranean organs, but in rain forests the roots of many plants possess an aerial or sub-aerial character. The adaptation of roots to an aerial environment is facilitated by the high relative humidity of the air and the exclusion of a great amount of direct sunlight in rain forests. These two conditions, therefore, are probably factors of considerable importance in the production of buttresses.

The prevalence of the buttress phenomenon in trees whose roots have assumed a definite aerial character is exemplified in the epiphytical species of fig trees (*Ficus*), which are so common in Queensland rain forests. In all the large specimens . . . which the writer has seen the flattening of the roots in a perpendicular plane near the surface of the soil was prominent.

It is also possible that hereditary factors are active, as several species of buttressed trees . . . tend to retain their buttressed character when planted in parks and gardens away from their natural environment of the rain forest. In these cases, however, the buttresses are not so large and conspicuous as in trees of corresponding sizes in the rain forests.

7. Breathing Roots

Tropical trees growing in swampy or muddy places often develop breathing roots. These are porous, peglike structures rising vertically into the air from the underground root system. Surface holes and numerous passages through their spongy tissues permit air to move freely to the roots below.

Similar structures, commonly called knees, on bald cypress[41] trees in the southeastern United States probably served this aerating purpose at one time, but evolution seems to have destroyed their usefulness, for their tissues today are hard and woody. Meanwhile the cypress has found another way to get air to its root system. Instead of being a straight cylindrical bole, the base spreads almost to conical shape and develops a skirt at normal water level which is constantly aerated by the slap, slap of wavelets. This seems to satisfy the tree's needs. The American ecologist R. F. Daubenmire[42] says:

> Certain trees that grow on soil subjected to long periods of inundation produce excrescences that rise vertically from their lateral roots at points where the roots occasionally rise to the soil surface. They are typically cone-shaped but laterally flattened, and in North America they are called knees. The possibility that knees are useful in permitting gas exchange between submerged roots and the free air is doubtful. . . .
>
> Knees are produced only where the soil is periodically exposed to the air, and their height growth depends upon wetness and aeration to the extent that, although they may attain a height of three meters, they never project above the highest level of wave action. Well established bald cypress trees can endure partial submergence for periods of many years, but since seedlings are killed by submergence it is evident that stands owe their origin to periods of low water levels during which establishment is possible.

The breathing roots with which this section is primarily concerned are those which really do supply oxygen or carbon dioxide to the buried lateral roots. Daubenmire points out that trees which usually dwell on land are so adjusted to the high oxygen content of the air that when they take to the water they must make special provision for aeration. They quickly develop tissues containing air holes and air passages. These are the true pneumatophores or breathing roots that characterize many tropical trees in wet areas.

Conspicuous examples are the various kinds of mangrove trees that grow all over the world on the swampy edges of rivers and bays in slack salt water near the ocean.[43] Similar growths are produced on a myriad of fresh-water swamp trees.[44]

On all these, special root branches grow erect until they emerge above the poorly aerated rooting medium. They usually have a well-developed intercellular system of air spaces continuous with exit apertures so that they are of unquestioned value in gas exchange.

8. *Flowers and Fruits Underground*

Reproduction is perhaps the strangest of all root functions. In the few trees in which this seems to occur, underground structures give rise to both flowers and fruits. The reproductive "roots" are really long slender branches from the base of the stem; they develop only scalelike leaves. Since they burrow into the soil they come to resemble roots. At their nodes, the points from which the scale-leaves arise, they produce true adventitious roots. The fruits develop in the axils of the scale-leaves, not from the actual roots.

Anyone who has cultivated peanuts (or ground nuts, as they are sometimes called)[45] is familiar with their habit of burrowing into the ground to produce their fruit. This example makes it easier to understand the earth figs, strange *Ficus* trees found in Malaya. However, the figs are more complicated. The flowers are inside the structure that becomes the fruit, so both flowers and fruit are produced underground. Corner[46] explains it thus:

> By the edge of the forest . . . there are . . . thickets of small bushy trees ten to twenty feet high, that have all the appearance of fig trees . . . yet they never seem to bear flowers or fruits. Such are the earth figs. And if we look at the base of their stems, slender, string-like or rope-like runners can be seen to emerge from various heights on the trunk, but mostly from the base, and pass into the ground. The shorter of these may bear figs above ground but the others appear to be sterile until, on gently pulling them, the bunches of figs come to the surface. These runners . . . may stretch for several yards and

commonly they proliferate new shoots which, taking root . . . grow into small trees beside their parent; hence the earth figs grow in thickets of a kind. But the main function of the runners is to bear the figs which they do, in small bunches that are covered by the humus. How the figs are pollinated underground and whether they are uprooted by animals, we do not know.

One of the most remarkable examples of fruit-producing roots is *Polyalthia hypogaea* of Malaya; it is a forest tree to one hundred feet high, which produces runners about one-fourth inch thick from the base of the big cylindrical trunk. These run into the humus and produce flowers at ground level and fruit in the humus.

Why? Undoubtedly this fruiting at ground level represents the downward accumulation of nutrients in the tree, possibly under the influence of growth hormones. If so, fruiting stolons arise from the parts of the trunk with the highest concentration of nutrients.

FOUR

Even the Leaves Are Queer

The leaves of the tree were for the healing of the nations.
—Revelation 22:2

In this chapter we can forget about trees whose leaves are green in color or commonplace in size and shape. Here is the story of the trees that either got cheated when leaves were being distributed or were overburdened with decorations, and trees whose leaves are a peculiar color, or an unlikely shape, and trees with fantastic leaves that produce young.

Here too are leaves that, instead of being born tiny and gradually increasing, are completely formed when they appear. In some trees, like the African *Musanga*, a club-shaped growth develops on the tree; this suddenly unfurls like a flag to display a full-blown leaf. In others, like *Brownea* of northern South America, the growth is a long, limp, fast-growing tassel which suddenly unrolls lengthwise to disclose several full-sized leaves, delicate red or purplish pink in color, prettily mottled with white. These pick up chlorophyll in a few days, turn deep green, and rise to a starched horizontal position, but they are fully grown before they emerge from the tassel.

1. *The Tree with Two Leaves*

In Africa there dwells a tree that has only two leaves to start with and never acquires any more.

Not everyone would call *Welwitschia* a tree, for its trunk is hardly a foot in height. But this trunk may be 3 feet or more in diameter, it is hard and solid as that of the tallest sequoia, and its life span runs to thousands of years. What else could it be but a tree?

When the two leaves first emerge from deep grooves in the broad, squat trunk they are appropriately small. As they lengthen they become wide and thick, also leathery and heavily ribbed. Throughout the years and centuries, even millennia, they continue growing, piling up in endless folds on the sand as they keep pushing out from the base. Their greenish-brown coloring never fades; they never drop from the plant. In time the desert winds rip them lengthwise; but the same two leaves keep growing on forever from the trunk. Carbon-14 tests show that one welwitschia, at least, is two thousand years old. (Younger plants can be seen in many botanical gardens.) This curious plant was found a century ago, growing in limited numbers in the sandy soil of arid regions in South-West Africa where rain almost never falls. The natives called the tree tumbo,[1] which means "Mr. Big."[2] The man who discovered it was a German botanical explorer, Friedrich Welwitsch, and when specimen plants were received at Kew Gardens in England Sir Joseph Hooker named the tree[3] after its discoverer.[4]

In its native home "tumbo" sends a hard, dark taproot sometimes fifteen feet into the ground. The trunk makes its greatest growth sideways, till it becomes like a round surface-cracked table up to 4 feet across. One observer said it looked like a burned crust of bread. The erratic curling of the torn leaves as they lie on the desert sands makes a well-developed tree look like a trash heap.

Hooker[5] remarked that every part of the plant exudes a transparent gum, and he described the curious flowering habit: erect scarlet cones on branches that rise about a foot above the rim of the tabular trunk. "Flowers" are borne on the scales of the cones. The single seed that develops from each flower in a female cone is broadly winged.

All sorts of questions arise about this living trash heap of the desert, and these have been answered by Emil Jensen, a botanist who lived at Walvis Bay, South-West Africa, and observed and photographed these desert dwellers for the readers of this book. He wrote:

> The leaves are tough bundles of fibre, and to the touch are like boards. The natives call the plants otji-tumbo (= "Mr. Big") or Otji-hooro (= the plants from Haigamkab, which is the location where Baines,[6] South African botanist and explorer, found them.
>
> The plants grow only on the west coast, beginning near Mossamedes in South Angola, where Dr. Welwitsch found them. From here the growing area extends southward along the coast to "the turning circle" in the bend

of the Kuiseb River in the Namib desert of South-West Africa. The growth area begins thirty miles inland and extends another fifty miles eastward, as far as the fog off the ocean drifts, for it is from this fog that the plants obtain their only moisture. The plants are scattered over the desert and are never in colonies. Where suitable conditions obtain they take root, one here and one there. All the photographs were taken along the Swakop River near Haigamkab. The plant has no commercial use. The dry wood burns like charcoal, without any smoke, and lasts longer than our camel-thornwood.[7] The trunk of the tree is not really wood; it is a dark brown material without annual rings, but so extremely hard that one can scratch it only with a nail. It is believed that the trunks store water but nobody knows. When the plant is green it sinks in water; when dry, it floats.

2. *Leaves of Odd Sizes and Shapes*

Nothing illustrates the existence of an infinite intelligence more clearly than the diversity of movement, shape, size, pattern, and construction of leaves. It is incredible that some leaves keep twisting themselves all day to point their edges toward the sun and thus resist evaporation.[8] The intricate pattern of the leaves of some trees, such as those of the Malayan *Trevesia*, is beyond man's comprehension, particularly when the next leaf on the same tree fails to repeat the design. The wide difference in size of leaves on the same tree[9] can be explained but not necessarily understood.

For sheer uniqueness, perhaps no tree can produce leaves as astonishing as those of a small Indian evergreen of the mulberry family that is often grown in Florida as an ornamental. It is commonly called *Ficus krishnae*,[10] for the Indian god Krishna, who is supposed to have formed the leaves for use as drinking vessels. Each leaf, 8 or 9 inches long, is doubled back on itself at the base so that it forms a cup which will hold a half pint of liquid. The upper surface of the leaf is on the outside of the cup.

For size, no simple leaf (except that of *Welwitschia*) begins to measure up to those of the traveler's-tree,[11] a Madagascar native much cultivated in Florida. This banana relative is distinguished by four remarkable characteristics:

1. *It grows in a flat plane, like a gigantic fan.* As the tree gets older it develops a palmlike trunk, and the huge fan of evergreen foliage is pushed far aloft, often to 40 feet. Feature writers say the fan always points due north and south like a compass. This is not true. In the author's garden stands a twenty-five-year-old clump of these trees, with six tall trunks up to 18 inches in diameter, and not one of the overhead fans points either north or south. Hundreds of these trees have been grown from seed, and not one ever pointed north.

ABOVE, LEFT: This club-shaped projection contains a fully developed leaf of one of the parasol trees (*Musanga cecropioides*) in tropical west Africa. ABOVE, RIGHT: The club-shaped holder has split and the leaf is emerging, still much creased. BELOW: The fully expanded leaf of the parasol tree—often 2 feet or more across. (Photos: Francis Hallé.)

LEFT: A female *Welwitschia bainesii* plant in South-West Africa. Its age, determined by carbon tests, is about two thousand years. All the trash at the right comprises one leaf, sliced to ribbons by time, folded on itself, frayed at the ends. The other leaf is at the left. Trunks or "bowels" of other trees have been piled here too. BELOW: A male *Welwitschia* about one thousand years old. (Photos: Emil Jensen.)

BELOW: Male flowers of *Welwitschia*. BELOW, RIGHT: Ripe female cones of *Welwitschia* before they begin to lose their seed pods from wind action. (Photos: Emil Jensen.)

The traveler's-tree (*Ravenala madagascariensis*). (Photo: Paul Root.)

LEFT: This podocarp (*Dacrydium kirkii*) is called "monoao" by New Zealanders. Mature leaves appear at the top, juvenile ones at the bottom. BELOW, LEFT: A New Zealand tree (*Pseudopanax ferox*) with two kinds of leaves on the same branch; the juvenile form appear as spikes at the base and at bottom right. (Photos: Douglas Elliott.) BELOW, RIGHT: The Hawaiian silversword (*Argyroxiphium sandwicensis*), which belongs to the sunflower family. Tiny white hairs on the leaves look like silver glistening in the sun. (Photo: Ray J. Baker.)

ABOVE, LEFT: South Africa's silver-tree (*Leucadendron argenteum*), with the metallic luster that appears even in a picture. (Photo: Douglas Elliott.) ABOVE, RIGHT: On this big, bronze-green *Phyllobotryum* leaf, in Nigeria jungles, appear the flowers of the tree. (Photo: G. K. Berrie.) BELOW: The magnificent golden bell-flowers of *Sophora tetraptera*, which have brought it recognition as New Zealand's national tree. (Photo: Douglas Elliott.)

2. *The leaves are simple, oblong in form, and the blade may be ten feet in length.* They are used for thatching houses in Madagascar. Often they are shredded by high winds, but this fails to spoil their beauty.

3. *The traveler's-tree is reputed to be a source of water for thirsty wayfarers.* A hole drilled in the thick green base of a leaf stalk is said to gush palatable water. Often the result is only a weak trickle of juice.

4. *The round black seeds, which are edible and about the size of garden peas, have a bright blue patch like velvet attached to one half of the surface;* botanists call this an aril. The only other species of traveler's-tree, *Ravenala guyanensis* Steud., grows in Colombia, South America. Its seeds are exactly the same except that the aril is bright orange.

The leaves of many other trees are of astonishing size. The Panama-tree,[12] which gave its name to the Republic of Panama, has tiered branches like a hundred-foot candelabrum. The leaves on the lowest layer are often 40 by 20 inches,[13] ascending layers having successively smaller leaves until those at the top of the tree are smaller than a man's hand. A remarkable thing about these accordion-plaited peltate leaves is that they are arranged so that none shades the leaves below it.

The cabbage-trees[14] of west tropical Africa, members of the buddleia family, also have exceptionally big leaves. One, *Anthocleista talbotii*, has upper leaves about 14 by 5 inches, while those on the lower branches may be 6 to 7½ feet long.[15]

The foregoing are all simple leaves; that is, they are not divided into separate segments, or leaflets. When compound leaves are considered (those that are divided all the way to the midrib), the palms take first place with leaves 20 feet or more long.

Alfred Russel Wallace[16] wrote of the jupati,[17] a Brazilian feather palm:

> Its comparatively short stem enables us to fully appreciate the enormous size of the leaves, which are at the same time equally remarkable for their elegant form. They rise nearly vertically from the stem, and bend out on every side in graceful curves, forming a magnificent plume seventy feet in height and forty in diameter. I have cut down and measured leaves forty-eight and fifty feet long, but could never get the largest.

Describing the inaja[18] palm on the Amazon, he wrote:

> The leaves of this tree are truly gigantic. I have measured specimens fifty feet long; and these did not contain the entire petiole, nor were they of the largest size.

Cooke[19] says:

> Of the fan palms the most magnificent are the leaves of the talipot palm[20] of Ceylon, which are used as umbrellas and for tents, a large one being sufficient to cover fifteen persons from the sun and rain.

48

3. The Phenomenon of Juvenile Leaves

Many trees when young have leaves entirely different from those produced when they reach maturity.

Just what is meant by juvenile leaves? In New Zealand the flora is exceptionally rich in trees which go through two distinct phases during their lives. The juvenile phase may persist for as long as eight or ten years; the plants grow but they keep their baby foliage and baby habits. Then, like teen-agers, they suddenly develop in several directions; the leaves change size, shape, and sometimes even arrangement, and the trees reach maturity. The wide difference in the physical appearance of the trees in these two stages has misled many competent observers into thinking the young and old were different species. A California nurseryman who had some young New Zealand Christmas trees to sell wrote his customers: "We must ask you to go elsewhere if you would like to see what you are getting in *Metrosideros*." He meant that his small plants did not look a bit like adult specimens of the same trees.

The lancewoods[21] in New Zealand are striking examples of extreme diversity between the juvenile and mature forms. In the taller species, for fifteen or twenty years the leaves are stiff and deflexed, and they surround the top of the tree like the ribs of a half-opened umbrella. They are thick and leathery but extremely narrow (usually ½ inch wide), and sometimes three or more feet long with sharp tips, and teeth around the edges. The midrib of the leaf is highly developed, occupying one-third of the surface, and the blade has a black metallic color, underlaid with green. After a long period, these ribbon-like simple leaves are replaced by dark green compound leaves with three to five leaflets. Then comes the mature stage. The leaves become simple again. They are only 4 to 6 inches long, linear, hard and thick, and not toothed.

On the savage lancewood (*Pseudopanax ferox*) pictured on page 46, the first leaves are 12 to 18 inches long and toothed, with the tips turned downward toward the stem. On mature trees the leaves are only 3 to 5 inches long, thick, rigid, pointed, and without teeth.

The kowhai,[22] whose magnificent golden-bell blossoms at maturity bring it recognition as New Zealand's national flower, starts life as a very different-looking plant from the mature form. Its interlaced young stems are tangled like vines, and the very tiny leaves often persist for years; at this stage they are evergreen. When the tree matures the stems straighten out, the leaves become much longer, and the tree becomes deciduous, although for a year or two after reaching maturity it drops its leaves only when it is about to flower in the spring.

The monoao,[23] also of New Zealand, is a conifer that retains its juvenile foliage for twenty years or more, but during that time produces adult foliage at the ends of the branches like a Lawson cypress.

The pokaka[24] gets mature foliage after ten or fifteen years and then is just as likely as not to send out juvenile shoots from the base. The juvenile leaves are irregular in shape, sometimes serrated on tangled branches. Adult leaves are regular, 1½ to 3 inches long, crenate with rounded teeth or serrate, sharply toothed.

Other New Zealand trees with very marked differences in juvenile and adult foliage include the ribbonwood,[25] whose juvenile form is a bush to 6 feet or more with slender, interlaced, zigzag branches; at maturity this is a tree to fifty feet. Also important is the kaikomako,[26] on which the interlaced young foliage may persist for many years before the adult takes over and the bush becomes a 30-foot tree.

Many distinguished botanists have been led astray by these foliage differences. The Dutch botanist Van Steenis[27] reports many instances of misidentification of trees by botanists. Among others he notes that *Sterculia polyphylla* is a juvenile stage of *S. foetida; Ficus basidentula* is merely the juvenile form of *F. callosa;* the type specimens of *Dacrydium junghuhnianum* Miq. from Sumatra consist of juvenile specimens of *D. elatum.* These are all because of the exceedingly wide divergence of plant forms in young and old specimens.

Eucalyptus seedlings have leaves that differ in size, shape, color, and arrangement from those of a mature specimen. The result is that nobody can identify a young Eucalypt. Among Eucalyptus species a conspicuous example of the wide difference in juvenile and mature leaves is *E. perriniana* Herb. Its silvery-white juvenile leaves are of remarkable form— silver discs one above another, the branch passing through their centers. When dead, many leaves become detached from their stems and rotate in the wind. This oddity has given the tree the name spinning gum. In late years, mature leaves of conventional shape and position develop on the branch and there is no more spinning.[28]

Corner[29] reports that a breadfruit relative[30] has sapling leaves with finger-like lobes. Eventually simple adult leaves appear, but it is not difficult to find trees 20 to 30 feet tall with juvenile leaves on the lower branches, adult leaves at the top, and intermediate leaves on the middle branches. Sapling and adult leaves may even appear on the same twig. In the Jahore jungle Corner found a sapling whose leaves were "so extraordinarily dissected they looked as if a pixie had been snipping patterns from them." C. J. Taylor[31] reports many examples of the change-over from juvenile to adult leaves in the forests of Ghana.

4. Off-Color Leaves

Leaves turning red or yellow at the end of the growing season are commonplace in the Temperate Zone but rare in the tropics, where there is no autumn. Two notable exceptions are the tropical almond[32] from Malaya and the west African tree known as *Combretodendron africanum*, with foliage that turns bright scarlet before dropping. The phenomenon of leaves flushing red when they first appear is common in the tropics,[33] unusual in the Temperate Zone.

Leaves of a pronounced gray color occur in many plants, particularly if they grow near the sea, for the gray fuzz is an armor against salt spray. Conspicuous trees of this kind in Florida are the sea-lavender[34] and the silver buttonwood,[35] and there are similar trees near all beaches. These, however, are only cheap imitations of the intensely gray trees, so fully covered with bright, whitish-gray hairs that they glitter in the sun like silver.

First of these is a robust Hawaiian plant of the sunflower family, commonly called silversword.[36] Maybe it is just an herb, but its woody trunk makes it a tree in this book. After several years of development in which the plant becomes a silvery ball two feet across, it suddenly throws up a central flowering stalk five to six feet high that carries one hundred to two hundred (rarely five hundred) nodding heads of flowers. The magnificent plant that is native to Haleakala, says Otto Degener,[37] is one of five kinds of silversword, all endemic to the islands of Maui and Hawaii, thriving in volcanic cinders mostly at elevations above five thousand feet. The entire plant almost always dies after production of seed. Degener wrote:

> The plant owes its color to a dense covering of hair which . . . repels some of the penetrating rays of the sun . . . more intense at high elevations than at low. The hair also guards the plant from too rapid loss of moisture by evaporation through its leaves.

Where acres of silverswords once grew on Haleakala, today there is scarcely a plant to be seen. Insects have been a factor, but man's vandalism has caused this plant to become nearly extinct.[38]

The other outstanding metallic-leaved beauty is the silver tree[39] from the Cape of Good Hope, familiar to many Americans because fine examples are seen in some California gardens. It is a magnificent 30-foot tree whose 6-inch leaves are densely covered with silvery, silky hairs.

No trees with all gold leaves have turned up yet, but some like those of the satin-leaf[40] are gold on the lower surface.

For black leaves, see lancewood in the preceding section.

51

5. The Sexy Leaves

The last of the marvels in this aggregation of leaf peculiarities is the capacity to produce flowers and fruits. Leaves of this sort seem to have learned all about the birds and bees and have confused the roles of breadwinner and parenthood.

In Africa there are two trees whose leaves not only provide shade, make chlorophyll, and concoct sugar to nourish the plant but also produce the flowers and the seeds. Because these trees are rare, they have no English common names. The natives of Madagascar call one of them harahara. Botanists call them both *Phylloxylon*,[41] and the two species have been termed "among the most remarkable trees on the whole island."[42] The reason is that the branchlets of this tall, hard-wooded tree produce what look like leaves but are actually flattened stems (like those of some *Acacia* species). Scientists call these phylloclades, meaning leaf-branches. They are leaflike, rather thick, bright green on both sides, about four or five inches long, less than one inch wide, and quite stiff, with a few tiny thorns scattered on their edges. Suddenly out of the side of one of these structures sprouts another phylloclade, appearing as though one leaf were popping out from the side of another. Then, as they thus multiply, the edges of all of them put out bright purple, sweetpea-like flowers about one-third of an inch long. These are followed by rough pods one and a half inches long.

The second kind of tree whose foliage gives rise to flowers, fruits, and seeds bears genuine leaves. When young these are reddish, but turn bronze-green as they mature.

Phyllobotryum,[43] which grows in Nigeria and the Cameroons, is a sparingly branched shrub or small tree to 12 feet high. Its huge simple leaves, up to 40 inches long and 7 inches wide, are bunched at the ends of the branches. They are broadest near the tip and taper gradually toward the base.

The leaves alone are striking enough, but the crowning peculiarity of the tree is that the multicolored flowers, each about ½ inch in diameter, are clustered on top of the leaves, all along the midrib. The sepals and petals are purple or mauve, the stamens cream, the ovary light red, and the style a deep purplish red. The fruits are small red capsules containing about five white seeds. "*Phyllobotryum* is pretty enough to deserve a place in your book, and surely an oddity," wrote Geoffrey K. Berrie, professor of botany at University College, Ibadan, Nigeria. "It is a rare tree and very local in west tropical Africa."

Fruit-forming leaves occasionally develop on the maidenhair-tree.[44] Hui-Lin Li[45] wrote: "Among the [*Ginkgo*] trees in Japan, there are cases of abnormal fruit formation, observed as early as 1891 by Sharai. On certain trees, fruits are produced on the surface of ordinary leaves of the tree. This kind of tree was recognized by Makino[46] as var. *epiphylla*. No such trees have been observed in either Europe or America."

These phenomena are not entirely unique in the plant world. The ornamental centipede plant[47] from the Solomon Islands is a tender ever-green shrub, on which the young branches are flattened like long many-jointed leaves, and the tiny white flowers, red in the bud, have the strange habit of growing on the extreme edges of these false leaves. A similar plant is the butcher's broom[48] of the lily family, the stiff, spiny branches of which are familiar as brightly dyed Christmas decorations.

FIVE

The Flowers Are Twisted

The flowers appear on the earth. —Song of Solomon 2:12

Among the trees of the forest are many with flowers that astonish. Some of the blossoms are peculiar in form. Extra-curious are the trees that display their wares in unaccustomed places. Some string their blossoms on long ropelike stems that dangle under the tree like fishing lines. Others put their flowers right on the tree's trunk, occasionally in such profusion that the trunk looks as if it were wearing a long skirt. A few trees actually produce their flowers underground.[1]

And last in this parade come the symphonic trees which no one can understand. When several of them are growing in one neighborhood, they all come into bloom the same day, as if signaled by a baton. Why? Nobody knows.

Some of these queer trees are cultivated. Some bear important crops of fruit. Others play a part in religious celebrations. Some even rank among the world's most beautiful shade trees. Whatever the role, the flowering of all is quite unlike the performance put on by ordinary trees.

1. *The Mexican Hand-Flower*

The first sight of a Mexican hand-flower tree[2] in bloom inevitably sends chills down the spine, for the blossoms have an uncanny resemblance to human hands stretched out in all directions. Their blood-red color makes

54

them sinister rather than beautiful. Small wonder it is that Indians in the highlands of Mexico venerate the tree and once gave it special significance in their religious ceremonies.

This 100-foot monarch of the chocolate family, with a trunk up to 7 feet in diameter, grows abundantly in the wet mixed forests of the mountains of Mexico and Guatemala at heights of six thousand to ten thousand feet. Its flowers, as big as a man's fist, sit in a leathery cup three to four inches across. From its base project the wrist, fingers, even finger-nails. This stiff mimicry stands away from the foliage, and usually lasts two weeks before it begins to fade. One turns from the tree with a shudder. In the cup the flower secretes a quantity of liquid that tastes like toast and water.[3] Julian Steyermark[4] wrote after seeing the tree in bloom:

> The resemblance to a hand is so marked that no person observing the flower could fail to be impressed by it. Inevitably this character was looked upon with awe. For a long time the inhabitants of the Valley of Mexico knew of but one tree, growing at Toluca, from which seeds were taken for propagation in the preconquest botanical garden of the City of Mexico, but it was found later that the tree was plentiful enough in some of the mountains to the southwest.
>
> In Guatemala the tree may well be more abundant than in Mexico, and presumably all the wetter, upper or middle slopes of the high mountains were covered with forest in which the tree was dominant. . . . Many of the trees are huge . . . with massive but low trunks close together. Their branching is irregular and the limbs are thick and heavy and often covered with epihytes. They flower abundantly, and the fallen flowers often carpet the ground. The blossoms apparently may be found at almost any season of the year.

2. *The Pin-Curl Tree*

First to pick up the beauty-shop twist is a small tree from Madagascar in the genus *Strophanthus*.[5] This name, derived from two Greek words meaning twisted-cord-flower, represents an effort to explain that the five petals of the funnel-shaped blossoms are elongated into strings that hang down 12 inches or more. This is true of the twenty-eight kinds of *Strophanthus* found in Africa and southern Asia, but all except this one are vines.

The flowers of this exception take the beauty honors for the family because the petals are broader, instead of being stringy and dangling, and they look as though just out of curlers, or like five bright-orange cork-screws. These flowers, clustered along the branch tips, put on a considerable show at blooming time.

3. Drumstick Trees

Like a woman holding some distasteful article at arm's length till she can get rid of it, a *Parkia*[6] tree dangles its malodorous balls of flowers at the ends of long ropes that hang down under the trees. About thirty kinds of *Parkia* trees have been described in the tropics of both hemispheres (mostly in Brazil[7]). The African species, called locust bean, produces leathery pods up to 2 feet long of which both the pulp and the seeds are edible. *Parkia* trees are usually large, and according to Dr. Adolpho Ducke "most of them are very beautiful." He adds, "Among the Amazonian species, some are eminently ornamental and should be introduced into cultivation for park use."

Although the trees themselves are of lovely form—great spreading shady monarchs with finely cut, drooping fernlike foliage—the flower heads make *Parkia* a conversation piece. The individual blossoms are tiny, but they are put together in dense heads, after the manner of *Acacia,* and these resemble nothing so much as the club the bandsman uses to beat the bass drum in the big parade. Often as big as a man's fist, they are bright red or yellow in color, and they hang down underneath the tree on long strings.[8]

Ducke wrote of *Parkia pendula*: "A large or even huge tree, magnificent, and outstanding due to its dark green, very wide crown, shaped like a very flat parasol, below which during a large part of the year hang, on long threads, the innumerable peduncles. [Drumsticks to you!] The dark red flower heads exude an unpleasant odor."

Dr. David Fairchild[9] considered *Parkia* one of the most striking features of the west African landscape.

Another spectacular tree that suspends its flowers on dangling ropes is the red lily-tree[10] or lantern-tree, from southern Chile. It has been cultivated in England for more than a century but has not been established in the United States. The lily-like or urn-shaped flowers, of solid rose crimson, are produced in profusion in May and June, so that the plant resembles "a bewildering assemblage of quaint miniature glowing lanterns."[11]

4. Cauliflory

In the tropics many trees produce their flowers at the tips of short stems that spring directly from the trunk or largest branches. Occasionally, without stems of any sort, the blossoms appear on the surface of the trunk as if they had been pasted there. This peculiarity is known as cauliflory.

It is a phenomenon that does not appear to be related to environment. W. R. Philipson,[12] exploring in northern South America, wrote:

Above this overgrown landslide were several small trees with feathery leaves, like *Mimosa*, and their flower clusters confirmed that they were in fact close relatives, being known as *Pithecellobium*. The most striking feature of this tree was that the flowers were borne on the bark of their trunks, and not on the twigs.

In the tropics many woody plants produce their flowers, and of course their fruits, on their old stems, or even, like this *Pithecellobium*, on their trunks. The cacao is a familiar example of a shrub which bears its flowers and fruits on its principal branches; we found several wild species of this genus, and greatly enjoyed the sweet, chocolate-flavored mucilage which surrounds their seeds. Even some of the largest trees, as for example *Couroupita*, a relative of the Brazil-nut tree, flower from the old bark of their massive trunks and later their enormous round fruits hang in clusters from the trunks. A relative of the humble violet, *Leonia*, is a large tree whose trunk is quite hidden by the long spikes of cream-colored flowers, and from time to time we met other trees whose rough trunks suddenly burst into a mass of feathery blossom.

It is difficult to understand why this habit of flowering from old wood should be favored by a warm climate. It looks strange even at first glance, but closer examination only emphasizes its oddity. The flower buds form deep within the tissues of the tree and then burst out through the bark. Our orthodox ideas about growth, based on the study of plants in temperate climates, are quite upset by this manner of growth. To call it abnormal is wrong; it is normal in the jungle. It is something we cannot explain, but which may be the visible expression of differences which go very deep.

A. R. Wallace,[13] who explored the Amazon in Brazil, wrote:

There is a type of tree in the Amazon valley sparingly represented near Para with the stems either quite simple or emitting only a few long wand-like branches, which are naked except at the continually lengthening apex, where they bear a few crowded leaves, often of such enormous length as to give them at a distance the aspect of palms. In their season, flowers spring from the naked trunk or branches, generally in clusters, and often noticeable from their size and beauty, as in *Gustavia fastuosa*, which has large roselike flowers sometimes seven inches across. Some of the handsomer Melastomes (*Bellucia, Henriettia,* etc.) are of this type.

An outstanding example of cauliflory is the jackfruit[14] tree, whose enormous fruits, following the flowers, dangle from the trunk and largest branches. (See Chapter Six, section 7.) Many *Ficus* trees have the same habit.[15]

A Puerto Rican tree with this habit, often seen in Florida, is *Chamaefistula antillana*. This is peculiar in another way too: in Puerto Rico it is a vine; in Florida, a tree.

5. *The Chocolate-Candy Tree*

The most important tree crop in the world is produced not on the branch tips but on the trunk and directly on the bark of the main branch. The inconspicuous pinkish flowers of the tree that provides cocoa and chocolate[16] are followed by woody, elongated, cantaloupe-sized pods containing the beans that everyone loves. They are an outstanding example of cauliflory. Paul Allen[17] wrote:

When we enjoy a cup of hot chocolate on a cool afternoon, munch a chocolate bar or relax by the radio and reach for a chocolate cream, few of us stop to consider that this rich quick-energy food confection was not always on Everyman's table and fewer still would recognize the plant from which it is obtained. For chocolate is the product of a tree of the deep tropics, and few who have not visited the wet warm lowlands of countries near the equator have ever seen it, though a few specimens have been brought to maturity in Florida at Chapman Field.

The bulk of the world's crop today comes from tropical Africa, with secondary centers of production in Costa Rica and Ecuador in our hemisphere, where the species originated. Early writers such as DeCandolle thought that its home was probably the basin of the Amazon, or the Orinoco, but what appear to be wild trees are frequent in the lowland rain forests of northern Honduras. Whatever its original habitat, primitive Indian agriculturists had watched its tiny but complex flowers transform into plump golden pods, filled with sweetish pulp and stimulating nourishing seeds, and had scattered the species far and wide, from Peru to Mexico in pre-Columbian times.

Although chocolate in its many forms ranks today as Big Business, and plantations of pedigreed clones are being developed in Central America for better flavor, disease resistance and higher yield, its potentialities as a cash crop were not recognized by the first Europeans.

It is, perhaps, too much to expect that a man be wiser than his time, but it is interesting to speculate on how closely fortune can sometimes pass, and yet remain unrecognized. Columbus, in 1502, on his fourth and last disastrous voyage to the New World, seeking shadowy Asiatic kingdoms, sighted and captured a great sea-going Mayan trading canoe near Roatan, one of the bay islands on the north coast of Honduras. He looked in vain among the various items of cargo for evidence of that wealth which alone would justify the expenses of his voyages in the eyes of the Spanish crown. Instead of gold or precious gems there were only textiles, copper axes and bells, pottery jars filled with a strange sort of maize beer, and a considerable quantity of some odd "almonds" which the Indians seemed to value highly. How could he know as he fingered these curious red, bean-like seeds . . . that here was the foundation of a great plant industry? . . . .

Seventeen years were to pass before Europeans saw chocolate again, but this time there could remain little doubt in their minds as to its importance, at least to the American Indian. Bernal Diaz del Castillo, one of the intrepid

LEFT, TOP: The flower cluster of *Boerlagiodendron*, as big as a bushel basket. Bright orange flowers rise above the bunches of fruit beneath. (Photo: Frank Caldwell.) LEFT, CENTER: The blossoms of *Napoleona leonensis*; they appear on the old wood. (Photo: Francis Hallé.) LEFT, BOTTOM: The Mexican hand-tree. (Photo: George Farnham.) BELOW, RIGHT: The unfolding flower of the cannonball-tree (*Couroupita guianensis*). (Photo: Francis Hallé.)

BELOW: The long petals of the flowers on this *Strophanthus* tree in Madagascar are so twisted that each flower makes a cluster by itself. (Photo: J. Bosser.)

ABOVE: The West Indies shower (*Chamaefistula antillana*)—a vine in its native Puerto Rico, but in Florida a 15-foot tree with cauliflorous habits.

ABOVE: The flower clusters of *Parkia*, like tennis balls hung on strings from the branches. Each ball is made up of thousands of tiny flowers. Most are yellow, but this (*P. filicoidea*) is red. (Photo: Robert Pichel.)

BELOW: The intensely red urnlike flowers of the red lily-tree (*Tricuspidaria lanceolata*) from Chile. (Photo: J. E. Downward.)

60

ABOVE: Flowers of the jaboticaba (*Myrciaria cauliflora*), made up principally of clusters of white stamens, on the trunk and larger branches. (Photo: P. Nogueira-Neto.) BELOW, LEFT: Fruits of the jaboticaba, growing directly on the trunk, look and taste like grapes. (Photo: Nixon Smiley.) BELOW, RIGHT: Cacao pods hanging on the tree's trunk. The tiny flowers on the stems just above the opened pod are inconspicuous. (Photo: American Cocoa Research Institute.)

soldiers who followed Cortez on the unbelievable conquest of Mexico, tells us that the Aztec Emperor, Montezuma, consumed the contents of fifty golden goblets of chocolate daily, prepared in the Indian manner, mixed with vanilla or other spices, beaten to a froth and served stone cold. Torquemada asks us to believe that the royal household used over two hundred million pounds of chocolate yearly, and while such a figure is obviously preposterous, nevertheless the seeds were an important item of tribute from the provinces, were pictured in the Codices, passed everywhere as a sort of currency and were occasionally counterfeited by having the paper-thin shells filled with clay, and were to the Aztec nation of tremendous economic importance.

Cortez, a superb showman, brought a quantity of the seeds with him on his triumphal return to Spain in 1528, where, besides describing its use by the Mexicans, he did not neglect to suggest that such a marvelous food, combining nourishment with the stimulating effect of an alkaloid, must have been created expressly by the Divine Providence, and that the tree had doubtless been one of those in the Garden of Eden, placed there for the enjoyment of men and the gods. Perhaps influenced by this sage opinion, the great Linnaeus when he described the plant in 1735, called it *Theobroma*, signifying "food of the Gods," with the specific epithet *cacao* as most nearly approximating the unpronounceable Aztec name "Cacahoatl."

It is not known when sweet chocolate, served hot, as we know it, was first made, but this marked improvement over the bitter, frothy, cold Mexican drink appeared some time during the sixteenth century while Spain held a tight monopoly on the products of the New World. In the homeland and in the colonies, the drink became so popular that it produced learned discussions among high authorities of the church as to whether it might properly be taken on fast days, since it was both stimulating and nourishing.

Fashionable ladies of Chiapas had chocolate served to them during Mass, to the scandal of their good bishop, who passed an edict, threatening any of his flock who indulged in such worldliness with excommunication. He was subsequently poisoned for his pains, or so Thomas Gage, the English-American friar, tells us.

Such a popular drink could not long remain the exclusive property of any one country, and by 1657 Samuel Pepys in London could record in his diary: "To a coffee house to drink jocolatte, very good."

6. *Jaboticaba—the Grape of Brazil*[18]

An outstanding fruit tree that produces its crop on the trunk instead of out on the branches is the jaboticaba[19] (pronounced *zha*-bo-ti-*cab*-a, with chief accent on first syllable, secondary accent on penult). It is Brazil's finest fruit tree; actually three different but closely allied trees with similar fruits are known collectively as jaboticaba.

These evergreen trees, to 35 feet, upward branching from near the ground, bear clusters of short-pediceled white flowers with conspicuous stamens, produced directly from the trunk and branches. These are followed by thick-skinned grapelike fruits that are 1 to 1½ inches in diameter, the pulp a pleasing vinous flavor suggestive of the muscadine grape. Each fruit contains 1 to 4 oval seeds.

Christian Halbinger Frank of Mexico City, who has been growing jaboticaba there, wrote: "M. *jaboticaba* takes five years until fruiting and M. *cauliflora* thirty years, but M. *cauliflora* has better fruit."

Harry Blossfeld, plantsman of São Paulo, Brazil, writes of these trees:

> Some two hundred miles west of São Paulo is a city named Jaboticabal which got its name from the fruit tree. In that city there are thousands of trees in all back yards and orchards. People stream to the city at harvest time and orchard owners charge an entrance fee for which you can pluck as many fruits as you can eat. Or they charge another fee for each five-gallon can you take out with fruit. Jaboticaba jelly is most popular with us and any suburban piece of land offered for sale is charged an additional price for each Jaboticaba tree standing on it. It takes from twelve to fifteen years to get a plant from seed into first fruiting, but by grafting on a more vigorous variety here known as "Paulista" it is possible to get young trees to bear fruit three years after grafting, or six years after sowing the seed.

7. *Symphonic Flowering*

Gregarious flowering is the term applied to the phenomenon, occasional in the tropics, of trees of a certain kind all coming into bloom the same day, like a gigantic symphonic orchestra. Similarly, they stop blooming the same day. The cause is attributed by various scientists to a long series of factors including sudden drops in temperature, certain humidity conditions, thunder storms, and even sudden diminution of sunshine. However, no extended research has been done on the subject, and nobody really knows what creates the incidence.

The Australian explorer Hill[20] reported gregarious flowering in *Eremophila*, a genus of Australian trees and shrubs. He wrote:

> It was noticed that usually the bushes have buds and fruits but no fully expanded flowers—very tantalizing for the collector. Then one day all the bushes of one species will be in flower, but after a few days they revert to their usual dull appearance. Time did not permit an investigation of this phenomenon, but I think the flowers tend to open on dull days. In the Australian desert the only way they can avoid desiccation before fertilization is by opening only on a dull day, and these are few and far between.

Corner[21] reported on Angsana[22] trees in Singapore:

> The inflorescences develop in the axils of the young light-green foliage, but the Angsana is peculiar because its flowering is not continuous. In any one neighborhood, the trees which are ready to flower will burst into blossom on

the same day; the petals will rain down the next morning, laying the familiar yellow carpets by the road, and then there will be an interval of several days before all such trees in the neighborhood flower again: and so the trees continue in fitful bloom until their inflorescences are exhausted. In full flower, the crowns seem painted yellow and the air is pervaded with fragrance. It appears that the trees require a special stimulus to open their flowers. The incidence of dry weather causes the leaf changes and the development of the inflorescences, but some other factor makes the flowers open: unless this factor arises, the buds remain rudimentary. It seems that the flower buds, like those of the Pigeon Orchid, are stimulated to develop by a sudden drop in temperature, as is caused by a heavy storm, when all the trees which are ready to flower and which lie within influence of the storm, blossom together after the necessary interval for development: the interval appears to be three days for the Angsana.

Of the Malayan chewing-gum-tree[23] Corner says: "All the trees of a district change their leaves and flowers simultaneously."

Corner cites similar phenomena in *Eugenia*. Discussing how these various kinds of trees flower once, twice, or three or more times a year, he continues:

Of these last, the Sea Apple[24] is the best example. In the south of the [Malayan] peninsula, where it is a common roadside tree, it flowers about the middle of March to the middle of April, from the end of July to the middle of August, and about the end of December to the middle of January. Sometimes it has small flowerings too, about the middle of June, the end of September, and the end of November. As the flowering is gregarious, many trees being affected at the same time over a wide area, it must be a climatic phenomenon that is dependent, perhaps, on some alteration of dry and wet, or hot and cool, weather too subtle to be detected by ordinary meteorological methods. Some years the trees flower earlier or later than is their wont, exactly as the change of the monsoon is unpredictable, and some flowerings are poor. Indeed, two good flowerings are seldom consecutive. The March flowering is the most regular and generally the most striking. Every tree will then flower for ten to twenty days, although the height of flowering, when the crown is whitened as with snow, lasts in each case only four to five days or a week.

Richards[25] discusses this phenomenon in some detail, noting that tropical plants which flower gregariously are not an uncommon feature in the rain forest flora. He quotes Richard Spruce,[26] who says of the Amazonian Myrtaceae:

They are remarkable for their simultaneous and ephemeral flowers. On a given day all the myrtles of a certain species, scattered throughout the forest, will be clad with snowy, fragrant flowers; on the following day, nothing of flowers appears save withered remnants. Hence it comes that if the botanist neglect to gather his myrtles on the very day they burst into flower, he cannot expect to number them among his "laurels."

Corner[27] comments further on the subject:

Well known examples of gregariously flowering species are various bamboos which flower at long intervals and die after ripening their fruits, and species of *Strobilanthes*. *S. cernuus* Blume in Java flowers gregariously about every nine years.[28] *S. sexennis* Nees in Ceylon flowers about every twelve years.[29] The tree *Fagraea fragrans* Roxb. flowers gregariously at Singapore every year in May with great regularity; there is a second less conspicuous flowering in October and November. R. E. Holttum[30] has shown that the chief flowering period occurs about four months after the break in the rainy season, which is usually in January; variation in the date of this break was closely correlated with variation in the time of flowering over a period of some eight years. In Mauritius, Vaughan and Wiehe[31] find that gregarious flowering of *Homalium paniculatum* Benth. follows severe cyclones. The best investigated examples of gregarious flowering are in the pigeon orchid *Dendrobium crumenatum*. . . . Flowering nearly always occurs after a thunder shower following a dry spell. The interval between the shower and the flowering may be eight, nine, ten, or eleven days, according to the species; for some species it varies by one or two days. Experiment has shown that the effect of thunder showers is not due to the direct action of rain or to any electrical phenomenon, but to the sudden fall of temperature. . . .

The gregarious flowering of tropical trees and orchids seems to have much in common with the flowering in "pulses" of temperate species of *Juncus*[32] in which all the individuals of the same species in the same district open their flower buds together at intervals of a few days without any obvious relation to changes in the weather.

SIX

Strange Fruits and Nuts

The tree is known by his fruit.   —MATTHEW 12:33

Everybody visits the State Fair. In the Fruit and Nut Pavilion is always assembled the year's harvest, prepared by nature to look beautiful. In a world tree exhibition, most of the displays worthy of a blue ribbon would not be fit for the palate—only for the eye. None but a limited few ever find their way to an epicure's table. Here are the prize winners.

1. *Nuts from the Seychelles*[1]

If you were to stand under a Seychelles palm nut tree[2] just as one of the nuts is about to drop, you would be lucky to escape. The solid fruits weigh anywhere from 30 to 40 pounds, and there are as many as 70 such blockbusters clustered on a single tree. Each one measures about 3½ feet around, and they take six years to ripen. The result is the biggest seed in the plant world—but not the biggest fruit (see Jackfruit in section 7 of this chapter).

Some persons make the mistake of calling this the double coconut, but it is not a coconut. It grows on a fan-leaf palm with sexes on different trees; the coconut grows on a feather-leaf palm with both sexes on the same tree. The outer husk of the Seychelles nut is smooth, brown, and less than 1 inch thick, and it splits off; the thick greenish-yellow shell beneath is not double but lobed. The fruit is usually two-lobed, sometimes three-lobed, and very rarely six-lobed.[3]

66

When the fruit is ten to twelve months old it has reached its maximum size and at this stage it is frequently eaten. Its jelly-like interior "is much appreciated throughout the Seychelles. It is colorless, practically tasteless, save sometimes for a slight nutty flavor. .*. . From this stage onwards, the the soft, jelly-like endosperm gradually sets to a very hard tissue resembling ivory."[4]

For centuries this nut, sometimes called coco-de-mer, was a mystery. Because it is heavier than water, it sinks; but when the husk has been shed and the interior has rotted, it will float. Sailors of long ago picked them up on the shores of the Indian Ocean, but medieval sages could not say whether they were animal, vegetable, or mineral. Tales persisted that they came from the Maldive Islands,[5] three hundred miles south of Ceylon; or that the trees grew in submerged gardens near Java but disappeared when sailors dived for them; that when the trees did extend above the water, a griffin lived in them and devoured any humans that chanced by. (When not so occupied, the griffin flew to the nearest land and ate elephants.)

The nut was highly prized. Superstition credited it with being a precious talisman, a universal panacea for all ailments, an antidote for all poisons, a protection against enemies, and a powerful aphrodisiac. Hooker[6] says some kings were so greedy for the nuts that they offered to give a loaded ship in exchange for only one. Common folk were forbidden to possess one. Rudolf I of Hapsburg offered four thousand gold florins for a single nut.

All this nonsense blew up when the palms were discovered on Praslin (one of the Seychelles) in 1742, and an enterprising merchant dumped a whole boatload of the nuts on the market in India. The price collapsed. Today the nuts can be purchased in Singapore, Bombay, Karachi, and other ports.

Seychelles palms do not bear till they are one hundred years old or more. No one knows how old the biggest palms on Praslin are, or what age they finally reach.

To germinate the seed, men husk the nuts, allow them to dry for several months, and then place them on the surface of the ground in a moist place. Four months after germination has begun, a shoot or "sinker" 6 inches long and about 1 inch in diameter has grown through a soft spot in the crotch of the lobes. The tree embryo is at the tip of this sinker, not in the nut. This shoot, if it meets no obstruction, penetrates the soil. If, however, it strikes a rock or other hard surface, it will travel horizontally for some distance and try again. A hard-pointed sheath develops at this point, and nine months later the first leaf sprouts at a forty-five-degree angle from the root. It is closely folded, has a smooth hard surface, and ends in a sharp point. When about two feet above the surface, it expands. Nine months later another leaf follows, coming up the grooved surface of the midrib of the leaf which preceded it, and so on at intervals of nine months, each succeeding leaf becoming larger in size. All these leaves cluster together and support each other, no stem appearing above the ground. From the age of fifteen to twenty-five the tree is in its greatest beauty, and the leaves of this period are much larger than they are subsequently.

Bailey[7] describes the curious construction of this palm:

> Unlike the coconut trees, which bend to every gentle gale, and are never quite straight, the Coco-de-mer trees are as upright as iron pillars, undisturbed in their position by the heavy gales and violent storms so often occurring in tropical regions.
>
> The arrangements . . . for the roots . . . are of a most peculiar nature, quite distinct from those provided for any other known tree. The base of the trunk is of a bulbous form, and this bulb fits into a natural bowl, or socket, about two and a half feet in diameter and eighteen inches in depth, narrowing towards the bottom. This bowl is pierced with hundreds of small oval holes about the size of a thimble, with hollow tubes corresponding on the outside, through which the roots penetrate the ground on all sides, never, however, becoming attached to the bowl; their partial elasticity affording an almost imperceptible but very necessary "play" to the parent stem when struggling against the force of violent gales.

One of the strangest aspects of this Seychelles palm is the way it sheds water. Durocher-Yvon describes the leaves, which are enormous—the petiole (leaf-stalks) eight to twenty feet long and the fan-shaped blades ten to sixteen feet long and five to eight feet wide. Three or four of these are enough to thatch the roof of a house. The number of leaves on a tree ranges from twenty to thirty but never exceeds those figures even on forty-year-old specimens. He continues:

> The leaves with their deeply-channelled petioles direct the flow of water [in a rainstorm] down the trunk of the tree. This water prevents the vegetative bud in the center of the crown from drying out and also supplies the base of the palm with moisture for the roots. During rain, except for the area immediately surrounding the base of the palm, there is a large area within a circumference of fifteen feet or more which is left completely dry. Outside this area raindrops fall from the drooping ends of the leaves.
>
> During heavy rains the palms growing along the Grand Anse-Baie St. Anne's road afford excellent protection to passersby. I remember having stood under the crown of a palm when it was raining heavily, and yet kept quite dry as if . . . indoors.

2. *Dangerous and Delicious*

The durian[8] is not only the world's most dangerous fruit—especially if a ten-inch, ten-pounder, covered with thorns, drops on your head—it is also probably the only fruit in the world so prized by those who love it for food that they risk their lives to get one.[9]

The durian grows on a tall, broad, heavily buttressed Malayan tree, and is famed for its odor, which is highly offensive, at least on first acquaintance. Corner[10] says:

> The odor of the fruit in season attracts wild animals from afar. The elephants, it seems, have first pick, the tiger, deer, pig, rhinoceros, seladang [a wild buffalo], tapir, and monkey enjoying what is left. In those parts of Pahang where durians are common in the forest . . . Malays and Sakai build shelters in the trees, above the reach of elephants, whence they can descend by a ladder to pick up the fruits as they drop. Tales there are of Malays who have gathered a fruit only to be gathered in turn by an elephant.

The round or egg-shaped fruits, weighing 6 to 8 pounds or more, grow on stringlike stems from mature branches. They have thick, hard rinds covered with stout, thickly set, sharp-pointed, half-inch spikes. Corner says: "The fruit takes about three months to develop and is not fully ripe till it has dropped from the tree; it then begins to gape into five pieces."

Reaction to the luscious-looking, custard-like pulp which surrounds the one to four seeds in each section is widely divergent. Malays love it. In *Tropical Planting and Gardening*, Macmillan[11] says it is also esteemed by some Europeans who acquire a taste for it after learning to ignore the smell. It has been described as "resembling blanc-mange, delicious as the finest cream." Alfred Russel Wallace[12] felt the sensation of eating durians was "worth a voyage to the East." He wrote: "A rich custard, highly flavored with almonds, gives the best general idea of it, but there are occasional wafts of flavor that call to mind cream cheese, onion sauce, sherry wine, and other incongruous dishes. Then there is a rich, glutinous smoothness to the pulp which nothing else possesses, but which adds to its delicacy. It is neither acid, nor sweet, nor juicy; yet it wants none of these qualities for it is in itself perfect. The more you eat of it, the less you feel inclined to stop."

Less complimentary opinions of the durian's odor could be quoted. One compared it to "French custard passed through a sewer pipe."

When dried it is delicious even to the Occidental palate.

3. Fruit on the Wrong Tree

Preconceived notions of what a fruit tree should look like, based on lifelong experience with apples, cherries, and peaches, may be upset when edible fruits seem to be hanging from the wrong trees.

Dates and coconut are common accessories in every American kitchen, but the idea of picking edible fruits from palm trees still seems to us bizarre. And yet two other palm species are cultivated for their fruits in their native lands. One is the peach palm[13] of Venezuela, the other the gingerbread palm[14] of Egypt.

The peach palm's 60-foot trunk is armed with exceedingly sharp, needle-like spines which keep animals from getting to the ripening fruit first. Even the big feathery leaves carry spines. The egg-shaped fruits, about the size of apricots, are borne in large drooping bunches like enormous grapes. They may be bright scarlet or orange yellow, with no difference in taste. The fleshy outer portion of the fruit contains starch and, when boiled a long time in salted water, tastes like chestnuts and is delicious. Sometimes the fruits are roasted and eaten with molasses. An agronomist at Turrialba, Costa Rica, reported that the fruits, known there as pejibaye, are rich in vitamins. Natives of that country are encouraged to cultivate and eat them. In many Latin American countries they are a prized article of food.

The gingerbread palm is strange in another way; it has branches, often three or four on a 30-foot tree; proper palms simply do not grow that way. Each branch terminates in a big splash of fan-shaped leaves, and from these clusters emerge the flowers with the sexes on different trees. The female trees develop long hanging bunches of beautifully colored and highly polished yellow-brown fruits, often two hundred in a cluster. In upper Egypt, where the tree is usually called the doum (or doom) palm, these fruits form a large part of the food of the poorer classes.[15] The part eaten is the fibrous, mealy husk which tastes almost exactly like gingerbread, though its dryness does not add to its palatability.

Another edible fruit that seems to be on the wrong tree is the muli,[16] which is borne up and down the culms of an evergreen bamboo in India and Burma. (Although bamboos are grasses, their woody stems and potential height—100 feet in some—make certain of them at the same time trees.) The smooth, straight, thin-walled stalks of this bamboo, rising 30 to 70 feet, are strong and are extensively used for building, for paper pulping, for rafts to float heavy timbers downstream, and for many other purposes. The plants spread rapidly by means of underground rhizomes

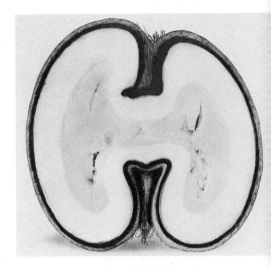

ABOVE, LEFT: The largest seed in the world is the so-called double coconut, which isn't a coconut at all, but the fruit of the Seychelles palm. It may weigh forty pounds. (Photo: Ward's Natural Science Establishment, Inc.) ABOVE, RIGHT: A cross-section of the Seychelles palm nut, showing the meat after it has solidified to an ivory-like hardness. LEFT: A Seychelles palm. Each leaf develops along the inner grooved midrib of the preceding leaf. (Photos: Courtesy L. H. Bailey Hortorium, Ithaca, New York.)

BELOW: Each durian dangles at the end of a long string. (Photo: Department of Agriculture, Bangkok, Thailand.)

ABOVE: This durian fruit weighs about 8 pounds. The thorns are as vicious as they look. (Photo: Indian Council of Agricultural Research.)

BELOW: The gingerbread palm (*Hyphaene thebaica*)—unique because it is one of the few palms with branches.

ABOVE: Fruits of the gingerbread palm. (Photo: The Palm Society.)

ABOVE, LEFT: The brilliant red fruits of *Cnestis ferruginea*, clustered at the branch tips. This tree is a native of west Africa from Gambia to Ghana. (Photo: Francis Hallé.) ABOVE, RIGHT: The clustered fruit of the peach palm, known in tropical America as *pejibaye*. (Photo: Joe DuMond.) BELOW: The bright pinkish-red fruits of the akee (*Blighia sapida*). Hanging on Florida trees in December, they look like Christmas ornaments; they pop open as they fall.

ABOVE LEFT: The scimitar-like seed pods of Oroxylon, which grow 2 to 4 feet long and 3 inches wide. (Photo: Soedjana Kassan, Bogor.) ABOVE, RIGHT: Brightly colored pods of the lipstick tree (*Bixa orellana*). They are usually a burnt red with green undertone, but vermilion and golden yellow forms are known. (Photo: Paul Root.) BELOW, LEFT: Seed pods of *Heterophragma adenophyllum*, a Malayan tree; they are coiled so that they writhe when the wind blows. The large leaves here are 20 inches long. (Photo: Julia Morton.) BELOW, RIGHT: Seed pods of *Monotes*, a genus of large timber trees in central Africa; the pods are surrounded by red calyx lobes that resemble flower petals. (Photo: Edward Ross.)

RIGHT: Female trees of *Ruprechtia coriacea* from Venezuela; these are showy in seed, for the calyces have turned bright red in clusters. Flowers on the male trees are inconspicuous. (Photo: Ricou.) BELOW: The 2-inch-wide flowers of the candle tree (*Parmentiera cereifera*), borne directly on the trunk and followed by dangling yellow fruits like yellow candles. (Photo: Paul Root.)

Chinese lanterns (*Nymania capensis*), a tree of the Cape of Good Hope. These inflated 2-inch fruits are red, pink, yellow, or green. (Photo: Dr. L. E. Codd.)

75

LEFT: Cannonballs hanging from "strings" attached to the trunk of the cannonball tree (*Couroupita guianensis*). (Photo: Julia Morton.) BELOW, LEFT: In western Africa this *Omphalocarpum anocentrum* is called the maiden's-breast tree. (Photo: Debray, Ivory Coast.) BELOW, RIGHT: A jungle tree (*Durio testudinarum*) of Borneo, with its fruit hung around its skirts at ground level. (Photo: D. I. Nicholson, Sandakan, Sabah, Malaysia.)

ABOVE: The sausage-tree (*Kigelia pinnata*) of Africa has velvety, deep-red, 3-inch flowers, usually opening one at a time. (Photo: Paul Root.) RIGHT: the tree's sausage-like fruit. (Photo: Ray J. Baker.)

BELOW: The common calabash-tree (*Crescentia cujete*). RIGHT: Maracas (rattles) made by emptying the calabash of seeds and pulp and inserting pebbles or lead shot. (Photos: Julia Morton.)

77

ABOVE, LEFT: A breadfruit tree growing not in the South Seas but at Bal Harbour, Florida, where William Whitman has established exotic fruits from many tropical areas. (Photo: Nixon Smiley.) ABOVE, RIGHT: A papaya or tree melon (*Carica papaya*). BELOW: A jackfruit (*Artocarpus heterophyllus*) from India, photographed in Miami. It is first cousin to the breadfruit, but it grows much larger, sometimes to 20 pounds, and hangs on the tree's trunk instead of from the branches. (Photo: Paul Root.)

and where tree growth has been destroyed by shifting cultivation the area is quickly taken over by a veritable sea of this giant grass that is often hard to stamp out. Kurz[17] says this bamboo flowers usually gregariously,[18] only at intervals of thirty to thirty-five years, but the culms are so numerous that fruit is plentifully produced.

Troup[19] says the smooth green fruit is large, fleshy, and pear-shaped, 3 to 5 inches long and 2 to 3 inches broad, with the stalk inserted at the thick end and the apex terminating in a curved beak. The fruits are filled with starch, and they are readily devoured by cattle, elephants, bison, rhinoceros, deer, pigs, and other animals. Flowering takes place in December or January. Soon after, the leaves wither and fall and the culms turn yellow. The fruits form rapidly, ripening and falling from April to June. Though large numbers of fruits fail to mature, often eight or ten ripe ones may be found hanging in clusters around each node down the whole length of the culm. The fruits perish rapidly, and if they are sent any distance they must be packed carefully in dry sand or charcoal. Young crops of this bamboo are extremely dense; seed produces several shoots to 10 feet tall the first year, to 20 feet the second year, and to maximum height the fifth year, still thin and crowded. At this time the extending rhizomes start producing new plants at points about 2 feet apart.

4. Colorful Seed Pods

The seed pods of many plants are far more conspicuous than their flowers, and many are used for landscape effects. In the Temperate Zone the hollies and firethorns are indispensable ornaments. Fewer trees than shrubs make displays of this kind, but in the tropics are several outstanding tree examples of such harvest-time elegance.

The sun-fruits, which include ten species of *Heliocarpus*, growing from Mexico to Paraguay, have minute yellow or green flowers in clusters at the branch tips. The tiny fruits which follow are made conspicuous by beautiful radiating bristles. Tamayo[20] says of the Venezuelan species,[21] which is a small erect tree: "The ornamental part of this tree is not the flowers . . . but the reddish or rosy fruits, borne in large masses and of a form reminiscent of drawings of the sun with its rays."

A daisy-tree from Transvaal called *Vernonia*[22] bears large clusters of white, mauve, or yellow flower heads in December. These are not showy, but they are followed by a brilliant display of small, hard, golden-yellow fruits, each containing a single seed. Dr. L. M. Simonson has a 30-foot tree in his garden at Lantana, Florida.

The seed pods of the lipstick-tree[23] split open like clam shells, displaying small seeds coated with a moist, bright orange-red dye called annatto. It is wonderful for children wanting to play Indian.

The pods resemble chestnut burs except that their bristly exterior is soft; they are usually green and the bristles red. Very bright red, burnt orange, and yellow forms are also known. The coloring matter around the seeds is extracted commercially in South America for use in coloring cheese, margarine, and other products. Certain natives color their entire bodies with this dye.

The specific name *orellana* commemorates a Spanish explorer who went to Peru with Pizarro and later descended the river now known as the Amazon. His wild tales about women warriors called "Amazonas" gave the river its name.

In central Africa is a group of medium-sized timber trees whose hard round fruits are surrounded by five spreading calyx lobes that persist; these look like red or yellow flower petals, each one measuring 1½ by 3 inches. *Monotes* is their botanical name.

In tropical west Africa *Heisteria*[24] has similarly noteworthy fruits. Aubreville[25] says the calyx "enlarges considerably and is transformed into a sort of corolla with four or five lobes of rosy violet, one and a half inches across."

Of *Aptandra*[26] the same author says: "The fruit is remarkable. The very small calyx is considerably enlarged, becoming a sort of funnel with undulating edges, of a magnificent old rose color, about two and a half inches in diameter. In the center is the little ellipsoid fruit of dark blue."

In Central and South America the showy fruits of *Triplaris* and *Ruprechtia* look like flowers, even at close range. The female trees put on great clusters of red or pink winged seeds. The male tree's flowers are inconspicuous. Both of these exotics have been planted on the South Florida toll road called Sunshine Parkway.

In western Africa both J. M. Dalziel[27] and David Fairchild[28] were struck by the beautiful crimson velvet fruits of *Cnestis ferruginea*. Dr. Fairchild wrote of a "splash of crimson among the dark green foliage of the road-side, a color even more brilliant than that of the red maple as it stands out against the dark spruce trees of Nova Scotia—the fruits of *Cnestis*." This is a shrub or small tree with insignificant flowers. The almond-shaped, two-inch fruits are in clusters at the branch tips.

Bright and decorative baubles like Christmas tree ornaments feature a small South African tree called Chinese lanterns or klapper.[29] Palmer and Pitman[30] wrote:

Passing through the Karroo in Spring, travellers often pause in astonishment at splashes of pure and vivid color among the dun scrub on koppie slopes.

These are the famous Chinese lanterns. If this little tree or bush could be easily cultivated, it would be well known because so uniquely ornamental (Unfortunately it is a difficult, short-lived plant.) The flowers are comparatively insignificant pink and somewhat bell-shaped but they develop into inflated fruits with a papery covering like those of a large gooseberry, sometimes nearly two inches in diameter, in rosy red, pink, and green, and every gradation of color between. These fruits are thickly clustered, remain on the tree for weeks, and such a tree grows splendidly against what is often a drab and monotonous background. When the seeds within are ripe, the airy inflated capsules are blown far and wide.

The akee[31] tree from Guinea, widely cultivated in Florida and the West Indies, bears bluntly triangular pear-size fruits that are first green, then pink, then bright red. A tree covered with these dangling ornaments is exceptionally handsome. At maturity the fruit splits three ways at the bottom, and flares back to expose jet-black, shiny, cherry-size seeds. The edible part of the fruit is the aril—a firm, cream-colored mass attached to the base of the seed. Fried in butter and seasoned, these are delicious. Canning and shipping them is now an industry in Jamaica. If the arils are underripe (when the fruit has not yet opened), they are poisonous; if overripe, eating them is said to be equally risky.

5. Dagger-Like Seed Pods

Dagger-like or snaky seed pods, hanging from a tree, never fail to excite curiosity. Among the most threatening are those of a Malayan forest monarch of sixty feet or more that Corner[32] calls "the tree of Damocles."[33] The saber-like pods 2 to 4 feet long and 3 inches wide, with a scimitar curve at the bottom, are suspended at the extreme tips of leafless branches. Their weight is sufficient to bend down the stems.

In Malaya also grows a dagger-tree[34] with 18-inch pods in bunches all up and down its 90-foot height. At first green, these turn brown in ripening.

The snake-tree[35] of Malaya gets its name from the 2-foot dangling pods which are twisted into a loose, extended coil.

When the cloth-of-gold tree[36] of the Transvaal goes to seed, it is covered with so many two-foot pods that, according to Palmer and Pitman[37] it appears to be weeping long thin sausages. But it is redeemed by the yellow flowers that blanket it in profusion, making it "one of the most conspicuous of all trees."

The candle-tree[38] is a 20-foot Panama evergreen bearing two-inch white funnel-shaped flowers directly on the trunk or older branches. These are followed by many dangling, cylindrical, smooth, fleshy, white or yellowish fruits which may be 40 inches long, though only 1 inch in diameter. Cattle relish them.

The horseradish-tree[39] gets its name from the taste of its root, though it is no kin to the table relish. This brittle Indian tree is remarkable in Florida because it bears locust-like white flowers every day in the year, followed by three-sided, dagger-like seed pods 12 to 18 inches long. When young these are eaten in India as a vegetable, like okra.

The hanging seed pods of another Malayan tree called *Heterophragma*,[40] occasionally seen in Florida, give the observer a creepy feeling, for they are half-twisted into a curl so that they seem to writhe all over the tree when the wind blows. They are 2 feet or more long. The large yellow cup-shaped flowers are unattractive.

6. Oversize Seeds and Seed Pods

Some tree seeds are excessive in their girth; some seed pods are giants worthy of a circus side-show.

A potful of soup can be made from one bean, if you pick it off a mora[41] tree. This is the biggest bean seed in the world; the pod usually measures about three by ten inches and contains one bean that weighs about four ounces. Each bean measures about 2½ by 4½ inches, Sturtevant[42] says, but Cooke[43] maintains they are sometimes twice as large. Brown,[44] who lived in the wilds in British Guiana, reports that the natives there boil and grate them, then mix them with cassava (tapioca) meal to eat. The taste is sweetish.

The mora-tree, however, does not produce the largest bean pods in the world. That privilege is reserved by *Entada* vines. The St. Thomas[45] or elephant creeper from southern Asia and Oceania has pods up to 6 feet long and 5 inches wide. Other *entada* vines in tropical America, Kenya,[46] and Australia[47] produce similar pods.

The button-tree[48] from Nigeria, 50 feet tall, decorates its trunk with fruits like gigantic buttons, often 10 inches in diameter and 4 inches thick. These grow flat against the bark, all up and down the trunk. When a fruit is picked, Kennedy[49] says, a thick juice exudes from the stem end, with a smell reminiscent of a brewery. Unwin[50] says the fruit contains about sixty seeds and is eaten by "elephants and other animals, porcupines especially." A related tree in the Cameroons has fruits so plump that it has acquired several vernacular names meaning "maiden's-breast tree."[51]

Just as remarkable in a different way is the skirtlike fruit crop produced by *Durio testudinarum*, a tree of the North Borneo jungle. The tree's fruits are clustered as though sitting on its lap, practically at ground level.

Although in appearance they closely resemble the edible durian, these related fruits are not for eating.

In every tropical botanical garden, the sausage-tree,[52] the calabash tree,[53] and the cannonball,[54] are conversation pieces. The mature fruits of all are inedible.[55]

The sausage-tree is so named because its fruits, suspended on long ropes under the branches, resemble great bologna sausages, usually about 2 feet long and 4 inches in diameter. The flowers which precede them hang in candelabra-like clusters, but ordinarily only one red funnelform blossom opens at a time, and then does not last, so the flowering is inconspicuous. The fruits take a year to ripen, and may not form at all unless the flowers are hand-pollinated.

The name calabash-tree[56] is ordinarily reserved for a dense, thirty-foot evergreen, rather dumpy and confused in its growth, and certainly not worth cultivating except to provide the big globular or egg-shaped fruits that cling to the branches under the foliage. Standley[57] wrote that in Central America these reach a maximum diameter of 12 inches, and continued:

One wonders at first how a tree can support such a load of fruits, that suggest pumpkins, although they are green rather than yellow. The shells of the fruits have been of great importance in household economy since the earliest human settlements, for they are used almost universally in Mexico and Central America for making cups, bottles, and all sorts of kitchen utensils. The cups, particularly those formerly used and still so employed in some localities for drinking chocolate, often are ornamented with intricate designs, and such cups must have been one of the first noteworthy articles to greet the eyes of Spanish explorers.

One of the commonest uses for calabashes today in Central America, is to make maracas—the seed-filled gourds with a handle used by Latin-American orchestras to accent their rhythm.

The fruit of the calabash-tree has been confused by many writers with the fruit of the common gourd[58] (creeping or bottle gourd), which is a vine.[59]

The cannonball is a timber tree of British Guiana but is cultivated in many tropical countries because of its curious flowers and fruits. The 6-inch blossom is an ornamented, fat, yellow, 3-inch pincushion flanked by six fleshy pink petals (see picture on page 59). It looks like a mousetrap or a comb-and-brush set. The flowers always emerge directly from the trunk. When flowering time comes, the trunk sprouts little special branches for the blossoms and these grow longer and longer from year to year as more and more flowers are added to the inflorescence. Hundreds of these

83

big blossoms cover the trunks of mature cannonball trees. The fruits, or seed pods, which follow are round balls 4 to 7 inches in diameter, reddish brown, loosely suspended on stout strings from the trunk. When the wind blows and the hard-shelled cannonballs start pounding against each other and the trunk, it is easy enough to think of cannonading.

One other fat, inedible seed pod is the fruit of the false nutmeg,[60] a tropical African tree to 80 feet. Battiscombe[61] says the very hard, smooth, woody, black, globular fruits are up to 1 foot in diameter. Hiern[62] reported that the fruit ranged from orange size to "as big as your head."

7. Chock-Full of Eatables

One curious feature of the Brazil-nut tree[63] and its cousin, the sapucaya-nut tree,[64] is the pod which contains the nuts. It has an extremely hard shell about ½ inch thick. In size and shape it somewhat resembles a husked coconut weighing 3 or 4 pounds, though in some trees the pods may be 8 inches in diameter and 15 pounds in weight. At the lower end of each pod there is a round trap door about 3 inches across. When the sapucaya nut is ripe, that trap door opens of its own accord and dumps the nuts on the ground. But on the Brazil-nut tree, the door stays shut. This sounds as if the nuts should be plentiful and cheap. They would be if monkeys and other animals did not get to the trees first. They are keen competitors for every nut, and they know how to open the trap door.

All of these trees are giants of the forest, reaching 100 feet or more, often 60 feet to the first limb. The Brazil nuts grow, of course, in Brazil. The others are scattered throughout northern South America, where the forty or more kinds of *Lecythis* trees are not well known, even to botanists. All of these trees, collectively, are called monkeypots because the fruits are used to catch monkeys. The monkey puts his hand through the trap door, grabs a nut, then cannot get his loaded paw out and will let himself be caught rather than release his grip.

One other thing curious about the monkeypot trees is the way the nuts are packed in the fruit, like sardines in a can, very systematically, yet, like olives in a bottle (or kisses from a pretty girl), get one . . . the rest come easily.

Melon-like fruits that grow on trees and are good to eat, are not entirely strange to epicures in the United States, for the papaya[65] has gained wide acceptance. These fruits are often larger than a football, though the best-flavored ones are small.

Another, a starchy fruit, is a leading article of diet with more people in the world than any other food, though to people of this country it is largely unknown. This is the breadfruit[66] which grows on a medium-sized ever-green tree native to the South Seas but is cultivated in tropical countries everywhere. The mutiny on the H.M.S. *Bounty* grew out of Captain Bligh's efforts to procure breadfruit trees in the Pacific for planting in the West Indies. Bligh had the plants on board and was headed for Jamaica when his troubles began. The trees were lost, but a second expedition succeeded.

The female flowers of the breadfruit, in a club-shaped formation, grow together in the course of several months after pollination, until they form one large fleshy mass that becomes the fruit. It is thus formed in exactly the same way as a mulberry, but in the breadfruit starchy material takes the place of the sugar and juice in the mulberry. These fruity heads are 5 to 12 inches thick, round or oblong, green when unripe, yellow brown when ripe. The exterior is usually studded with small hexagonal knobs, but some fruits are warty, scaly, or prickly, and a few varieties are smooth. The pulp inside is whitish to yellow, firm when unripe, soft and pasty when ripe. Roasted when unripe, the fruit has little flavor, though it has been likened by some to a baked potato. Half-ripe fruits are used for poi, ripe fruits for pudding. The best varieties of the breadfruit are seedless, and propagated vegetatively. Seeded breadfruit provide edible seeds as well as pulp. The figlike leaves of the tree are 1 to 2 feet long and deeply cut into several pointed lobes.

First cousin to the breadfruit is another melon-like creation, the jack-fruit (or jakfruit).[67] It is too big to hang out on the branch ends of a tree, so is usually borne directly on the trunk or stoutest limbs. In construction, it is like the breadfruit but much larger. It is usually barrel- or pear-shaped, one to three feet long, and from 10 to 20 inches in diameter. Corner[68] calls this fruit "the biggest and one of the most complicated in creation." Its color when it is ripe ranges from cream to golden yellow.

The jackfruit is fast growing, sometimes bearing at three years of age when it may be 30 or more feet high. The tree's leaves are not lobed like the breadfruit's, and are rarely larger than 3 by 7 inches.

The jackfruit is a native of India but is cultivated in all tropical countries. Though said to be insipid in flavor, it is a favorite food among East Indians, and they also roast and eat the plentiful seeds which are buried in the pulp.

Another tree with extremely large fruits is the African breadfruit[69] which belongs to the same family. Dalziel[70] says that the fruit attains eighteen inches in diameter and up to thirty pounds in weight.

PART II

Trees That Are Peculiar All Over

SEVEN

Desert Preparation for an Astronaut

Behold, I am a dry tree.   —Isaiah 56:3

Gasps of astonishment could come from explorers who wander across the surface of the moon and the planets. They may well be featured by bloated and grotesque vegetation.

Right here on earth are striking examples of such tortured scenery, particularly in the dry wastes of parts of Mexico, Madagascar, and South-West Africa, and about the Persian Gulf. The absence of rainfall in those areas turns the trees and shrubs into terrible, misshapen things beyond everyday experience. In order to survive, they become what are called succulent plants, which means they are cactus-like, having juicy tissues in which they store moisture under the protection of a tough hide. Often their leaves have been reduced by the hostile surroundings to mere points or scales or thorns that cut evaporation in the face of a broiling sun. Environment has prepared them for a desert existence.

1. The Elephant-Trees

Traveling through some parts of Baja California, one might think he was viewing a moonscape. Among the unearthly-looking sights will be a curious plant that might as well be called the elephant-tree. Its scientific name is *Pachycormus,*[1] a combination of two Greek words signifying "thick trunk." (Does the reader remember Barnum's "ponderous pachyderms"?) Whether the plant's name of "thick trunk" refers to the stem of a tree or to an elephant's nose piece makes no difference, for the tree really looks like a tired, distraught elephant.

The nineteenth-century explorer J. A. Veatch[2] found this short-trunked, very crooked tree in 1859, on stony slopes of desert mountains, its low-hung branches hugging the ground. He was astonished by such a monstrosity. Ignoring its kinship to poison ivy, he wrote:

> When loaded with its bright red flowers, the effect is strikingly beautiful, particularly when hundreds of the trees stand near each other, intertwining their boughs, and forbidding ingress to the mysterious space they cover and protect. The trunk divides into several ponderous branches that shoot off horizontally and are bent and contracted into grotesque resemblances of the flexed limbs of a corpulent human being. These huge branches often terminate suddenly in a few short twigs covered with a profusion of red flowers, reminding one of the proboscis of an elephant holding a nosegay. The resemblance is heightened by the peculiar brown skinlike epidermis that forms the outer bark, which splits and peels off annually, accommodating the increase of growth.
>
> The branches of the larger trees often shoot out to a horizontal distance of 20 feet from the trunk, thus covering an area of 40 feet in diameter. Smaller subordinate limbs spring upward from the upper side of the large boughs, and in this way give a neat oval appearance to the outline of the tree.
>
> The leaves are minute and fall off before the blossoms are fairly developed. The young tree looks a good deal like a huge radish protruding from the ground.

Howard E. Gates[3] likened *Pachycormus* to an old gnarled apple tree with the dropsy, but noticed that on the west coast where constant winds blow off the ocean, the branches point inland from the trunk for 15 or 20 feet and rise only a foot or two above the soil. He said the flowers, varying from pink to orange, are small but borne in such abundance that a flowering tree could be spotted for a mile. The tree is too tender for southern California's climate.

Another so-called elephant-tree[4] of the southwestern deserts of the United States, distantly related to the first, is a smaller tree, usually 4 to 10 feet high, with a trunk up to 2 feet in diameter. It occurs on the southern fringe of the Borrego Desert in southwestern Arizona, southeastern California, and northwestern Mexico—a hot, arid section. The tiny leaves appear after the fall rains, if any, and last as long as moisture is available. Stands of the plant are sparce and scattered. Actually the tree seems scarcely more than a shrub, although the caliper of its trunk is very

ABOVE, LEFT: The boojum tree (*Idria columnaris*) of Lower California. The flowers are borne at the tips of the tiny branchlets. (Photo: George Lindsay.) ABOVE, RIGHT: The ocotillo (*Fouquieria*), not infrequent in the deserts of the southwest United States. (Photo: T. MacDougall.) LEFT: The elephant-tree (*Pachycormus discolor*) of Baja California, which offsets its grotesque shape by bearing beautiful bright red flowers. (Photo: George Lindsay.)

BELOW: *Euphorbia* tree in Kenya, a striking example of candelabra branching. (Photo: Mrs. Karl Nibecker.)

ABOVE: Unidentified species of *Alluaudia* in Madagascar, with a pair of succulent leaves under each thorn. (Photo: Francis Hallé.)

BELOW: These cardon cacti (*Pachycereus pringlei*) of Baja California resemble the saguaro (*Cereus giganteus*). (Photo: Ralph D. Cornell.)

ABOVE: The writhing, thorny arms of *Alluaudia humberti* in Madagascar. (Photo: J. Bosser.)

ABOVE, LEFT: *Pachypodium lealii* in flower near Navindombe, Angola. The natives call it "bumbo." (Photo: J. B. Teixeira.) ABOVE, RIGHT: Trunk of the *Fagara* tree, with its knobby protuberances tipped with sharp thorns. (Photo: Francis Hallé.) BELOW, LEFT: The ghost man (*Pachypodium namaquanum*), covered with thorns. At its top it carries a tuft of wavy leaves. BELOW, RIGHT: The ghost man at flowering time, shoving aside the leaves with a burst of blossoms. (Photos: C. K. Brain.)

ABOVE, LEFT: A flask tree (*Moringa ovalifoliolata*) on a granitic mountain in the Tsumeb district of South-West Africa. (Photo: H. A. Lueckhoff.) ABOVE, RIGHT: Cucumber-trees on a dry, stony hillside of the island of Socotra in the Indian Ocean—the only member of the gourd family that becomes a tree. BELOW: *Adenium* trees on Socotra; they have their own self-contained water reservoirs in order to survive the long dry spells. (Photos: Douglas Botting.)

ABOVE: *Adenia pechuelii* in the chalk and granite mountains of the Namib Desert, South-West Africa. (Photo: Emil Jensen.) BELOW: *Pachypodium* tree in Madagascar. Looking like a lichen-covered boulder, it is a complete "tree" with woody base and short branches sprouting many leaves. (Photo: Francis Hallé.)

large for its height. The reddish bark is smooth and aromatic. When it is scratched, a red latex exudes.

2. The Boojum Tree and the Ocotillo

In the wizard's garden of Lower (Baja) California, grows a bizarre nightmare that is commonly called the boojum tree.[5] Some observers have likened it to an upside-down carrot. Its maximum diameter at the base is rarely 3 feet; it ranges upward as a slim pole sometimes as high as 70 feet. The trunk and branches are covered helter-skelter with short, thorny, leafless branchlets at the tips of which appear in season little yellowish-white flowers.

Thousands of these trees flourish in a two-hundred-mile belt on the eastern side of the Lower California peninsula, several hundred miles south of the United States–Mexican border and quite inaccessible. Most of the trees grow straight up, single spired. A few of them, high up, suddenly decide to have two or three branches straight up or at fantastic angles. Or the whole tree may arch clear over, put its top in the ground, and take root also at that end of its incredible trunk.

Walker[6] reported that bees frequently build hives inside hollow boojum trees and that "some residents of the town of Punta Prieta in the heart of the cirio country make their entire livelihood by robbing boojum hives, and they report that a big tree will frequently contain over one hundred pounds of honey." Center[7] reported that the desert Indians cut a plug from the side of the bee tree with a machete, remove the honey, then put the plug back and wait for the bees to fill the hollow again.

Joseph Wood Krutch[8] satisfied a lifelong ambition in visiting the boojum forests. He was able to compare ten-year-old photographs of the trees with the current appearance of the landscape to check the trees' rate of growth. He wrote:

> Growth is so extremely slow that in most cases ten years make no immediately obvious change . . . certainly none in the general pattern of the tree. In one case a specimen which had several very slender branches near the summit seemed, as the result of a fairly accurate estimate, to have grown about 18 inches on several of these branches or about 1.8 inches per year. Since so many of the apparently old boojums are nearly or completely unbranched, it is possible that branching is usually the result of an injury.
>
> Idria may be a relict. But there are at least two facts which seem to make that assumption improbable. For one thing, it flourishes abundantly in the one place where it does grow and is obviously reseeding itself since young plants from 6 to 8 inches up to 6 or 8 feet tall are not uncommon.

Notoriously, rodents attack seedlings; and if there are many rodents, none may survive. Perhaps boojum seeds germinate whenever conditions are favorable to them but survive only if, for several years following, the rodent population is at a low level. That would explain the fact, obvious enough in Baja, that young specimens are found in groups of about the same apparent age, some groups being composed of individuals apparently years older than those of any other group while none of intermediate size can be found. This certainly suggests that successful reproduction takes place only at intervals separated by several—possibly a considerable number—of years, as one would expect if the establishment of a new generation requires some unusual condition like a year favorable to germination followed by several unfavorable to rodents.

Standley[9] called the wood of the boojum trees "soft and spongy" and Father Francisco Clavijero,[10] who published the first account of them in 1789, recorded that the juicy trunk, even when dried out, was no good for fuel, although "in the mission of San Francisco de Borja they used to burn it for lack of other firewood."

Close kin of the boojum and almost as queer is the ocotillo,[11] with some ten species flourishing in the driest parts of Mexico and Arizona. These trees make clumps of thorny, arching, snaky stems, each clothed its full length after a rainy spell with leaves on short spurs and terminating in spring with clusters of scarlet tubular flowers that are startlingly showy for so ugly a plant. Krutch[12] calls attention to the curious spines on both the ocotillo and the boojum. These, he says, are produced in a fashion characteristic of no other family. He says:

> Look at the top of a branch which happens to be growing and you will notice that the new leaves are quite different from those on the older parts of the plant. Instead of being sessile (or sitting) right on the stem itself, they have, like most leaves, a stem, stalk, or, as the botanists call it, a petiole. But when the time comes for one of these new leaves to drop, a very odd thing happens. Instead of falling with the leaf in the usual fashion, the petiole remains attached to the main stem, develops a sharp point, and hardens into a thorn. When next the leaves come out on this branch, they will be sessile at the base of the thorn, which will never again be produced at that point.

3. The Thorn Trees

In the deserts of southern Madagascar, East Africa, and southwestern United States, grow three quite unrelated kinds of thorn trees—so-called here because all of them have little or no foliage. Presumably because of the extremely dry climates where they grow, thorns have largely taken the place of leaves, as they allow less moisture to evaporate.

Perhaps the most horrible of these plants, because of their writhing, contorted branches, are four kinds of *Alluaudia* trees at the southern tip of Madagascar. Even scientists know very little about them; a few scholars call them *Didierea*.[13] They dwell in a hostile, barren land, and as though in supplication for relief from torture they reach skyward 20 feet. They are fit ornaments for the moon.

Southern Madagascar has never been explored thoroughly by botanists and many plants there have never been described. The first specimens of an *Alluaudia* were brought back to England in 1880 and botanists at Kew had a difficult time trying to place it in the right family of plants. It looked like a *Euphorbia* but there were too many differences. Later, other botanists decided it should be included in the soapberry family (*Sapindaceae*), but it was a misfit there too. Scholars who have studied the subject most recently have created an entirely new family for it, the *Didiereaceae*.

The photographs of these strange Madagascar trees (page 90) immediately suggest to Americans the thorn trees of their own southwestern deserts and nearby Mexico, the gigantic organ cacti. Best known is the saguaro,[14] a tree of 20 to 60 feet in Arizona and Mexico, usually single-stemmed, strongly ribbed, sometimes with one or more branches. Similar but smaller and less frequently observed is the related cardon[15] in Lower California. Ordetx Ros in *Flora Apícola de la America Tropical* says it takes these trees 30 years to reach a height of 4 feet; thereafter they grow about 3 inches a year. They rarely live more than a hundred and fifty years.

These American monstrosities have their counterparts among the *Euphorbia* trees in tropical Africa and Madagascar, which are usually provided with pencil-like or spiky branchlets, sometimes tipped with green leaves. Although they often bear bright flowers, nobody would ever suspect that the plants were cousins of the poinsettia.

Some of these branch like normal trees.[16] Others branch like enormous candelabra; one of them,[17] in the mountains of East Africa, reaches a height of 90 feet. A smaller tree of the same style of growth[18] reaches 40 feet and is found growing on ant hills all over central Africa. Another of these strange thorn trees,[19] usually seen growing on escarpments, has branches that are curved like a bow. All are big trees.

4. *The Grapple Tree*

Another Madagascar contribution to the array of ugly desert succulents is the grapple plant.[20] The snaky branches of this distorted tree stretch out over the ground and are often partly buried. From these come upright leafy stems bearing bright yellow or pink flowers, quite handsome.[21] The vicious part of the plant is the seed pod which follows the flowers. This is a shell-like capsule, 5 inches across, constructed like so many interlaced fish hooks and designed to fasten itself to any creature that touches it. It is dangerous to people and animals alike.

Just how horrible these pods can be was depicted by a South African naturalist.[22] He wrote:

> A springbok, leaping and curvetting in the gladness of his heart, sets his foot down upon the capsule. The curved arms, elastic as whalebone, give a little, and the hoof comes down upon the tough seed-vessel. The hooks catch on all round the buck's hock and every kick and scuffle drives them farther into the flesh. The luckless beast is fairly shod with this grappler, and many a weary mile must he limp along in torment before he has trodden the thing into pieces and poached the seeds into the ground. And this is the way, at cost of much weariful agony to the antelopes, that the grapple plant ensures its seasonal life from year to year.

5. *The Knobby Tree*

On the eastern seaboard of South Africa and in the Transvaal, the knobby tree or knobwood[23] grows in moist forests. In less polite circles its vernacular name in Afrikaans is *perdepram,* literally "horse's teats." All the names arise from the terrific 3-inch knobs that stud the trunk; these are usually tipped by sharp thorns.

Lueckhoff[24] wrote of this tree:

> *Fagara* is a common tree in the temperate, evergreen forests which occur in the summer rainfall areas. The tree reaches a maximum breast height diameter of perhaps 18 inches and a height of 70 feet, but is generally much smaller. The knobs on *Fagara* vary greatly. They can be very pronounced and abundant to relatively small and scattered. They are always more abundant in the lower parts of the bole and thin out rapidly higher up the stem. In the crown they are generally absent or very poorly developed.
>
> The knobs on *Fagara* are modified thorns but their purpose is obscure and I am not aware of any theories having been advanced. Thorns are more commonly found on trees and shrubs in drier areas and their purpose is presumably to protect them from grazing animals. This is not the case in *Fagara* which grows in fairly moist, dense forest where it is in no danger from grazers.

Verdoorn[25] reported seeing the bowl of a pipe made of one of the conical protuberances which stud the bark.

Palmer and Pitman[26] give "fever tree" as another common name and describe it:

A tall knobwood, with a brown trunk studded with knobs like small stout horns, is an extraordinary and unforgettable sight. . . . These knobs are part of the bark only and do not show as knots in the wood as might be expected; yet, like the trunk of the tree, they have distinct annual layers. They are fairly easily broken off the trunk (which is left intact) and are light in weight.

6. The Half Men or Ghost Men

So frightening and grotesque are some of the *Pachypodium* trees that grow in Angola and South-West Africa, that the natives call them ghost men, and avoid by night the desert areas where they grow. Their fears go far back in their tribal history.

E. J. Alexander[27] says the twenty species have short-lived leaves, and large showy flowers—white, pink, or reddish. These monstrosities go to extremes: some are excessively thorny, their trunks and branches completely covered with spines; others have no prickles at all.

Most astonishing are the ghost men.[28] Findlay[29] wrote:

This is a most fantastic plant and its origin is the basis of an old legend. The creator, taking pity on a band of Hottentots fleeing across the desert and wishing to protect them from their enemies, changed them into plants which could withstand the pitiless desert. As they were fleeing northwards, the Half Men or Ghost Men as these plants are called locally, always grow with their crown of leaves facing towards the north, that is, towards the sun in the Southern Hemisphere.

Gaunt and eerie they grow as silent sentinels of the desert, yet in early September they blossom as the rose, their leafy crowns being covered with tubular reddish-brown flowers, presenting an unforgettable spectacle to those daring to visit this remote area. The spiny stems may be 5-6 feet high and can be often a hundred years old.

Although the type locality is cited as Sperlingputz in South-West Africa, more plants occur in the arid, mountainous areas south of the Orange River than to the north of it. The Half Man does not take kindly to cultivation away from his native habitat and in South Africa, unless planted under specially constructed shelters, tends to rot off at the base and die.

Pachypodium namaquanum is now protected by law and removal or damage to plants is punishable by a heavy fine. Fortunately, however, much of the area where they are found is harsh rugged country, some of it falling within the forbidden diamond areas.

An amazing thing about the ghost men is the intense and penetrating odor of the flowers. Brain[30] reports that the blossoms are so strongly scented of jasmine that he has smelled them a quarter of a mile away.

Hutchinson,[31] exploring in East Africa, found a similar, very thorny species[32] growing as a low, fleshy bush about a foot high with spirally arranged, narrow, hairy leaves.

F. J. Chittenden[33] refers to *Pachypodium* species as shrubs, but this classification is inept. They have woody trunks, and few of them branch from the base. Corner[34] calls them cactus-like trees without internodes, the small leaves occurring only on the top of the stem.[35] Even the extra peculiar star-of-the-Lundi[36] (the Lundi is a river in Southern Rhodesia), described in section 10 of this chapter, is woody.

Another misshapen *Pachypodium* tree was discovered by Welwitsch[37] a hundred years ago in Angola. The natives there call it bumbo.[38] It is a small tree, ranging from 10 to 18 feet high with a curious cactus-like habit. Its trunk is 8 to 16 inches in diameter at the base, and bristled on all sides with three-pronged purple spines. The trunk is conical, tapering rapidly, and toward the top it branches sparingly and without obvious pattern. The juice exuded from a wound on the trunk is watery and sticky with a resin, but not milky. The fragrant flowers are large, handsome, bicolored (rosy purple and white), and borne in clusters at the branch tips while the tree is bare of leaves, which is practically all the year, although Welwitsch reported that the tree bore fruit only in summer.

Elsewhere in South-West Africa are forms of *Pachypodium* that have no thorns at all on their stems, although they are very fat and ugly like many of the other species. Conspicuous among these is a low tree,[39] described from this German territory as long ago as 1885. Another of these misshapen monstrosities[40] grows in Otavi in the northern part of South-West Africa. The flowers of this species are larger than in the others and much ruffled on the petal edges.

7. The Flask-Tree

A tree's best friend in the desert is the soft wood of its trunk because it will absorb and store enormous quantities of water when the rains come, and make it available to the tree over a period of months when drought prevails. A good example is the flask-tree (*Moringa*)[41] that grows in the mountains of South-West Africa. In the driest areas its trunk becomes enormously swollen; in moister areas the trunk is still soft and spongy but does not attain gargantuan form.

This tree is closely related to an Indian tree[42] cultivated in Florida as an ornamental. The misshapen African tree also is occasionally seen in both Florida and southern California, but the probabilities are that with adequate rainfall it will not develop an overfat trunk.

The botanist[43] who described this species of *Moringa* said it was a tree 2 to 6 meters (20 feet) high and 1 meter thick, but in the wild many of them are much larger. The bark is a smooth, light gray and the wood very spongy. Dinter called it *"sehr schwammigen."* The tree is not hollow, but its soft wood stores water, as do true succulents, and the wood has no commercial use. Dinter found the tree growing on granite mountains at Okozongominja and in several other localities. He wrote: "I find the taste of the leaves and the flowers much more resembling Capuchin cress than those of *Capparis."*

8. *The Cucumber-Tree*

The island of Socotra is a red dot on the map where the Gulf of Aden meets the Indian Ocean off the east coast of Africa. It is a mysterious mountain land of cave-dwelling aboriginal people, a land of strange and primitive forms of plant life, a land of Bedouins, among whom, despite the influences of Mohammedanism, witchcraft prevails.[44]

It is from this faraway land that two trees rise up to embellish our moonscape, two of the strangest trees in the world and fit subjects for lunar gardens.

The first is the cucumber-tree.[45] It is the only tree in the gourd family, and an astonishing individual it is with its fat belly, thorny leaves, and bristly fruit much like the common cucumber. Douglas Botting[46] wrote of it:

> Undoubtedly the most spectacular and characteristic forms of life on Socotra are the trees which give the mountains the appearance of a strangely fertile moonscape. Toadlike cucumber-trees crowd the lower hill slopes, their grey trunks distended with milky sap like elephantiatic limbs, surmounted with a brief fringe of stiff crinkly leaves. These trees produce a small yellow flower and a small useless fruit—a cucumber, I suppose.

Both Sir Isaac Bailey Balfour[47] and A. Lemée[48] have provided detailed technical descriptions of the plant.

The cucumber-tree never attains great height, but its soft, bare, gouty stems, surmounted by a few slightly pendent branches, give it a weird look. Wellsted[49] says:

> The most singular among the trees are two varieties which are called, in the language of the island, Assett and Camhane; both grow in very rocky places, and derive nourishment from soil lodged in cells and cavities. The whole diameter of their trunks consists of a soft, whitish cellular substance so easily cut through that we could divide the largest of them with a common knife. Camels and sheep feed on the leaves of the Camhane, but reject those of the Assett. A milk-white juice exudes from the trunk and leaves of both, the nature of which is so acrid, that if it penetrates to the eyes the pain is almost intolerable. Several stems branch forth from the same family of roots, and the Assett trees mostly divide, at a short distance from the ground, into

several branches. From the relative proportion between their height and diameter, and the few leaves of foilage borne by them compared to their bulk, the most singular and grotesque appearances are often produced; some are not more than 5 feet in height, while their base covers a greater extent in diameter. Both varieties, during the northeast monsoon, bear a beautiful red flower.

Balfour[50] quotes this paragraph from Wellsted, expresses the opinion that the "Assett" trees are not cucumber-trees at all but Adenium (q.v.), and insists that the cucumber-tree's flowers are yellow, not red.

9. The Adenium Trees

Nothing could be uglier than the Adenium[51] trees that grow on the island of Socotra. Contrariwise, nothing could be lovelier than the flowers of some of the Adenium species found in central Africa.[52] This is a strange group of highly succulent trees, with excessively fat trunks and few leaves.

Botting[53] found the Adenium trees on Socotra spectacular—enormous growths on the rocky hillsides. Like the toad-swollen cucumber-trees, Adenium became more abundant higher up in the mountains, and as Botting saw them, "even more bloated and grotesque." He wrote:

Often two or three squashy trunks will spring from the same base, each with a crest of stiff, formal leaves which begin to fall when the red blossom comes.

The milky juice of the roots of some species of Adenium in tropical Africa is used in preparing the arrow poison used by many bush tribes. This is especially true of one[54] found in the Otavi, in northern South-West Africa.

A curious tree, much like Adenium in appearance, but related instead to Ficus, is a Dorstenia[55] on the island of Socotra. It has the same stout stem, with leaves clustered at the ends of thick branches. The plant bleeds freely when wounded, yielding a yellow, viscid juice that soon hardens into a yellowish-brown cake.

10. The Anomalous Trio

Three trees that may not be trees compose the final sketch in this discussion of succulents. They have huge woody bases or trunks that do not branch from the bottom, which certainly entitles them to classification as trees. But if the reader disagrees, let him decide; if they are not trees, what are they?

The first is a dry mountain plant of South-West Africa called *Adenia*.[56] It has a fat bottom and it grows upright. Alexander[57] wrote:

There are numerous species of *Adenia* with huge, swollen, stem-bases seated on the ground or half buried, with upright, sprawling or even climbing annual stems arising from the crown. These stems, which are usually succulent, are sometimes very thorny, at other times smooth or angled, and they bear orange or yellow funnelform flowers, followed by berries of a similar color. Strangest in the family is *A. pechuelii*,[58] which grows on vertical cliff walls in Damaraland, South-West Africa. The plant is composed of 20 or 30 swollen, fleshy, globular heads, fused at the base into a single body, which is anchored into rock clefts by a single tap root. Each head is topped by a tuft of short, twiggy branches with tiny narrow leaves and equally tiny flowers in the leaf axils. The mature plant is said to weigh a half ton.

The second monstrosity is a dwarf tree, 2½ feet high, that looks like a fat white dog, with too many legs, lying on its back. This Angola native is a species of *Cissus*.[59] Its succulent, fat, bulblike, woody trunk has a smooth green bark over which, as the tree gets older, grows a whitish-brown skin that peels, in the manner of a white birch. The inconspicuous yellowish-green flowers with fleshy petals are followed by red-violet fruits the size of a pea. Chittenden[60] calls this a greenhouse plant "of little beauty."

The third monstrosity harks back to *Pachypodium*, of which several kinds were described in section 6 of this chapter. The kind called star-of-the-Lundi[61] in central Africa "is a succulent shrub or very short tree with a much enlarged bole, often rising little above the ground, resembling a lichen-covered boulder, from which the spinous branches spring irregularly and rather unnaturally."[62]

EIGHT

Obesity among Trees

They are inclosed in their own fat. —PSALMS 17:10

Perhaps a clinic should be established for the benefit of overfat trees. Up to this time the obese of the arboreal world have had no one to sympathize with them, and no prospect of a reducing diet to lower the waistline. The fat trees have been ostracized, put in museums, and excluded from cultivated gardens. Nobody loves a fat tree. (But they are eye-catching!)

Perhaps these ponderous plants dream of slim figures, willowy shapes, and svelte lines. If they ever achieve such a miracle, they can show their grandchildren the following pages from the memory books of five distinguished inflated tree families, and the youngsters can point to the funny pictures and howl, "O, look how fat Mama was!"

1. *The Baobab Trees*[1]

In many ways the baobabs are among the most remarkable trees in the world. The chief African species[2] and the northern Australian giant[3] are cultivated everywhere in the tropics for their several peculiarities. They are famous for four things:

(1) They live to incredible ages. Michael Adanson, a botanical explorer in Senegal, for whom the genus was named *Adansonia*, found a tree in 1794 that measured 30 feet in diameter. He calculated its age as 5150 years. Alexander von Humboldt called the baobab "the oldest organic monument of our planet." Palgrave,[4] however, says that the great age of the baobabs is debatable, as there are no annual rings.

(2) The diameter of the tree, often 30 feet, is out of all proportion to its height, which is usually 40, and but rarely 60 feet. Ernest ("Chinese") Wilson found old trees, when bare of their leaves, to be fascinatingly ugly, like "a gigantic crow's nest." In *Aristocrats of the Trees* he wrote:

> It is the bulky trunk that is so imposing, being often 100 feet in girth and clothed with a smooth bark. Thick as is the trunk, a bullet from a rifle of high velocity will pass right through it, for its tissues are soft and pulpy. On an island immediately above the Victoria Falls of the Zambezi River, the missionary explorer, David Livingstone, carved his name on a baobab tree when he discovered this eighth wonder of the world.

The wood is soft, and subject to the attacks of fungus which destroys its life, and renders the part affected easily hollowed out. This is done by the natives, and within these hollows they suspend the dead bodies of those who are refused the honor of burial. There they become mummies— perfectly dry and well preserved—without any further preparation or embalmment. Livingston speaks of a hollow trunk of a baobab, within which twenty to thirty men could lie down with ease. Palgrave says: "The vitality of these trees is amazing, and even when the interior has been burned out by veldt fires, the trees still flourish. If bark is stripped off, it grows again. Owing to the habitual lack of water in the areas where the trees grow, their roots often extend one hundred yards from the tree."

(3) All parts of the tree are exceedingly useful to the native populations. The bark of the baobab furnishes a fiber which is made into ropes, and in Senegal woven into cloth. The fiber is so strong as to give rise to a common saying in Bengal: "As secure as an elephant bound with a baobab rope."

(4) The most astonishing thing about baobab trees is that they do not continue to get larger year after year. Sometimes they get smaller! G. L. Guy, an experienced forester at the National Museum, Bulawayo, Rhodesia, has been keeping records on a plot of baobab trees for thirty-five years. He shows that "Tree No. 6" when measured for girth at breast height, made these changes:

Year:	1931	1938	1946	1949	1953	1966
Girth in inches:	222	220	212	216	221	214

Guy attributes the shrinkages to droughts, and the expansions to wet years, though he has not yet completed the correlation of all data involved.

The baobab in Africa is the most valuable of vegetables. Its leaves are used for leaven, its bark for cordage and thread. In Senegal the natives use the pounded bark and the leaves as we do pepper and salt. The leaves are eaten as a vegetable, often mixed with other food, and are considered cooling and useful in restraining excessive perspiration. The fruit is much used by the natives of Sierra Leone, on Africa's western coast. It contains a farinaceous pulp full of seeds—which taste like gingerbread—and has a pleasant, acid flavor. The seeds in Angola are pounded and made into meal for food in times of scarcity.

One of the most astonishing things about baobab trees is that they get chopped down and eaten—completely consumed—by elephants. They might be termed the greatest of animal snack bars. W. Robertson-Bullock, senior ranger of the Northern Rhodesia forest department, wrote of seeing almost every baobab along an inspection route damaged by elephants. Some of the trees had been felled and almost completely eaten, from leaves and twigs down to the trunk. The fine, damp inner fibers of the trunk had been dropped to the calves by the cow elephants.[5]

Anton-Smith[6] of Northern Rhodesia wrote:

> It is not known why the elephants rip the trees. The theory is put forward that their habitat is changing and they are seeking additional sources of a certain nutriment, as it is only within the past ten years that this has been noticed in Northern Rhodesia.
>
> One game guard reported that he had found a skeleton of an elephant beneath an uprooted baobab; his idea was that the elephant had attacked the tree so savagely that it had fallen on him and crushed him.

2. The Revered Ombú

The perfect tree for public parks has been found in South America. It never has to be replaced because it seemingly never dies. It makes lots of shade for its great branches extend up and out 50 feet or more. Insects dislike the tree, so those who relax in its shelter are never bothered by ants, flies, gnats, or mosquitoes. Best of all, the gigantic roots of the tree protrude well above the soil to form ponderous benches all around. It is probably the only tree in the world that provides seats for those who want to sit in its shade. And then, as a special boon to park administration and police, the tree at night gives off a vile odor[7] that keeps loiterers and spooning couples from using it as a rendezvous. What more could be expected of a park tree?

These points add up to describe a rapid-growing tree called ombú or umbú.[8] It grows wild in Argentina, Uruguay, Paraguay, southern Brazil, and Peru, and has become naturalized in many parts of the Old World. It is an oversize edition of the common American pokeweed, and is more like a gigantic herb than a tree. Its trunk has no annual rings because it consists of loose, fibrous layers, often several hundred of them. The living trees are unaffected by grass fires, for their trunks and branches are 80 per cent water. Hence, when green the tree will not burn at all; but when dry it can be consumed by fire like newspaper without giving off heat.

The ombú is beloved by Argentine people above all other trees, and it figures conspicuously in their history, legends, literature, and even mythology. It withstands heat and drought, it is undamaged by the violent windstorms that sweep the pampas, it provides excellent shade in regions where other trees will not grow, and although a hard freeze knocks off its leaves they are quickly replaced.

Plenty of flowers are produced by ombú trees, but the males are on one tree and the females on another. Because birds and bees avoid the trees, they depend on vagrant winds to achieve pollination. This method is highly ineffective because ombú trees are notably solitary; they never grow in colonies, and the nearest possible mate is usually far distant. When seeds are produced and fall to the ground, they almost never become established. Either the ground under the ombú tree is too dry to permit germination, or if the seed germinates the plants are killed by drought, too much shade, or too severe frosts.

Walter L. Swindon[9] wrote of the traditional respect this tree inspires:

> Probably the criollo affection for it is to be found in the fact that it serves as a traveller's guide, by which name it is often known, indicating as it does the situation of some native ranch or more pretentious dwelling where one is certain of receiving unbounded hospitality. . . . The Ombú has been planted, by unknown hands, in almost every part of Argentina.

Allan W. Eckert[10] wrote that no one has ever seen an ombú dead of natural causes, diseased, decayed, or dried with age. Although an ombú is extremely long-lived, there is a constant rejuvenation of its outer surface.

"All of the inside of the massive trunk is lifeless," Eckert remarked, "including the root portion going far underground. Yet the surface is as strong and fresh as it was hundreds of years ago and even the dead portion is believed used as a reservoir for water storage. . . . Although the tree may look incredibly old if viewed from a distance, actually it is a young surface enfolding within itself all the past generations of life."

3. Bottle-Trees

The dictionary says a bottle is a hollow receptacle with a narrow neck and no handles. This almost fits what Australians call their bottle-tree,[11] except that is is built like a Thermos,[12] with compartments.

The bottle-tree really looks like a bottle, being broadest in the middle. In the lower part of the tree, between the inner bark and the wood, is a compartment that holds a considerable quantity of water. This is important to travelers because the tree grows only in the drier parts of northern Queensland, never in the rain forests.

RIGHT, TOP: A baobab tree (*Adansonia gregorii*) in northern Queensland. (Photo: Australia News and Information Bureau.) RIGHT, CENTER: An enormous baobab tree of northern Australia, believed to be two thousand years old. Its hollow trunk was once used as the town jail. (Photo: Courtesy of *The Age*, Melbourne.) RIGHT, BOTTOM: The ombú tree (*Phytolacca dioica*) of Argentina, which provides its own bench. (Photo: Geronimo Sosa.)

LEFT: Kapok trees in Ecuador. (Photo: Ward's Natural Science Establishment, Inc.) BELOW, LEFT: A bottle-tree (*Brachychiton rupestris*). This Australian tree stores water in its trunk and can go for long periods without rain. (Photo: Australian News and Information Bureau.) BELOW, RIGHT: The Cuban belly palm (*Colpothrinax wrightii*). (Photo: Russell Seibert.)

108

There is a second reservoir in the middle of the tree. According to Audas,[13] this contains "a great quantity of sweet, edible, juice-like jelly which is wholesome and nutritious." Just imagine! A cafeteria in the middle of the desert! E. E. Lord[14] goes farther and says that this gummy substance, also the young roots and the fruits, are all valued native foods while the leaves make excellent fodder for domestic animals.

The bottle-tree, whose trunk is sometimes 6 feet in diameter, is also called the barrel-tree. It reaches 50 feet in height and is crowned with a large, dense head of narrow, 3-inch leaves. The foliage is rather variable and resembles that of the related tree which the Australians call kurrajong.[15] The tree is frost-tender when young. Audas says that from the bark of this much-loved, curious tree the natives obtain a useful fiber.

4. Kapok—the Pillow Stuffer

The kapok-tree,[16] which provides silky fibers for stuffing pillows and life preservers, is native to tropical America, but it grows in all tropical countries. Chief supplies of kapok pillow stuffing come from Java.[17] In Africa, according to Dalziel,[18] the kapok has become the biggest of all trees. In some places it is called the silk-cotton tree.

In its habits it is thoroughly disorganized, for some trees (chiefly young ones) have spiny trunks, others smooth; some branches may be leafless, some may hold the old foliage, and others may be sprouting new foliage, all on the same tree. Similarly, trees in the forest may produce flowers progressively on different branches, or only on some branches, in any year. Some trees have spiny branches and some have smooth; the fruits vary in size and shape, and the floss may be white or tinted. Some fruits pop open when ripe and dump their floss on the ground; others do not.

The most conspicuous feature of the kapok is its enormity. With a possible height of 150 feet, it has a trunk sometimes 40 feet in circumference, often with huge buttresses. These start 12 to 15 feet up on the trunk and extend far out in all directions—15 feet or more—but they are invariably of uniform thickness, usually 6 to 12 inches.

The kapok has small, unattractive, dirty-white tassel-like flowers, which appear ordinarily every other year. Rendle[19] says of it:

> The silk-cotton tree drops its leaves in the late autumn or winter months, but flowers only in alternate years. In a flowering season the leaves drop off usually in November or December, and immense quantities of blossoms appear in January or February at the ends of the branches. The seed-pods are well developed, sometimes even ripe, before the young leaves appear

again in April or May. In the following season, when flowers are not produced, the young leaves appear as early as the end of January, so that in this
case the tree is not without leaves very long. This alternation usually affects
the whole tree, but sometimes one side of the tree flowers, while the other
is full of leaf without flowers, and vice versa the following season. The leaves
occasionally fall as early as the end of July.

The flowers are followed by 4-inch capsules filled with a silklike cotton
in which are embedded numerous small brown seeds. The trees are
planted in many places for their shade. Standley[20] calls it one of the
most celebrated trees of tropical America, and one of the three or four
largest trees of Central America, noteworthy for its ample, depressed
crown. He notes further:

> The cotton is employed in vast quantities in Europe and North America. . . .
> The greater part of the commercial kapok is exported from western Africa
> and the East Indies. The wood . . . is pinkish white or ashy brown, weak
> and soft, but firm and rather substantial considering its light weight. It is not
> durable. The oil expressed from the seeds has been utilized in some regions
> for illumination and for soap making.

Dalziel[21] says:

> In life-saving apparatus, kapok is superior to cork, which has a weight-sup-
> porting capacity about one-fifth that of kapok. A lifebelt stuffed with 2
> pounds of kapok has a carrying capacity of 50 pounds. In retention of
> buoyancy kapok suffers a loss of only 10 per cent after immersion for thirty
> days, and after drying it fully regains its original supporting power. The
> floss, both of *Ceiba* and *Bombax*,[22] is used as tinder with flint and steel;
> for this purpose it must be perfectly dry, and it is obtained by roasting the
> pod, the carbonized fibre being kept carefully in a leather pouch or in a
> hollow hard-shelled nut. The dry floss is very inflammable, and villages with
> many silk-cotton trees have sometimes had to be abandoned owing to the
> danger of fire. In India it is used in the manufacture of fireworks.

5. The Cuban Belly Palm

The inelegant common name of belly palm[23] has affixed itself to a curious
palm in Cuba. About halfway up, its tall trunk is swollen like a snake
that has swallowed a guinea pig.

In Cuba the utilitarians manufacture casks, beehives, water troughs,
and even small boats out of the first available belly palm. The trees grow
extensively on the Isle of Pines and on the sandy plains of western Pinar
del Río, often in association with pines. This palm so far has been a
challenge to growers; it has not yet been successfully cultivated in Florida
or elsewhere.[24]

NINE

The Lily Hexapod

I am . . . the lily of the valleys.   —Song of Solomon 2:1

The lily family is one of the biggest in the plant world—and cosmopolitan. Some of the nearly four thousand kinds are trees. A few have been on earth for a million years, and look it! The present generation, straggling down through unnumbered aeons, is rather the worse for wear. The senior citizens of the group are really antiques and do not belong in the Space Age. They should be pressed between pages of a book, then filed in the archives of history to remind future generations what the world looked like when dinosaurs prowled.

Unfortunately in this book there is room to describe only a few of these strange relics of the past.

1. *The Black-Boys*

The world's first plastics factories antedated the du Ponts by a million years. Remnants of those manufacturing enterprises are still operating in Australia without benefit of patents, patronage, or publicity.

In scattered areas all over the down-under continent, grow lilylike plants that in Western Australia are called black-boys,[1] in Queensland grass-trees, and in South Australia yaccas.[2] About a dozen species are known, ranging from 4 to 20 feet in height. Their scientific name, *Xanthorrhoea*, means literally "yellow flow," a recognition of the thick yellow sap that exudes around the bases of the 3-foot, lilylike leaves that arise from the heart of the plant. Chemists call this sap an acaroid resin, which puts it in the group of modern plastics that are used to make domes in aircraft.

On the black-boys, this sap is thick and does not run far. It forms a coating around the leaf bases and then solidifies. When the plant gets ready to develop new leaves, they must rise above the previous crop, so they push upward from the center, or heart, of the plant. Around their bases a new layer of resin oozes forth and hardens. This continues year after year, the resin piling up until it becomes, in effect and function, a tree trunk. It is not a trunk in the normal sense; its interior consists of fibrous leaf bases frozen into the resin. And there is no bark. Nourishment passes to the treetop through the heart. That column of solidified resin, or plastic, is harvested (by chopping down the tree, of course) and utilized in the manufacture of sealing wax, varnish, dyes, and picric acid. It has even been used in making candy.[3]

How long it takes for this original plastics factory to pile up a harvestable crop, is a matter of dispute. The Australian News and Information Bureau[4] maintains that "a 10-foot tree is 1,000 years old." One Australian botanist[5] says: "Stems over 5 to 6 feet may be 50 to 100 years old."

Another[6] spent twelve years trying to determine the age of living grasstrees. He learned that mature plants grow fairly rapidly, "but the rate of growth of young plants up to, say, 5,000 years old is much slower and variable." He continues:

Methods used have now been reduced to a check of leaf growth. Mature trees are classed as those having a "trunk" above ground level. The "trunk" consists of a fibrous core, surrounded by thickened leaf bases, lying close together, radiating almost horizontally. It is comparatively simple to count the 8,000 or so leaves on such a tree, measure the rate of growth of the leaves, and by calculation, from their number and the dimensions of their bases and the "trunk," to arrive at an approximate growth rate for the tree. Such a calculation for a tree three feet high gives a growth rate of about one foot in 120 years. . . .

It has been found that the rate of growth does not proceed at the above rate until the tree's "trunk" grows above ground level. Observations are therefore being concentrated on plants having no such "trunk."

An interesting feature of young plants is that only their leaves project through the soil, in vertical growth from the crown, usually between 3 inches and 11 inches below soil level. It has not been determined whether the plants germinate at soil level or at a depth. Observations support the proposition that soil accumulation accounts largely for their depth. . . .

Plants having from seven to 1,400 leaves have been checked; the average annual linear rate or growth of their leaves is 452 mm. and the annual increment is approximately 2½ leaves. . . .

It is possible to calculate the approximate ages of such plants, but between their ages and the ages of old plants, there is a wide gap where nothing is known.

The plant with 1,400 leaves was a very young plant, the youngest plant that could be found in an area. Its crown was 280 mm. below soil level. . . . Its growing crown was 25 mm. above its root crown and all its leaves, both living and dead, were counted, totalling 1,400. . . .

Assuming that its average annual increment was as high as 2½ leaves . . . an age of 560 years would apply. Its height of 25 mm. was one-twelfth of the distance it had grown towards the present soil level. It could therefore be 6,720 years old by the time it reached maturity at soil level, but in 6,160 years from now, where is the soil level likely to be? There was nothing unusual about the situation of the plant. The soil was sand and the site was the top of a hill.

Lord[7] wrote: "No record of Australian shrubs would be complete without reference to these extraordinary plants. . . . The flowers are on a stout spike 5 to 10 feet long, resembling a giant bulrush. Established specimens will not transplant. Beekeepers avoid the plants as their heavy deposits of resin at the base of the leaves is collected by bees and is undesirable. A curious thing about the flowers is that they always open on the north side first."

In describing the Australian bushland, Audas[8] noted that in several districts, grass-trees form a conspicuous feature of the landscape, the tallest species, Xanthorrhoea arborea, attaining 20 feet or more. Flowering is irregular, he said, and usually takes place after a bush fire.

2. The Dragon's-Blood Trees

Weirdest of all the lilies in the world are the dragon's-blood trees[9] of Socotra, an island in the Indian Ocean. They get their name from the blood-red resin that oozes from their trunks. Botting[10] called them the most spectacular of all the eerie trees on that island,[11] with an appearance as strange as their name. He found them everywhere, dotted along the skyline, projecting precariously from every crag, looking "like umbrellas blown inside out."

The Socotra tree is closely allied to dragon's-blood trees in Somaliland, Abyssinia, and the Canary Islands. They are all very ancient relics in the liliaceous genus called Dracaena. Some forty species have been described and a few are cultivated in Florida and California gardens, but the trees in these four places are unique in exuding bloody splashes of resin on their trunks. Botting explains:

The Socotrans refer to the cinnabar-like resin[12] that exudes from these trees as the Blood of the Two Brothers, a reference that recalls an old Indian Legend from which the Socotrans themselves probably derived it. According to this legend dragons were always fighting elephants. They had a passion for elephant's blood. They used to twine themselves round the elephant's trunk and bite behind the elephant's ear. Then they drank all the blood in one gulp. But on one auspicious occasion the dying elephant, falling to the ground, crushed the dragon beneath it. The matter exuding from the dragon together with a mixture of the blood of the two animals was called cinnabar and the name was applied to the rich red earth where the red sulphide of mercury occurred, and later to the gum of the dragon's-blood tree. This legend accounts for the English popular name given to the resin of the tree—dragon's blood—and for the Socotran name—Blood of the Two Brothers.

According to the Hindu religious tradition the elephant and the dragon were closely related: the members of the Brahman triad were Brahma (the Creator, in the shape of an elephant), Vishnu (the Preserver) and Siva (the Destroyer, usually in the shape of a cobra, equivalent to a dragon). The combat between the elephant and the dragon, between the Creator and the Destroyer, the forces of life and death, was eternal. The fact that a reference to this Hindu concept occurs in Socotran mythology establishes that Indian contacts with Socotra must have been much closer in the past than they are now, an hypothesis for which there is plenty of other evidence.

The dragon's-blood trees in the Canary Islands[13] are unique in having their lives divided into three distinct periods—juvenility, maturity, senility. The first stage usually lasts twenty-five to thirty years. The second stage, in which reproduction occurs, is of indefinite extent, perhaps hundreds of years. In this period the scars of fallen leaves disappear, the thickness of the trunk is increased, and branches form. The senile stage may last indefinitely, and is marked by the formation of aerial roots and excrescences of resin. This "dragon's blood" has been found in the sepulchral caves of prehistoric men in the Canaries and has hence been supposed to have been used by them in embalming their dead.

The most famous of the Canary Island trees once grew in the town of Orotava. It was a giant among plants of this kind; Willis[14] in his dictionary says it was 70 feet high, 45 feet in girth, and supposed to be 6000 years old. Without mentioning a figure, Lindley and Moore[15] estimate its antiquity as "at least greater than that of the pyramids." These authorities continue:

The trunk of this tree was hollow and might be ascended by a staircase in the interior up to the height at which it began to branch. Duc found it to be 79 feet in circumference. Humboldt mentions that when he saw it, it had the same colossal size (15 feet diameter) which it had when the French adventurers, the Bethencourts, conquered these gardens of the Hesperides in the beginning of the fifteenth century (a lapse of 400 years). A tree like this, of slow growth, which for centuries changed so little, may well be believed to have possessed great antiquity.

This tree was destroyed by a hurricane in 1868.

The oldest existing tree in the Canary Islands, said to be 2000 years old, is at Icod, and a close second in size and age grows at La Laguna.

Many dracaenas are treelike and often of grotesque form. In Northern Rhodesia *Dracaena steudneri* is a woody plant to 40 feet high, and sometimes even 60 feet, much resembling an overgrown century-plant. Each of its few stout branches ends in a tuft of 3-foot, lilylike leaves.

3. *The Story of the Three Bears*

Once upon a time there was a landscape nurseryman whose name was Goldilocks. He liked pretty things to ornament his garden, and he traveled far to find plants different from those in the neighbor's yard next door. His obsession for the unique carried him as far west as the Arizona desert and into Mexico, and right there is where our story begins.

He was out in the wide open places where live the three bears—Papa Bear, Mama Bear, and Baby Bear. They all look alike, as bears should, with their hair hanging down in their eyes, but of course Papa Bear is a great big fellow with a fat stomach, slick hair, and much dignity as becomes the head of a family. Mama Bear is not so big; in fact, she is a bit dumpy, her hair is a tangled mass, and she is anything but pretty. Nevertheless she can still get up on her hind legs and look out for herself, as she has had to do all these years. Baby Bear is still an infant. He is small, but what attention he gets with his long hair! Instead of emulating his parents, he sits flat on the ground like any spoiled child, and makes the world come to him. He has a sharp tongue—almost saw-toothed.

The weather was hot and dry. Wandering around in sandy wastes was a bit exhausting and Goldilocks was tired. He thought of his lovely beds back home—flower beds, of course. He day-dreamed of how nice it would be just to stretch out in one of them and catch a few winks. About that time he saw what looked like a soft spot in the sun; he lay down, but the terrain was too rough. He found another spot, but it, too, was uncomfortable. Finally he dropped into a cradling nook that just fit him, and off he went to sleep, and he dreamed a dream!

Papa Bear had been on a binge to Miami Beach, and he brought back a photograph of himself in a flower bed near the sea, surrounded by a lot of lovelies (roses), all perfumed up. He thought Mama Bear would admire that snapshot of her beautiful Papa Bear, but he had miscalculated.

Papa Bear's real name in the dictionary is *Beaucarnea*,[16] but he never discussed this subject with Mama Bear, whose name was *Nolina*,[17] and he felt that names were not so important anyway so long as he had a Mama Bear around to talk to. Moreover, before her marriage Mama Bear was one of the Philadelphia Bigelows, and in a desert like Arizona's there are a lot of Nolinas and Mama Bear would not want to be confused with them. Papa Bear had heard there were other Beaucarneas in the neighborhood, but he had no time for them. They might claim relationship, after all, wasn't he one of those rich tourists who spend the winters in Florida?

This happy family group was disrupted by Goldilocks' excursion into the desert. When the three bears came home, Papa Bear grouched. "Who's been sleeping in my flower bed?"

And Mama Bear squealed. "Yes, and who messed up my bed?"

Whereupon it was time to hear from Junior. He had been christened *Dasylirion*,[18] because he made Papa Bear think of the stars. And our precious little constellation started screeching: "Who's messed up my bed? Gosh, there he is now."

The noise awakened Goldilocks. Thoroughly frightened, he took to his heels and disappeared over the border into California. Mama Bear turned furiously on her mate. "Next time you go to Miami Beach to show off," she said, scolding, "I'm going to send this baby picture along for your girl friends to see. They won't think you're so hot!"

"Now Mama," Papa Bear cooed, "if you are not real sweet to me, I might be tempted to look around at some of these other desert dancing girls called *Nolina*. I hear some of them are pretty nice."

Mama Bear grunted. "Come on to supper," she said.

4. The Aloe Trees

Most aloe plants are knee-high clumps of heavy, lily-like leaves, but a few of the sixty-five kinds in South Africa and Madagascar are trees. In Northern Rhodesia *Aloë excelsa* is a tree with a 20-foot trunk that is often 10 inches in diameter. At the tip of each branch is a tuft of lily-like leaves.

The widely branched tree *Aloë dichotoma*, pictured on page 119, is a feature of Angola deserts, for it stands 25 to 30 feet high. The leaves at the branch tips are 6 to 10 inches long, arranged in a spiral. Branched clusters of yellow flowers rise from the gray-green hearts of the spirals of leaves.

5. The Joshua-Tree

The Joshua-tree,[19] a giant yucca of the southwestern deserts of the United States, typifies this group of stiff-leaved, evergreen, frequently ornamental

ABOVE, LEFT AND RIGHT: Black-boys (*Xanthorrhoea arborea*) in western Australia. They grow 6 to 8 feet high and are topped by flower spikes. (Photos: Australian News and Information Bureau.)

BELOW: A mountainside grove of dragon's-blood trees (*Dracaena cinnabari*) on the island of Socotra. In the lower left-hand corner is a frankincense tree (see Chapter Seventeen on odoriferous trees.) (Photo: Douglas Botting.)

RIGHT: A *Beaucarnea* tree, growing in a Miami rosebed instead of the Arizona desert, where it belongs. This is the Papa Bear of the fantasy (pages 115-116). (Photo: Paul Root.) BELOW, LEFT: *Nolina* is the scientific name for Mama Bear. (Photo: Reid Moran.) BELOW, RIGHT: Baby Bear (*Dasylirion acotriche*) has no appreciable trunk. (Photo: Walter Singer.)

118

RIGHT: The *Aloe* tree in the Angola desert, Africa. It develops a considerable trunk and is frequently 25 feet high or more. (Photo: Edward Ross.)

LEFT: An old lily-tree (*Vellozia intermedia*) growing in the dry region of Goiás in central Brazil. (Photo: Harold Edgard Strang.)

RIGHT: *Vellozia incurvata* trees at Serro de Ouro Branco, Minas Gerais, Brazil. (Photo: G. Pabst.)

RIGHT: The southern yucca (*Yucca australis*). This Mexican tree (photographed in California) is probably the only yucca with hanging flower clusters. BELOW, LEFT: This Joshua-tree (*Yucca brevifolia*, since cut down), was 65 feet high, with a trunk diameter of more than 4 feet. It grew in Antelope Valley, near Lancaster, California. BELOW, RIGHT: Our Lord's candle (*Yucca whipplei*). It has the biggest flower display of any lily. (Photos: Ralph D. Cornell.)

120

lilies. It is not, however, cultivated in gardens, for too many other forms, easier to handle, are available in quantities. These are particularly useful in seaside gardening because of their resistance to salt spray and sand blasting.

Several kinds of yucca become treelike; of these the Spanish dagger[20] and the southern yucca[21] are best known.

When these tree yuccas appear in the wild, observers find difficulty in thinking of them as lilies. Many of them have magnificent flower spikes, although the handsomest yucca, called Our-Lord's-candle,[22] springs from an earthbound rosette of leaves and never becomes arborescent.

6. Vellozia

In the driest parts of South Africa, Madagascar, and Brazil grow about sixty-five kinds of woody, fibrous, erect, sometimes treelike plants called *Vellozia*, with lilylike flowers that may be white, yellow, violet, orange-red, or blue, and are often showy. As the plants grow taller, the upper part of the stems is covered with the fibrous sheaths of old leaves. The lower part becomes a mass of adventitious roots, and the whole constitutes a sort of trunk. These above-ground roots are capable of absorbing water like a sponge, and this faculty enables the plants to survive on the dew they accumulate. Rain rarely falls in the areas where they grow, and there is no moisture in the soil for roots to collect.

Dr. Harold Edgard Strang, director of the Centro de Pesquisas, Florestais e Conservaçao da Natureza at Tijuca, Rio de Janeiro, is the outstanding authority on *Vellozia* in the Western Hemisphere. He says[23] that these plants are popularly known in Brazil as *canela de ema* (ostrich's leg), and that they grow on rocky ground or on solid rock. The old name for this genus was *Xerophyta*, in recognition of the rainless existence of these strange lilies.

Except for their flowers these trees would never be recognized as lilies. Marianne North trekked by mule up four thousand feet in Minas Gerais, through appalling conditions caused by heavy rains, to see the flowers. She wrote:[24]

> At the top of the ridge I saw many strange plants for the first time. The *Vellozia*, a kind of tree lily peculiar to these mountains . . . had a stem like an old twisted rope, out of which sprang branches of the same, terminating in a bunch of hart pointed leaves like the Yucca; out of these again came the most delicate sweet smelling blue-grey flowers with yellow centres resembling our common blue crocus in shape. . . . There are many other *Vellozia*, all having the same dagger-like leaves; some send up long stems with bunches of green or brown flowers.

TEN

Gigantism

There were giants in the earth in those days.   —Genesis 6:4

Gigantism among plants is as difficult to explain as was Jack's bean-stalk, but in certain parts of the world, usually at high elevations and in the presence of continuous moisture that is sometimes excessive, some herbs of our gardens are found to have close relatives growing as trees.

This phenomenon is largely confined to half a dozen kinds of plants. Many lobelias and their kin are affected; we know them in the United States in the wild as Indian tobacco and blue lobelia, and the cardinal flower; other kinds are cultivated in our gardens. A host of daisies or sun-flowers exhibit this size abnormality. Other victims of gigantism include St. John's-wort (*Hypericum*), a few plants in the coffee family (*Rubiaceae*), and the heaths (*Erica*).

Huxley[1] wrote:

> In general, the size of trees diminishes as the height increases, as they decrease on approaching the pole. And, just as at St. Pierre and Miquelon, Newfoundland, there are dwarf forests whose tops one can touch, one meets on high mountains, in the form of stunted bushes, the proudest trees of low-altitude forests. Since, too, similar plants exist on mountain tops as in the Arctic, the plants in the crater of a snowy tropical volcano often resemble those of Greenland.
>
> Yet on the high mountains we sometimes find relations of quite humble plants which seem to have spent a sojourn in Brobdingnag and have become incredibly large, an unexplained phenomenon known as gigantism. At about 12,000 feet the South American paramos (a word meaning "desolate spaces")

are covered with large composites up to 10 feet high such as the Espeletias. . . .

In Madagascar, above the "lichen forest" and a deep carpet of mosses, grow the tree heathers. While the real trees, between 5,500 and 7,500 feet, barely reach 20 feet, on the higher slopes of Mount Tsaratanana these heathers emulate trees. They are surpassed in size and ruggedness by those which one discovers on the high mountains of equatorial Africa—Ruwenzori, Kenya, Kilimanjaro. These flowers are white or pink (*Erica arborea*) or greenish (*Philippia*). At around 7,500 feet they reign, queens of a realm where few other plants dare to grow.

Higher, the heaths give way to fabulous flora, different to that of the Andes of which it is the complement. In this zone rise the giant lobelias, in wide, damp, misty prairies, which also please enormous grasses and tree 'groundsels' 25 and 30 feet tall. One of these, *Senecio friesorum*, which even braves 13,500 feet, has protective leaves, like a muff, on top of rosettes formed by the other leaves.

The lobelias look not unlike yuccas; their straight, slender stems open out into a rosette of long, narrow leaves; from their centre springs a great spike, a column of flowers, long and narrow in *L. gibberoa*, the tallest which may reach 25 feet; stiff, waxy, symmetrical in several species; or clad in woolly bracts like some furry monster in the case of *L. telekii*.

Synge[2] filled a book with his adventures in the land of gigantism in central Africa, centered around Ruwenzori, a high mountain mass bisected by the equator on the boundary between Uganda and the Belgian Congo. As his expedition worked its way up the mountain, he pictured a camp scene:

With branches lit up from below with the golden light of the fire, we were reminded of the exquisite decoration of some stage fantasy or mysterious ballet. With the light below, the streaming lichens and the feathery foliage seemed golden-red and artificial. All the land here sloped steeply, and we had some trouble in finding and then enlarging enough flat ground for the tent. Even then 'Burnt Tree' was a camp in tiers. . . .

Gradually the bamboos diminished in size, dwindling from fifty feet to fifteen, until suddenly we emerged into a zone of tree heathers. Imagine a haunted wood composed of ordinary ling heather magnified fifty times; there were trees fifty feet high instead of bushes of one foot, twisted into weird shapes and gnarled so that each resembled a drawing by Arthur Rackham. Out of each trunk glared a face, sometimes benign, more often wicked and bearded with streamers of lichens and mosses.

Looking out between the tree heathers we could see far into the mountain across a wide expanse of ridges and gorges, but there were no signs either of the lakes or the snowfields which we had hoped to see. It seemed a wild and desolate expanse, in very truth a place where no man lived or would be likely to live. It was not only bare, but mysterious and unearthly. . . .

Even from the highest branches dangled long sulphurous yellow strands of the *Usnea* lichen, the old man's beard of many travellers, which Somer-

ABOVE, LEFT: *Trematolobelia necrostachys,* one of the many tree-form lobelias, in Hawaii. (Photo: R. J. Baker.) ABOVE, RIGHT: A red-flowered tree geranium (*Neurophyllodes arborescens*) of Hawaii. (Photo: Robert J. Badaracco.)

RIGHT: The hooded greyfriar (*Espeletia grandiflora*) in the Colombian Andes. (Photo: Robert Perry.) BELOW, LEFT: A giant lobelia in the foreground, with a clump of enormous groundsels (*Senecio*) behind. (Photo: E. Aubert de la Rüe.) BELOW, RIGHT: Tree heathers (*Erica* sp.) of Ruwenzori.

ville declared reminded him of the hair of Botticelli's angels, an extremely apt comparison in the sunlight. In the mist they resembled nothing so essentially happy, but appeared rather as some melancholy ghosts, not of the animal, but of the vegetable world, the lost souls of a past vegetable glory flapping their branches and stretching out to frighten the wretched man who dared to penetrate such places. It is, indeed, a place of mystery, haunting when these shapes stand out dimly from a background of swirling mists. Among these the stiff spikes of the lobelias barred our path like figures with upright lances. In present-day life such plants seem out of place: they are rather the complement of prehistoric man, or even the giant reptiles and pterodactyls.

When the sun shone, and it frequently did so for us, the aspect of the mountain changed very quickly and immediately became friendly. Everything then smiled at us; the pink and white everlasting flowers opened into a mass of colour. . . .

A golden *Sedum* of positively gigantic size first attracted my attention as it sprawled luxuriantly over a large rock. The Heather forest became more and more like the haunted wood of the old fairy tale. . . . A tree St. John's-wort (*Hypericum bequaertii*) next sent me into raptures. The flowers were nearly as large as tulips and hung delicately like orange lanterns from the ends of the branches. The sheer exuberance of the growth of the giant groundsels and the lobelias is astounding and thrilling. One rosette of *Lobelia bequaertii* would often be several feet across, and would have several bunches of closely-packed leaves, shining purple and radiating from the centre, where a drop of water would be enshrined like a jewel at the heart of the world. When this lobelia flowered it threw up a stiff green obelisk-like spike, monstrous and bizarre, but very much in keeping with the surroundings. The other dominating species was *Lobelia wollastonii*. Its spike is a glorious powder blue. When the sun touches the dewdrops on its blue flowers and grey bracts the whole spike seems touched with a silvery radiance. . . . It was just over 12,000 feet when we made our next camp by a small stream. . . . Two lobelias formed our doorpost, and the tent ropes were tied to giant groundsels. The mosses were thicker here than anywhere else on the mountain. To sit down and rest was like reclining in a feather bed, brilliant not only with greens, but also with orange and crimson.

Somerville called the valley 'Paradise Valley.' It was walled like a natural garden, with grey hills covered with everlasting flowers, heathers and tree groundsels. . . . Everywhere there were flowers, bushes of white and pink everlasting, powdery blue lobelia spikes, the purple of the *Lobelia bequaertii*, and the golden of the tree groundsels, yet it was an orderly, not a tangled riot as on the rest of the mountain. It was like a place imagined in dreams.

Roger Perry[3] explored the bleak desolate places of the northern Andes, extensive treeless plains at 10,000 up to 15,000 feet, and studied the 70 species of *Espeletia* there. The natives call them greyfriars because they stand shrouded most of the time in gray mists. Their range is from Colombia and Venezuela southward into Ecuador. They have adapted themselves to this environment where the air is humid, the ground is often saturated, and the rate of evaporation is slow because of low temperatures. The old leaves often remain as a cloak for the stem. Perry says young leaves are either waxy or covered with long protective bracts or layers of downy hairs. They conserve moisture this way, resisting excessive transpiration. *Espeletia* plants are often 20, sometimes 30, feet high. Most of the *Espeletia* have straight unbranched stems but one of them, *E. nereifolia*, in the upper cloud forest, is a many-limbed tree to 35 feet.

Under similar wet conditions in the mountains of the island of Maui, Hawaii, grows a red-flowered tree geranium[4] that reaches 10 feet or more with a trunk 5 inches in diameter. Degener[5] wrote:

The *hinahina* are small shrubs with the exception of one treelike type which grows to a height of ten or more feet. Most of them bear leaves that resemble in shape the individual scales of a butterfly's wing. These leaves are usually densely covered with hair which imparts to them a beautiful silvery appearance. In one kind of *hinahina* the flowers are red and bilaterally symmetrical in regard to the position of the petals; in all others they are white, often marked with purple, and always star-shaped. They invariably mature their stamens and their pistils at different times, thereby preventing a flower from being fertilized with its own pollen. . . .

The leaves usually stand erect and are about as silvery with hair as are those of the famous silver-sword occasionally found in the same region. This is probably a special adaptation to withstand the rays of the sun which are more active at higher than at lower elevations because of the lesser thickness of atmosphere which they must penetrate. Leaves that stand upright expose their surface far less directly to the sun than do those that lie flat. And leaves that are covered with white hair not only repel many of the sun's rays like a mirror from their surface but hinder the excessive evaporation of moisture through the epidermis.

Degener goes on to describe how some of these Hawaiian geraniums, growing in the Koolau Gap of the Haleakala Crater, are "enveloped and drenched by clouds for most of the day."

Alvin R. Chock[6] wrote of a similarly wet area on the Hawaiian island of Kauai, where the vegetation is exceedingly rich:

Surrounded by forests high in the mountains of Kauai is Kokee, located on the northwestern portion of that island. Nearby is the splendor of Waimea Canyon, Hawaii's 'Grand Canyon of the Pacific,' one mile wide and over a half mile deep, with its rugged, colorful slopes and cliffs. To the north and east is the wet and boggy Alakai Swamp, created by Waialeale, the wettest spot in the world, where the annual average rainfall is 460 inches.

Here, as in Africa, lobelias furnished examples of gigantism, with six endemic genera, all known to Hawaiians as "haha." Their flowers are conspicuous and attractive. The hahalua (*Cyanea leptostegia*) is palmlike in appearance, often 40 feet high and fairly abundant in Kokee. *Lobelia yuccoides*, "with its spectacular blue flowers, is a showy plant."

Dwarfism among trees, as opposed to gigantism, was mentioned by Huxley.[7] Toward the arctic regions, toward the seacoast, and toward timber line at high altitudes, the stature of trees is gradually reduced without any deformity. The ecologist Daubenmire[8] says this is caused by drying winds which produce an unfavorable internal water balance. In such trying locations, trees may be so dwarfed that "specimens a century old are no larger than a small shrub." This dwarfing is evident at many places in the high Rocky Mountains.

In arctic regions and high mountains of the Northern Hemisphere, dwarf willows with leaves that are measured in millimeters hug the ground on prostrate stems. Two of them, *Salix herbacea* and the bearberry willow, *S. uva-ursi*, grow as far south as the mountain peaks of New Hampshire. The latter may also be found in the Adirondacks.

ELEVEN

Cabbage-Trees of St. Helena[1]

I made me gardens and orchards, and I planted trees in them.
—ECCLESIASTES 2:5

Among the weirdest trees in the world are half a dozen kinds that grow in patches 2700 feet above the sea on the Central Ridge of the remote island of St. Helena in the south Atlantic. Collectively they are called cabbage-trees,[2] but they are not cabbages; they are daisies.

Why are these trees weird? Because in this jet age daisies are merely flowers of the field. But in St. Helena, where Napoleon cooled his heels and dreamed of a lost empire, life's tempo has dragged for centuries; here the pages of time have forgotten to turn, and the daisies are trees—big trees. They go back tens of thousands, perhaps millions, of years. St. Helena is over a thousand miles from the African continent; no planes can land there and only one ship a month stops by, northbound one trip, southbound the next. Not only are the daisy trees ornaments out of a dim and distant past, but it is difficult even to trace the affinities of St. Helena's indigenous vegetation to the plants of other lands.

John Hutchinson[3] called these strange plants "a fragment from the wreck of an ancient world," for

> When discovered over 400 years ago the island was entirely covered with forests, the trees drooping over the tremendous precipices that overhang the sea, a vivid contrast with present-day conditions. Now the bulk of the flora consists of exotic species which have assisted in the destruction of the native

128

plants. What a pity man and beast have almost destroyed this museum of antiquity.

Hutchinson continues:

About forty species of flowering plants were formerly known to be endemic in this island, but many of these have now disappeared, owing to cultivation and the voracity of the goat, which was introduced into the island in 1513, and multiplied so rapidly that in 1588 Captain Cavendish stated that they existed in thousands, single flocks being almost a mile long.

The Central Ridge of St. Helena, a comparatively small area of land above 2200 feet elevation, is the last stronghold of several of the endemic flowering plants and ferns. Commonly, the trade wind brings a cloud layer at about 2000 feet, and in consequence this ridge is frequently shrouded in mist, and is perennially damp. No figures for precipitation are available as no records are kept, but it is not so much the total quantity of the moisture as its regularity which accounts for the peculiar vegetation of the zone. The ridge can best be described in the two parts into which it is naturally divided.

Long Range to Sich's Ridge

This is much the larger part and includes the highest peaks, Diana's (2718 feet), Actaeon, and Cockhold's Point. Various maps published in the past hundred and fifty years differ in their nomenclature of these eminences, except that all seem to agree on which is Diana's. A Norfolk Island pine[4] a few yards west of its crest identifies it. One other peak has a similar tree, but on its highest point. In this area are growths of New Zealand flax,[5] which is invading the ridge and competing with the indigenous plants. The bramble[6] also is thick on the heights and it makes exploration extremely difficult on the steep, slippery slopes.

Most exciting of the indigenous plants are the tree daisies, commonly called cabbage-trees, of which half a dozen kinds survive. These arboreal relics from bygone ages are not unlike the tree daisies found in the mountains of eastern Africa and in the Andes.[7]

Most numerous of the indigenous trees which remain is the black cabbage,[8] which attains a height up to 20 feet. The very dark bark is usually covered with lichens, epiphytic mosses, liverworts, and ferns. Next most common of the strange trees is probably the he-cabbage.[9] The white-wood cabbage[10] and the dogwood[11] are less common, but are still found in fair numbers. All four seem to be smaller in size and fewer in number than when J. C. Melliss[12] described them in the nineteenth century.

Indigenous vegetation at High Peak on the island of St. Helena. (Photo: N. R. Kerr.)

BELOW, LEFT: Whitewood cabbage-tree (*Petrobium arboreum*) on High Peak. BELOW, RIGHT: A close-up of the he-cabbage (*Senecio leucadendron*) in its early growth. (Photos: G. C. Lawrence.)

RIGHT: These high peaks of St. Helena are the home of this spreading specimen of black cabbage (*Melanodendron integrifolium*). BELOW: Flowers and leaves of the black cabbage. (Photos: N. R. Kerr.)

ABOVE: Black cabbage trees in bloom on the Central Ridge of St. Helena. LEFT: Old gumwood trees at Longwood, Napoleon's residence. (Photos: N. R. Kerr.)

131

This more southerly part of the ridge, two miles in length, has a lower mean altitude and, though more openly exposed to the trade wind, a lower rainfall. The leeward slope is much less steep than the windward, and the main road to the south of the island passes along this lee side, parallel to the crest only a hundred yards or so distant from it.

The daisy trees are the most characteristic of the true St. Helenian plants. *Commidendron* and *Melanodendron* are peculiar to the island. Though the number of extant species has been reduced by at least three in the last four hundred years, the following six kinds of daisy tree are still found:

Gumwood (*Commidendron robustum*): The gumwood at one time covered many acres of the mid-altitudes from 1500 to 2000 feet, but now is reduced to about 250 specimens. The gnarled old trees in a hedge at Longwood, Napoleon's residence during the last six years of his life, are the last remnants of the Great Wood, which before 1720 covered some hundreds of acres. Seven trees survive at Thomson's Wood (probably a contraction of Tombstone Wood, from the large blocks of phonolite which litter the area). The largest surviving group of trees (about 200 in number) is near Peak Farm, at about 1800 feet, on the windward side. These trees are of different ages and the group seems to be well established. Individual trees vary considerably in leaf size and color, and when William Roxburgh[13] listed the plants of St. Helena he distinguished two species of gumwood which he called *Conyza gummifera* and *C. robusta*.

Scrubwood (*Commidendron rugosum*): The scrubwood is now the most widely dispersed and most numerous of the *Commidendron* trees. It grows on dry coastal areas and on cliffs and precipices of the coast from Flagstaff to South West Point, and inland at Coles Rock and on Lot. A large handsome bush more than 8 feet across, always in flower, survives on Longwood Plain within easy walking distance of Longwood. The largest number of plants is to be found about the cliffs of Man and Horse. In the areas from which goats are excluded young seedlings are now found, so there is some reason for hoping that the projected elimination of the ranging goat may encourage the spread of this very beautiful shrub.

Little Bastard Gumwood (*Commidendron spurium*): The little bastard gumwood, called by some of the botanists the "little cymose cabbage tree,"[14] is surrounded with some confusion because William Burchell[15] erred in numbering his specimens. However, his drawing of the "cymose cabbage tree" is clear enough to identify the species. The tree was described by Melliss as "very rare"; it is now on the verge of extinction. After considerable search about the ridge, Kerr found a single, sickly plant on the windward side of the Depot. A year later, he found eight bushes on a precipice on the southeast side of Mount Vesey. All are old and decrepit, and seeds collected from them have not germinated. It is very doubtful if the species will persist for more than a few decades unless efforts being made to propagate it prove successful. In earlier years this shrub probably occupied large areas of the windy slopes of the central ridge. Ranging goats have almost exterminated it.

Black Cabbage-Tree (*Melanodendron integrifolium*): The black cabbage-tree,[16] the only species of the genus, is a handsome, spreading tree whose black, almost bare branches carry at their tips large, shining, dark green leaves. Masses of greenish-white daisy-like flowers, each about ½ inch across, appear in October and November. The tree is fairly common in wet areas from Long Ground Ridge to Sich's Ridge. A few trees grow on the windward side of High Peak. None of the existing trees appears to be as large as those illustrated in Melliss's book, though several are obviously of considerable age. The bark of this tree is usually thickly encrusted with epiphytic lichens, mosses, and ferns. Flowers and seeds are produced freely and many seeds are fertile. Seedlings of different ages are fairly frequent near Diana's Peak, and there is good reason to suppose that this species will persist.

He-Cabbage Tree (*Senecio leucadendron*): At the tips of its almost bare branches, the he-cabbage tree has pale green, rough-edged leaves. From tufts of these leaves in June and July emerge the massed white heads of small, thickly clustered, daisy-like flowers which, in their earlier stages, resemble the curd of a cauliflower. The surviving trees, mostly 5 to 15 feet high, can be seen at Cason's, above the road by Bates Branch and beside the road on Sandy Bay Ridge. Finer examples are fairly common in association with *Melanodendron* on the slopes of the Central Ridge and in the valleys leading from it. It flowers freely but the seeds appear to be less fertile, as very few young trees can be found.

Whitewood Cabbage-Tree (*Petrobium arboreum* R. Br.):[17] The whitewood is more slender and has thinner branches than the black cabbage, and its smaller rounded leaves usually have purple stalks. It reaches a maximum height of about 20 feet. Clusters of 6 to 20 small, greenish-white, short-rayed daisy flowers appear from March to June. In Melliss's time this was the commonest of all indigenous trees on St. Helena, but now it is far less common than the black or the he-cabbage, though it is found in association with them at High Peak and along Cabbage-Tree Road. Most of the trees Kerr inspected were very unhealthy, with numerous dead branches apparently killed by attacks of a wood-borer. One tree had a number of irregular gall-like swellings. The species flowers and seeds reasonably well, but no young seedlings have been noted.

Cabbage Trees Extinct or Nearly So

The she-cabbage trees[18] appear to be extinct. Melliss described the young stems and leaves as being bright purple, resembling those of a red cabbage (garden variety). The clusters of white flowers hung down from the smaller branches in June. The slender, upright trees, 12 to 15 feet high, grew at altitudes of 2000 to 2600 feet on the Central Ridge, and Melliss called them the fourth most abundant tree. However, when Kerr searched the area he found none. It is possible that a few trees may yet persist on the densely covered slopes near Diana's Peak. The thick tangle of brambles on the leeward side and the slippery slopes of the windward side make a search of this area very difficult.

One other daisy or cabbage tree still survived in 1888. It was a lone specimen of *Psiadia*,[19] which apparently had no folk name. One report[20] read:

> Here we have a plant nearly allied, generally, to *Aster*, which forms a good-sized tree with spreading, naked branches, bearing small, stalked, spatulate, toothed leaves crowded towards the ends of the branches, and which leave when they fall very prominent cicatrices. The heads of flowers are borne in dense clusters. . . . Originally described by Sir Joseph Hooker, it was figured by Melliss in his work on St. Helena, and is mentioned by Hemsley in the "Report of the Botany of the *Challenger* Expedition."

This tree is now extinct.

Kerr believes that *Commidendron burchellii*,[21] closely allied to *C. spurium*, which also grew on the sides of the Central Ridge, is almost certainly now extinct. Melliss knew only a single plant near the old Picquet House, growing among *C. spurium*. Kerr's careful search failed to reveal a single specimen.

PART III

Trees That Cannot Live without Animals

TWELVE

Birds, Elephants, and Turtles

The voice of the turtle is heard in our land.
—SONG OF SOLOMON 2:12

In relationships between trees and animals, most commonplace is the dispersal of seeds by birds, monkeys, deer, sheep, cattle, pigs, and others,[1] but the connection is important here only as it involves the effect of gastric juices on seeds swallowed by animals.

Florida home owners are much annoyed by the Brazilian pepper tree,[2] a handsome, medium-sized evergreen which in December is so heavily laden with red berries among its dark green aromatic leaves as to suggest holly. For weeks the trees are beautiful. The seeds ripen and fall, but no seedlings ever come up under the trees.

When the robins arrive in great flocks, they land in the pepper trees with enthusiasm and gorge themselves on the tiny fruits. Then they run out on the lawn and dance under the water sprinklers. Before they depart in spring to spend the summer in the north, they all leave calling cards on Florida lawns. In the ensuing weeks, pepper trees pop up all over the place, especially in flower beds where the robin had spotted a worm. The tired gardener pulls up a thousand pepper trees to keep them from taking over. The robins' gastric juices did something to that seed.

All pencils were formerly made from the wood of cedar trees[3] that grew plentifully along the Atlantic coastal plain from Virginia to Georgia.

Soon the ravenous demands of industry eliminated all the usuable big trees, and another source of wood had to be found. A few little cedars persisted, however, matured, and began bearing seed—but here, too, no seedlings ever came up under the trees, which to this day are called pencil cedars.

But drive along any country road in the Carolinas and keep your eyes open; you can see millions of pencil cedars. They have been relocated in straight rows along every barbed-wire fence where they have been planted in the droppings of ten thousand sparrows and meadow larks. The re-establishment of the pencil cedars is assured. Without the help of these feathered intermediaries, the cedar forests would have been only a fragrant memory.

These services by birds raise a question: To what extent do animal digestive processes affect other seeds? Kerner[4] found that most seeds lost their viability after passage through animals. Roessler[5] obtained germination of only 7 out of 40,025 seeds from various plants fed to California linnets.

In the Galápagos Islands off the west coast of South America grows a large, native, long-lived, perennial tomato plant[6] which is of special interest because detailed scientific experiments[7] proved that less than one per cent of its seeds will germinate naturally. The scientists proved also that eighty per cent of the seed germinated when the ripe tomatoes were eaten by the island's giant tortoises and were retained in their digestive tracts two to three weeks or even longer. The experiments suggested that the giant tortoise might be an important natural agent not only in breaking the dormancy but also in effectively dispersing the tomato seeds. The scientists also concluded that the agency in the tortoise's digestive tract which speeded germination was enzymic rather than mechanical.

In Ghana, Baker[8] from California experimented with the germination of seeds from the baobab[9] and sausage[10] trees. He found that these seeds are very difficult to germinate without treatment, yet he observed that numerous seedlings were becoming established in rocky areas considerably distant from trees of either species. It became evident that these places were favorite roosts of the baboons, and remains of fruits revealed that they were being devoured by these simians. The extremely strong jaws of the baboons are adequate to crush the very hard, indehiscent fruits of these trees, and without such aid the seeds would have no opportunity for dispersal. The germination rate of seeds removed from baboon dung found at these sites was much improved.

The wood-oil-nut tree,[11] also called Zambezi almond and Manketti nut, is a large handsome tree in Southern Rhodesia bearing plum-sized fruits with a thin pulp surrounding a very hard nut—"edible, if you can crack it," a forester wrote.[12] The wood of the tree is only slightly heavier than balsa.[13] On a package of seed I received was written: "Collected from elephant dung." The seeds seldom germinate naturally, but sprout freely in the wild because elephants are exceedingly fond of the fruits. Passage through their digestive system leaves the nut apparently uninjured physically, although those I received and planted looked like gray pecans that were perforated all over with pencil-lead-size holes that were only surface-deep. Were these etched out by the elephant's digestive juices?

C. J. Taylor[14] has written that other species of *Ricinodendron* growing in Ghana bear seeds that germinate readily. But he adds that it is possible that the seed of the umbrella-tree[15] "requires to pass through an animal gut because germination in the nursery is extremely difficult, but natural regeneration is often prolific."

Although elephants do a great deal of damage to savannah woodlands in Southern Rhodesia, the spread of some plants is dependent upon them.[16] Elephants particularly like the pods of the camel-thorn[17] and eat large quantities of them. The seeds pass undigested through the elephants. During the rainy season dung beetles bury the elephant dung. In this manner great quantities of seed are inadvertently planted in an excellent seed bed. Thus the pachyderms compensate to a degree for the bark stripping and other damage they do to vegetation.

C. T. White[18] has reported that the seed of the quandong[19] in Queensland would not germinate until voided by the emu, which relishes the fleshy prunelike covering.

ABOVE, LEFT: Pencil cedars (*Juniperus silicicola*) grown from bird droppings along fences in South Carolina. ABOVE, RIGHT: Fiddle-leaf fig (*Ficus lyrata*) in Florida. A small wasp is responsible for its seed production. (Photo: Paul Root.) RIGHT: African elephant, whose fondness for fruit of the wood-oil-nut tree helps to perpetuate it. (Photo: T. Turnbull.)

LEFT: A Galápagos tortoise, involved in partnership with tomato plants. (Photo: American Museum of Natural History.)

THIRTEEN

The Wasp Trees

The fig tree putteth forth her green figs.—Song of Solomon 2:13

One of the most difficult groups of tropical trees to understand is the figs.[1]

Most of them come from Malaysia and Polynesia. In Florida and other warm areas, where some species are cultivated for ornament, they are called rubber trees, because a wound of leaf or bark brings forth a thick, white, sticky latex. This is not used to make rubber, and the trees are not even distantly related to the Brazilian rubber tree[2] of commerce. Corner[3] says:

In all members of this family[4] the flowers are small. In some, like the Bread-fruit trees, the Mulberries, and the Fig trees, the flowers become crowded into compact clusters, forming heads or spikes, which ripen into fleshy fruits. . . . In the Breadfruit trees and the Mulberries, the flowers are placed on the outside of the fleshy stalk that supports them; in the Figs they are, as it were, on the inside. The fig is made by the widening of the inflorescence-stalk and the arching over and contraction of the edge until a cup or vase is formed, with a narrow mouth, like a hollow pear, and the flowers turned outside in. . . . The mouth of the fig is closed by many small, interlocking scales. . . .

The flowers of Fig plants are of three kinds: male flowers with stamens, female flowers that set seed, and gall flowers, so-called because they contain the little wasps that pollinate the flowers. The gall flowers are sterile female flowers and they can be distinguished very easily on breaking open a ripe fig because they look like little, stalked bladders or balloons with a hole bitten on one side, which marks where the wasp came out. The female flowers can be recognized from the small, flat, hard yellowish seed which each contains, and the male flowers from the stamens. . . .

The pollination of Fig flowers is, perhaps, the most curious relation between plants and animals that has been discovered. Fig flowers can be pollinated only by these tiny insects called fig wasps (*Blastophaga*) so that the Fig plants are absolutely dependent on them for their reproduction. . . . If we plant an exotic Fig tree in a country where its special kind of fig wasp is absent, that tree will never propagate itself by seed. . . . The fig wasps, in their turn, are absolutely dependent on the Fig plants for their livelihood, because their maggots develop inside the gall flowers, the adults breed inside the figs and their only free existence is when the female wasps fly from the ripening figs on one plant to the young figs on another. The male wasps, which are almost or quite blind and wingless, live in the adult stage for only a few hours. If the female wasps cannot find a suitable fig tree, they have nowhere to lay their eggs and of necessity die. There are many kinds of these fig wasps, each being restricted, it seems, to one kind of Fig plant or to a few allied species. They are called wasps because they are distantly related to the true wasps, but they do not sting and their little black bodies are barely a millemetre long. . . .

When the figs on the gall plant ripen, the adult wasps hatch from the ovaries of the gall flowers by biting a hole through the wall of the ovary. The males and females mate inside the fig, and the males die shortly after. The females scramble out between the scales which close the mouth of the fig. The male flowers are generally placed near the mouth and just when the fig is ripening the male flowers open so that they shed their pollen on the female wasps as they escape. The female wasps, powdered with pollen, then fly to another tree of the same kind which is developing a new crop of figs and which they probably find by their sense of smell. They enter the young figs by working their bodies between the scales which close the mouths of the figs. This is a difficult process. . . . If the wasp has entered a gall fig, her ovipositor easily passes down the short style and reaches the ovule in which one egg is laid. . . . The wasp moves from flower to flower until her stock of eggs is finished; she then dies exhausted without having eaten any food since she hatched. . . .

FOURTEEN

Tree Flowers Pollinated by Bats

The fowls of the air lodged in the branches.   —Matthew 13:19

In the Temperate Zone we customarily depend on insects to pollinate our flowers, and the bee is reputed to be the busiest of them. In the tropics, however, particularly among night-blooming trees, bats of many kinds are the agents upon which fertilization depends. Scientists[1] have shown that these night-flying "flower-feeding bats . . . seemingly fill the same ecological niche that is occupied by hummingbirds during the day."

The phenomenon has been extensively studied in Trinidad, Java, India, Costa Rica, and elsewhere, and photographic records have been made by scientists in Ghana[2] as well as in the United States.[3] In all these observations, a few facts stand out:

1. Most of the bat-pollinated flowers have, for human beings, a highly unpleasant smell. This applies to *Oroxylon indicum, Adansonia digitata,* and species of *Kigelia, Parkia, Durio,* and others.

2. The bats range in size from species smaller than your hand, to giants with a four-foot wing span. The little ones can often hover or wrap their wings about the flower structure as they stick their long red tongues into the nectar. The big bats push their beaks into the blossoms, lap up quickly what they can before their weight carries them out of range, then try again.

3. The flowers that attract bats for pollination are confined almost

entirely to three plant families: trumpet-flower (*Bignoniaceae*), bombax or silk-cotton tree (*Bombacaceae*), and mimosa (*Mimosaceae*). Exceptions are *Fagraea* of the strychnine family (*Loganiaceae*), and the giant saguaro cactus of the southwestern deserts.

ABOVE, LEFT: A long-nosed bat (*Leptonycteris nivalis*) puts his tongue into the flowers of the saguaro cactus, and becomes covered with pollen, which he carries to other flowers. (Photo: E. L. Lendell and B. J. Hayward.) ABOVE, RIGHT: In Ghana a female bat visits the flower-heads of *Parkia clappertoniana*, the locust bean. (See Chapter Five.) (Photo: B. J. Harris.)

BELOW: *Freycinetia*, whose fruits are relished by field rats. The rats fertilize the nearby flowers as they climb over the plants. (Photo: Ray. J. Baker.)

FIFTEEN

The Rat "Tree"

These are a smoke in my nose. —Isaiah 65:5

The climbing screw pine[1] seen on islands in the Pacific is not a tree, though if it can find a support to grasp with its many clasping roots, it will stand erect enough to look like one. Otto Degener[2] wrote of it:

> *Freycinetia* is common throughout the Hawaiian Islands in the forest, especially at lower elevations. It is not known elsewhere, but thirty or more related kinds are found in the islands to the southwest and in the Orient.
>
> The *ieie* is very conspicuous along the highway from Hilo to Kilauea Crater during the summer when it is in bloom. Some plants climb the trees and reach their very tops, the main stem gripping the trunks with its slender aerial roots while the branches curve out into the sun. Other individuals trail on the ground in great masses, forming impenetrable jungles.
>
> The woody, yellow stems of the *ieie* are about one inch in diameter and ringed with the scars of fallen leaves. They produce numerous, long, adventitious air-roots of almost uniform thickness throughout, which not only gain nourishment for the plant but enable it to hold on to its support. The stems branch every few feet to produce terminal clusters of slender, shiny, green leaves. These are pointed at their ends and spiny along their edges and on the lower side of the midrib. . . .
>
> The special method that the *ieie* has devised to insure cross-pollination is so unusual as to be worthy of more detailed discussion.
>
> At flowering time the ends of certain branches of the *ieie* develop about a dozen bright, orange-red leaves called bracts. These are fleshy and slightly sweet near the base. Within them stand three brilliant cones, or inflorescences. Each is composed of hundreds of flower clusters, each cluster

consisting of about six united flowers of which nothing remains excepting their pistils firmly grown together. On entirely different individuals, similar showy bracts occur, also containing cones. These, instead of bearing pistils, bear only stamens that shed pollen. The *ieie* has thus prevented all possibility of self-pollination by bearing its two sexes on two separate kinds of plants. . . .

In viewing the matured flowering branches growing there, one will find them almost invariably mutilated—most of the fragrant, colored, fleshy bracts have disappeared. They have been eaten by rats which, in their quest for food, climb from flowering branch to flowering branch. In eating the fleshy bracts, the whiskers and fur of the rodent are covered with pollen, some of which undoubtedly rubs off on the stigmas of female plants visited later. The *ieie* is the only plant in the Hawaiian Islands and one of the very few in the entire world that uses mammals to effect pollination. Some of its relatives are pollinated by the flying fox, a kind of fruit-eating bat, that enjoys the bracts.

SIXTEEN

Ant Trees

The ants are a people not strong, yet they prepare their meat in the summer. —Proverbs 30:25

Certain tropical trees are infested with ants. This phenomenon is completely foreign to the Temperate Zone, where ants are just little black creatures that get into the sugar bowl.

In the tropics, innumerable ants of many kinds and sizes, vicious and voracious—ready to bite, sting, or otherwise destroy their enemies—are frequently encountered in the forests. Trees are their preferred abodes, and certain kinds are selected in many different plant families. Nearly all are commonly called "ant trees." When the relationships[1] of ants and trees in the tropics are examined, it appears that a mutually beneficial agreement has been reached.

(1) The trees house and often feed the ants. In some instances the trees exude globules of nutrients for the ants to devour; in others, minuscule scale insects feed on the plant and are fed on in turn by the ants. The trees are particularly important to ants in forest areas that are occasionally inundated, because they keep the ant's living quarters well above the flood.

(2) The trees undoubtedly get some nourishment from the detritus assembled in the ant nests; misplaced roots often insert themselves into the nests. And the ants protect the trees from marauders of all kinds—caterpillars, grubs, boring beetles, other ants (the leaf-cutters), and men.

Concerning this last point, Darwin[2] wrote:

146

The plant derives protection to its foliage . . . by the presence of whole armies of virulently stinging ants whose very minuteness renders them the more formidable.

Belt in his *Naturalist in Nicaragua* (p. 223) notices and figures the leaves of one of the Melastomae with swollen petioles, and he states that, besides the small ants always infesting them, he noticed, several times, some dark-coloured Aphides. He also suggests that these small virulently-stinging ants are of use to the plants by guarding them from leaf-eating enemies such as caterpillars, snails, and even herbivorous mammals, but above all from the omnipresent Sauba or leaf-cutting ant, which he declared he observed to be much afraid of these small species.

This cooperative arrangement between trees and ants is worked out in three distinct ways:

(1) Some ant trees have twigs that are already hollow, or that are filled with a soft pith the ants can quickly remove in preparing a nest. The ants find a hole or a spot of soft tissue at the base of the twig, bite their way through if necessary, and move in, often enlarging both the hole and the twig in the process. Some trees seem to have prepared the necessary entrance in expectation of the ants' arrival. In some thorny trees the ants live inside the thorns.

(2) Other ant trees house their tenants inside the leaves. This is accomplished in one of two ways. Usually the ants find or bite an entrance into the base of the leaf where the stem is attached; they move in, pushing the front and back surfaces of the leaf apart just as if they were ungluing two pieces of paper, and—presto!—they have a nest. Botanists say the leaf is "invaginated"—which merely indicates it has been blown up like a paper bag.

The second way of utilizing the leaf, much less frequently observed, is to curl the edges under until they touch, glue them that way and move in.

(3) Other ant trees do not themselves actually house the ants but act as supports for air plants and vines which do act as hosts to ants in exactly the same way that trees do. When you encounter an ant tree in the jungle, you are not going to stop to ascertain whether the ants are streaming out of leaves that belong to the tree or leaves that belong to a plant growing on the tree.

1. Ants in the Twigs

Spruce[3] wrote in detail of his experiences with ant trees on the Amazon:

Ants' nests in swellings of the branches are found chiefly in soft-wooded trees of humble growth, especially where the branches put forth at the extremity of a whorl; then, either at each leaf-node or at least at the apex of

LEFT: Close-up of ant galls on a whistling thorn tree (*Acacia*) in Africa. The common name comes from the noise made by wind blowing across holes in the galls. (Photo: D. I. Nicholson.) RIGHT: *Cecropia*, a weedy tree of swampy areas in Latin America. Its hollow stems provide flood-free accommodations for ants.

LEFT: *Cordia nodosa* twig-tip, destined as a home for ants. (Photo: Museu Goeldi, Belém, Pará, Brazil.) RIGHT: Bladder-like ant nests on *Dischidia collyris*, a vine that clings to a jungle tree in Malaya. (Photo: H. M. Burkill.)

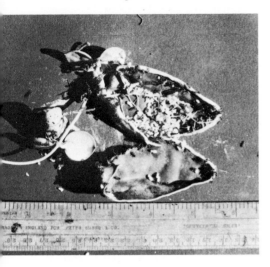

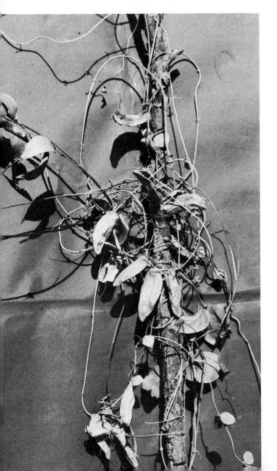

149

the penultimate branches, will probably be found an ant-house, in the shape of a hollow swelling of the branch; communication between the houses being kept up, sometimes by the hollowed interior of the branches, but nearly always by a covered way along their outside.

In *Cordia gerascantha*, at the point where the branches divide there is mostly a sac, inhabited by very vicious ants of the tribe called Tachi by the Brazilians. *Cordia nodosa* is usually tenanted by the small fire-ant, but sometimes by the Tachi. Probably the former was in all cases the original occupant, and the Tachi is an intruder.

All woody members of the knotweed order (*Polygonaceae*), Spruce continues, are infested by ants:

The whole of the medula of every plant, from the root nearly to the growing apex of the ramuli, is scooped out by those insects. The ants make a lodgment in the young stem of the tree or shrub, and as it increases in size and puts forth branch after branch, they extend their hollow ways through all its ramifications. They appear to belong all to a single genus, and they all sting virulently. They are known in Brazil by the name of Tachi or Tacyba, and in Peru by that of Tangarana; and in both countries the same name is commonly applied to any tree they infest as to the ants themselves.

Triplaris surinamensis, a tree of very rapid growth, common all along the Amazon, and *T. Schomburgkii*, a smaller tree, on the Upper Orinoco and Casiquiari, have slender elongated tubular branches, nearly always with perforations, like pinholes, just within the stipule of each leaf, which are the sallyports of the garrison, whose sentinels are besides always pacing up and down the main trunk, as the incautious traveller finds to his cost when, invited by the smoothness of the bark, he ventures to lean his back against a Tachi tree.

Nearly all tree-dwelling ants, although in the dry season they may descend to the ground and make their summer-houses there, retain the sacs and tubes above-mentioned as permanent habitations; and some kinds of ants appear never to reside elsewhere, at any time of the year. The same is probably true also of ants which build nests in trees, of extraneous materials, independent of the growing tissues of the tree itself. There are some ants which apparently must always live aloft; and the *Tococa*-dwellers continue to inhabit *Tococa* where there is never any risk of flood [see page 152].

Ant trees of many different genera are found throughout the tropics. Among the best known is *Cecropia peltata*, the trumpet-tree of tropical America, so-called because of the use made of its hollow stems by the Uaupes Indians.[4] The hollows are often inhabited by fierce ants (*Azteca*) which rush out if the tree is shaken and attack the intruder. These ants protect the *Cecropia* from the leaf-cutters. The internodes of the stems are hollow but do not communicate directly with the air. Near the top of each, however, is a thin place in the wall. A gravid female ant burrows through this and brings up her brood inside the stem. The base of the leaf-stalk is swollen and bears food-bodies on the lower side, upon which the ants feed. New bodies form as the old ones are eaten. Several other species show similar features. An interesting point that shows the adaptive nature of these phenomena is that in one species the stem is covered with wax which prevents the leaf-cutters from climbing up. In this there are neither food-bodies nor thin places in the internodes.

In some acacia trees, the stipules at the base of the leaves are replaced by large thorns, swollen at the base. In *Acacia sphaerocephala* of Central America, ants bore into these thorns, clear out the internal tissue, and make themselves at home. The tree provides them with nourishment, according to J. C. Willis:[5] "Extra floral nectaries occur on the petioles, and yellow sausage-shaped food-bodies on the tips of the leaflets." Willis adds that if any attempt is made to interfere with the tree the ants rush out.

The old riddle of which came first, the chicken or the egg, gets a rerun in the case of the black-galled *Acacia*,[6] or whistling thorn, in Kenya. The branches of this small shrubby tree bear straight, slender, white spines up to 3 inches long. On these thorns large galls are formed, soft and grape-purple when young, hardening and turning black and becoming inhabited by ants in age. Dale and Greenway[7] report: "The galls at the base of the spines . . . are said to be formed by ants, who hollow them out. When wind blows against the holes in the galls, it makes a whistling noise; hence the name whistling thorn. Research by Dr. G. Salt on the origin of galls in many *Acacia* has educed no evidence of their being stimulated to grow by ants; the plant produces the swollen bases and the ants make use of them."

An ant tree of Ceylon and southern India is *Humboldtia laurifolia*, of the pea family. On this, only the flowering twigs develop hollow spaces, and these are inhabited by ants. Non-flowering twigs, according to Willis, are normal in structure.

Regarding the South American species of *Duroia*, of the coffee family, Willis says that on two, *D. petiolaris* and *D. hirsuta*, the stems just below the inflorescences are swollen and hollow, and entrance for ants is obtained by two slits. A third, *D. saccifera*, has ant-houses on the leaves. The entrance, which is on the upper side, is protected from rain by a little flap.

Corner describes the various kinds of *Macaranga* called mahang by the natives, which are the chief ant trees in Malaya. He writes:

Their leaves are hollow and the ants live inside. The ants bite holes through the twig between the leaves, by which they come out and run over the surface, and in their dark galleries they keep multitudes of scale insects like herds of blind cattle. The scale insects suck the sugary sap of the twig and from its abundance they exude through their bodies a sweet excretion that the ants devour. The plants, moreover, form what are called "food-bodies," which are tiny white spheres (1 mm. wide) composed of oily tissue, which provide another article of food for the ants. . . . In all cases, they are in positions protected from the rain. . . . If a twig of one of these trees is cut, the ants run out and bite. . . . The ants obtain their entry into young plants through the winged females which bite their way into the twigs. The seedlings may be inhabited before they are a foot high, when they have curiously swollen, sausage-like internodes. The hollows in the twigs arise from the shrivelling of the wide pith between the nodes, as in bamboos, and the ants turn the separate hollows into galleries by biting through the partitions at the nodes.

J. A. Baker,[10] who studied *Macaranga* trees and ants, found that he could start a war by bringing two plants inhabited by ants into contact. Apparently the ants from each tree recognized each other by the peculiarity of the nest smell of the individual.

2. Ants Inside the Leaves

Richard Spruce's narrative[11] points out that the dilated tissues and membranes that furnish dwelling places for ant colonies exist chiefly in certain Melastomes of South America. Prominent among them is *Tococa*, which is numerous in both species and individuals along the Amazon. It grows principally in parts of the forest that are likely to be inundated by rivers, lakes, or heavy rains. In describing the sac that is formed on the leaves, he writes:

> The leaves in the majority of the species have but three ribs; a few species, however, have five- or even seven-ribbed leaves; but, in all, the origin of the innermost pair of ribs is an inch or so up the midrib from the base of the leaf; and it is this portion of the leaf, from the insertion of the inner ribs downwards, which is occupied by the sac.

This is where the ants make their homes. Spruce reported finding only one species, *Tococa planifolia*, without such inflated areas on the leaves, and this species, he noted, grows so close to the water that it is certain to be submerged for several months every year. This species, he explained,

> could never serve as a permanent residence for ants, nor consequently have any character impressed on it by their merely temporary sojourn; even if their instinct did not teach them to avoid it altogether, as they actually seem to do; whereas the species of *Tococa* growing far enough inland to maintain their heads above water even at the height of flood are thereby fitted to be permanently inhabited, and are consequently *never destitute of saccate leaves*, nor at any season of the year clear of ants; as I have reason to know from the

many desperate struggles I have had with those pugnacious little creatures when breaking up their homes for the sake of specimens.

Saclike ant-dwellings also exist in the leaves of plants of other families.

3. Air Plants and Vines as Ant Nests

Most important of the air plants which harbor ants on the high branches of tropical trees are the 18 species of *Myrmecodia*, found from New Guinea to Malaya and in the remote north of Australia where there are no white settlements. Often associated with these is another air plant, *Hydnophytum*, a genus of 40 species. Both are in the coffee family. Merrill[12] says some of these occur at low altitudes and sometimes even in the mangrove forests, while others grow in the primary forests at high altitudes. He continues:

> The basal part of these plants, sometimes armed with short spines, are very greatly enlarged, and this enlarged part is tunneled by a series of large passages, from some of which small openings to the exterior occur; within the greatly swollen bases of these plants myriads of small black ants find their abode. Springing from the top of the tuber-like, tunneled base are the vegetative parts of the plant, sometimes stout and unbranched, sometimes rather slender and much branched; the small white flowers and the small fleshy fruits are borne in the leaf axils or in the axils of fallen leaves.

Merrill continues with a description of some of the vines that are hosts to ants in the same manner:

> Perhaps the most peculiar of all, however, are those leaf adaptations noted in such groups as *Hoya*, *Dischidia*, and *Conchophyllum*, all vines with abundant milky sap belonging in the milkweed family (*Asclepiadaceae*). Some of these hang free, as epiphytes or semi-epiphytes, but in *Conchophyllum* and in some species of *Hoya* the vines may be closely appressed to the tree trunks or branches, while the circular leaves, one row on each side of the slender stem, are convex with their margins very closely appressed to the bark. Under each leaf many roots are produced from the leaf axil which often quite cover that part of the bark protected by the leaf, serving to hold the plant in place and to absorb moisture and nourishment for the needs of the plant; each of these ready-made homes under each leaf is occupied by colonies of small ants.

A curious pitcher-plant of southeast Asia, *Dischidia rafflesiana*, serves as host to ants. Some of its leaves are flat, others inflated as pitchers, which are thus described by Willis:

> Each is a pitcher with incurved margin, about 10 cm. deep. Into it grows an adventitious root developed from the stem or petiole just beside it. The pitcher . . . usually contains a lot of debris, largely carried into it by nesting

153

ants. Most contain rain water. . . . The inner surface is waxy, so that the water cannot be absorbed by the pitcher itself, but must be taken up by the roots.

Developmental study shows the pitcher to be a leaf, with its lower side invaginated.[13]

PART IV

Trees of Peculiar Behavior

SEVENTEEN

Sexual Curiosities

My beloved is unto me as a cluster of camphire.
—Song of Solomon 1:14

Sex plays an important part in making some trees peculiar. Leaves that take over the job of producing the next generation are odd enough; roots that give rise to flowers and fruits underground are even more peculiar. Now appear other abnormalities:

1. Certain trees switch sexes. The females, apparently tiring of life in that condition, convert to males. Similarly, some male trees, as though envious of the fair sex, switch over and become females.

2. Just as the human female uses perfume to attract the male, so certain trees use scented flowers as a lure. Or again, an odor may arise from the fruit, from a tree's bark, or from its wood. Apparently this aroma is keyed to the sensitiveness of certain insects or other creatures. Does the plant know that its scent attracts one particular animal, repels all others? Usually the creature drawn to it is a pollinating agent, but not always. Often the purpose of the smell is not clear to mankind.

3. Only one tree in the world[1] dies after giving birth to its young.

4. At least one natural "mule" has been produced in the tree world— a hybrid between two genera.

5. Two trees (and possibly more) reproduce their kind without any form of sexual union.[2] Is this a warning that males are becoming increasingly unimportant?

In addition to the abnormalities recorded here, see Chapter Twenty-three for the peculiarities of the ginkgo tree (*Ginkgo biloba*). Its sex life is different from that of any other tree.

1. *The Sex Switchers*

The Florida sago-palm,[3] which is not a palm but a cycad, and not a Floridian but a native of Indo-Malaysia, is a common dooryard plant in the Sunshine State. The true sago-palm,[4] which is somewhat hardier and comes from Japan, grows throughout the southern states as an ornamental. These plants are strictly dioecious, which means that one produces male flowers, another only female flowers. Pollen is carried by the wind. When the female flower opens, it unfolds long limbs that look like petals but are really leaves, and on the edge of these, each in a little individual nest, are the potential seeds.

In common practice, sago-palms are almost never propagated from seed; mature trees produce numerous offshoots on the trunk, which are easily cut off and rooted. These will always be of the same sex as the parent. When all the sago-palms in a neighborhood are females, their seeds are infertile and do not develop.

A Miami, Florida, woman[5] wrote to a newspaper garden editor[6] that a female cycad in her yard had suddenly developed an objectionable odor and a male inflorescence.[7] Her letter continued: "At one time we considered taking the tree down as it has leaned to one side [perhaps since Hurricane Donna] and we actually started chopping it down. It now has the scar of the ax marks. Could this cause the sex change?"

Mrs. Julia F. Morton, who conducts the newspaper's garden column, is a botanist of extensive experience with tropical plants. She replied:

> The elongated cone and the odor are certainly male features and I feel sure that the change was brought about by the chopping. It is interesting to recall that, while the papaya is a totally unrelated plant, the male papaya can be changed to a female by beheading. Sometimes a male papaya will undergo sex-reversal just from seasonal conditions; the female plant more rarely. . . . Stanley Kiem, Superintendent of the Fairchild Tropical Garden, said he had once before heard . . . that a sex change had possibly occurred in a local cycad but, since the individual had several specimens, it was assumed that he had confused one with another. As you have only one plant, you could hardly be mistaken.

Chamberlain,[8] probably the world's foremost authority on cycads, acknowledged skeptically that he had received reports of sex aberrations among the cycads, with this paragraph:

> No plants are more absolutely dioecious than the cycads. Schuster reports one case in *Cycas revoluta* where a plant was cut into two longitudinal pieces,

156

ABOVE: The female flower of the false sago-palm (*Cycas circinalis*) in its early stages—like a dish of vanilla ice cream. BELOW: Probably the only natural generic tree hybrid in the world—a cross between a New Zealand tree (*Myrtus bullata*) and an Australian tree of a different genus (*Eugenia myrtifolia*). It is called *Eugeniamyrtus smithii*. (Photo: Douglas Elliott.)

ABOVE: Mountain-pride flowers (*Spathelia simplex*). The cluster is 6 to 8 feet across. When the flowers fade and the seeds mature, the tree dies. (Photo: Ken Sharon.)

LEFT: Balsam (*Abies balsamea*), whose fragrance has a delicious tang. RIGHT: Foliage, flowers, and seed pods of the ylang-ylang tree (*Canangium odoratum*). The flowers are distilled in Malaya for their perfume. (Photo: Ricou.)

A myrrh tree, on the island of Socotra in the Indian Ocean. It resembles a low spreading cedar. (Photo: Douglas Botting.)

Parinari curatellaefolia (of the rose family), reported to emanate an exceedingly offensive odor on hot days in Rhodesia. (Photo: G. L. Guy.)

LEFT: The stink of the wood of this hackberry (*Celtis cinnamomea*) in Ceylon persists for days when a tree is cut. (Photo: T. B. Worthington.) RIGHT: The magnificent 5-inch white flowers of the Trinidad stinkwood tree (*Gustavia augusta*) offset the objectionable smell of the wood. (Photo: Trinidad Botanic Garden.)

which were taken to different places. It is claimed that one piece produced a female strobilus and the other, a male. On a lawn in Australia there were several plants of *Cycas revoluta*. It was reported to me that one of these produced a female strobilus and, a few years later, a male strobilus. It is also claimed that a bud from a female plant of *Cycas circinalis*, in the Garfield Park Conservatory at Chicago, reached the coning stage and produced a male cone. In 30 years of study in the field and in greenhouses I have never seen anything to indicate that the cycads are not absolutely dioecious.

John G. Williams has a false sago-palm in his orange grove on Taylor Lake, west of Tampa, Florida. It has been in his family's possession for sixty years and has always produced male cones. The 1962 freeze hit the plant very hard; when it had recovered and bloomed, the flowers were female and seed formed.

A *Ruprechtia* tree from Venezuela, which I had grown from seed and given to the Martin County Hospital, Stuart, Florida, some fifteen years ago, began blooming heavily in 1957, when it was about eight years old, producing great quantities of showy, bright red female flowers each December. In 1962 when a hospital annex was under construction, the tree was moved to a new location, cut back severely, and re-established. It failed to bloom at all in December 1963, but in December 1964 its branches were covered with tiny, inconspicuous male flowers.

Sex switches among papaya plants[9] have been studied extensively by geneticists in several countries.[10] They occur also in certain orchid genera.

Holly trees have been reported to change sex if growing conditions are unfavorable. Female trees that have borne berries heavily for years, if placed under duress, have been known to start producing male flowers instead.

Other trees, and a good many lesser plants, switch sexes.[11] Schaffner[12] found that ordinary hemp or marijuana[13] produces purely male and purely female individuals when planted in the field in spring, but that about ninety per cent of both male and female plants reverse their sexual expression when planted in a greenhouse during the winter. Observation showed that a difference of about six hours in the amount of daylight between winter and summer established a direct relation to the percentage of sex reversal in the plants. Other plants whose sex reversal was studied by Schaffner included ordinary field corn,[14] one of the meadow-rues,[15] a native aroid (Jack-in-the-pulpit),[16] and the white mulberry.[17]

Sex reversal in the normally dioecious yew tree[18] is causing considerable confusion in the nursery trade, for the bright-colored berries make the female plants more desirable. Propagators have been warned[19] to be on the lookout for plants which occasionally put on a single branch of the opposite sex. John Vermeulen, who introduced the heavy-fruiting Kelsey yew, says that a strongly upright male mutant is known to sport from this variety occasionally. It is believed that male mutants sport as often as female, but are less conspicuous.

2. Odoriferous Trees

All smelly trees are peculiar, because millions of their fellows have no perceptible odor. Our senses are tantalized by such tree products as cinnamon,[20] allspice,[21] cloves,[22] nutmeg,[23] mace, the tonka bean,[24] and others. We glory in the fragrance arising from crushed leaves of bay,[25] camphor,[26] eucalyptus, and others which contribute so heavily to cosmetics and medicine. But all these are commonplace in this book, to be laid aside for the consideration of trees that really are smelly. These are quickly divided by the nose into two groups: the bouquets and the stinkers.

The most important tree odors come from the resins that are exuded from the bark, sometimes naturally but more frequently as a result of physical injury to the tree. Can anything be more delicious and stimulating than the fragrance of a forest of balsam fir[27] on a hot summer day? Many of the conifers have this same sort of delightful aroma, but the vast majority of Temperate Zone trees fails to stir the olfactory sense at all.

Most famous of all resins in history, of course, are the frankincense and myrrh brought to the Christ Child by the three Wise Men. Botting[28] says that several thousand years before Christ the Arabians were getting as rich exploiting incense as are their descendants today developing oil wells. Vast quantities of incense were sold in all parts of the ancient world. Chaldean priests burned enormous amounts on the altars to Baal; the Babylonians used it for purification (instead of taking baths), and in Jerusalem giant garners were constructed to hold this gift to the Most High. All over Greece incense was burned to honor Zeus, and later a cargo-boat service was established to carry the product to Rome. The Egyptians burned more incense than any others for they burned it in worship, used it as a medicine, as an embalming agent, and as part of a religious ritual concerned with regeneration of the spirits of the dead. Botting continues:

> In his mercantile specifications of 1200 B.C. Rameses III laid down that the color of incense may vary from a cloudy amber-yellow to a jade-green as pale as moonlight, but that anything else was worthless. Such perfect incense was produced by the frankincense and myrrh trees alone, and for many hundreds of years it was brought overland from the region of Dhufar and the Hadhramaut in Southern Arabia, where these trees grow. Heavily-guarded camel caravans, loaded with the precious resin, made their way westwards through South Arabia to the Yemen where they turned north and

progressed slowly along the Red Sea coast till the incense route divided and one branch led west to Egypt and another east to Babylon and Syria. Each camel-load cost £100 and bore a 500 per cent profit by the time it reached its destination. It is therefore not surprising that the enterprising Egyptians should have attempted to reduce expenditure by cutting out the middlemen in the incense business. They decided to go and collect the incense themselves and, if possible, bring back the saplings of the incense trees for transplantation in Egyptian soil.

The first known Egyptian expedition to the incense-bearing countries, which the Egyptians called the Land of Punt or the Land of God, set out in approximately the year 3000 B.C. Little is known about this expedition, except that it brought back 80,000 measures of myrrh and 2,600 pieces of costly woods. From time to time during the subsequent hundreds of years, other expeditions sailed down the Red Sea to bring back from Punt the priceless incense. The last and greatest of these expeditions set sail in 1493 B.C. at the express command of the great Queen Hatshepsut. The fleet consisted of five large galleys, each with thirty rowers, and was away for an unknown period. Preserved on the walls of the temple at Dehr-el-Bahri are lengthy inscriptions and drawings of the homecoming of the expedition. . . .

Of all the unusual trees that grow on Socotra (an island in the Indian Ocean, off the mouth of the Persian Gulf), none has such exotic associations or has had such an importance in the past as the frankincense tree and the myrrh tree. In parts of the mountains, and in particular in the valley which leads down to the town of Qalansiya, these trees grow in abundance. In the summer they blossom and fill the entire valley with a magnificent scent.

The myrrh tree[29] (of which there are six species on Socotra) is like a low spreading cedar.

The frankincense tree[30] (of which there are three or four species on the island) looks like a decomposing animal. It has stiff low branches. The leaves are scanty, curly, and indented. A thick bark (which the local Bedouin sometimes make into buckets) and a tiny whitish peel cling closely round the trunk of a peculiarly blotchy color. The woody fibre of the tree, distended with sap, looks like rotting animal flesh, and the clear, yellowish-white resin comes from incisions with a strong aroma. The fruit is a berry the size of a marble and the flowers are few, red and geranium-like on the end of short spikes. The trees are not cultivated and only a little incense is collected, for local purposes, not for export.

The odor given off by flowers rarely travels far, at least in sufficient volume to be perceptible by humans, and it is not always pleasant. On a misty evening, with no wind, the fragrance of frangipani[31] or ylang-ylang[32] pervades nearby acres to the olfactory delight of all, but under the same circumstances the blossoms of *Jacaratia*,[33] *Oroxylon*,[34] and the *baobab*[35] are extraordinarily malodorous and can keep every sensitive nostril at bay. The flowers of one species of *Terminalia*[36] make it the "stink tree" of Queensland, and the blossoms of an Indian *Sterculia*[37] reek like a dead skunk. There are plenty of such undesirables. Familiar ones in the Tem-

162

perate Zone are the stinking fruits of the female ginkgo trees from China, and the highly offensive flowers of the female tree-of-heaven (*Ailanthus altissima*).

In the tropics some trees produce timber that has a delicious and lasting odor, usually produced by an oil contained in their tissues. Sandalwood[38] is a good example. It has been cherished for hundreds of years for its aromatic elegance. The wood of some eucalyptus and other myrtaceous trees has a pleasant fragrance, and any forestry school will supply a long list of others. Contrariwise, the smell of many tropical woods is highly unpleasant.

Consider the report of a forester in Southern Rhodesia about a tree that belongs, of all places, in the rose family:

> *Parinari*[39] on a hot day has a very distinct odor, but so far I have noted no reference to it in any biological works. I noticed it when I was out hunting with a friend of mine, and the deeper we got into the *Parinari* forest, the more I was convinced that my companion had not had a bath for some weeks. The deeper we got, the longer the period of my guess about his habits, until late in the afternoon I realized that no one could smell as bad as that without knowing it, and managed to trace the odor to the trees.[40]

Obviously such emanation from the trees may be seasonal; it may be noticeable only on a steaming hot day, or it may be strictly a local phenomenon.[41] Odors are so ephemeral that some which are offensive to one individual cannot even be detected by another. The physiological reactions of two sniffers are never identical. Any of these variables may explain an apparent contradiction of the above by another experienced botanist:

> My research student G. T. Prance, who has been working in *Parinari* for three years, cannot confirm the Southern Rhodesian forester's remarks about the offensive odor of *P. curatellaefolia*. I have lived in *P. curatellaefolia* forests myself and have never noticed an unusual smell. Prance tells me that the fresh wood is slightly malodorous.[42]

Bawang hutan[43] is the forestry department's official name for a big timber tree in Sumatra, Malaya, and Borneo. Translated, it means "forest onion." Corner[44] says this tree "stinks of bad garlic in all its parts and I have noticed the stale smell in Bornean forests where the tree is abundant." I. H. Burkill[45] says the timber has a garlic odor when fresh and a peppery odor when dry. Corner writes:

> *Pithecellobium jiringa* also smells of garlic in its tissues. Some rubiaceous small trees of *Coprosma* and *Lasianthus* smell of the most iniquitous ordure in bark, twig, and leaf, so that in brushing past them in the forests they can at once be identified. Many, if not most leguminous barks, when cut, smell of crushed bean pods. But few trees now known to me (other than

Scorodocarpus), give out a humanly perceptible smell without cutting or crushing the tissue.

An outstanding example of bad odor emanating from a tree is the ombú[46] in Argentina. Strangely enough, the smell is imperceptible to humans in daytime, but becomes extremely offensive at night. The scent is probably present, however, by daylight because birds, insects, and all other creatures avoid the tree both day and night. Man's olfactory sense just lacks this keenness.

The plant called mustard in the Bible[47] is a shrub or weak tree to 30 feet high which grows from central Africa northward into western Asia. A forester in Northern Rhodesia[48] reports that on a hot sunny day the tree gives off an acrid odor.

Out in the forests, trees with halitosis are frequently known locally as "stinkwoods." Among these are a Brazil-nut relative[49] in Mauritius, and a member of the laurel family in South Africa. The latter is an *Ocotea*,[50] and many of this genus grow in northern South America. G. L. Guy writes from Salisbury:

> It is the freshly felled timber that smells. Some years ago furniture dealers in South Africa imported imbuia (*Phoebe porosa*) from South America and sold it as genuine stinkwood to which it does bear some resemblance, but it lacks the rich golden glow which makes stinkwood one of the most beautiful timbers in the world. South Africa forestry officers were able to prove the difference by damping and rubbing disputed pieces of wood: genuine stinkwood was easily recognizable by the "stink" even many years after being utilized.

In southern Florida the white stopper[51] is often called skunk-tree because it is so easily identified by its odor as a person walks through the woods.[52]

In Ceylon there is a hackberry[53] known as stinkwood, but it is only the heartwood that merits the name. The Singhalese and Tamil names for this tree both mean "stink of ordure." A recently felled tree can be smelled many days at a long distance.

Another stinkwood has very handsome magnolia-like foliage and magnificent fragrant flowers, 5 inches across, the petals creamy-white or purple-ringed. It is *Gustavia augusta*, a tree of Trinidad and Brazil. Unfortunately, anyone walking under the tree becomes aware of the profoundly disagreeable odor, perhaps emanating from the leaves as well as from trunk and roots. When I grew some of these trees in Florida, I too found the odor repulsive.

When W. R. Philipson had returned from his travels in Brazil, he wrote:[54]

We were determined to leave the camp because a varasantha tree[55] fell across the clearing and everything was covered with vicious ants, and in addition an unpleasant smell that had puzzled us for days was at last traced to its source. We had searched in everything and under everything for some meat or other animal remains that might have been overlooked. At last we found that the smell was coming from the stumps of some trees of a kind of stinkwood that we had cut down in clearing the campsite. These small trees occur abundantly throughout the forests of tropical South America; their botanical name is *Gustavia,* and they belong to the same family as the Brazil nut. Though they bear the most exquisitely lovely flowers, not unlike white magnolias flushed with rose, the natives and colonists alike have given them repulsive names in all their languages and dialects. Flower of death, corpse tree, and stinkwood are examples that refer to the offensive smell of the freshly cut wood. We could not grub out the stumps, some of which were actually inside our kitchen and eating shelter, so that we were glad to know that we had only one more night to pass in these surroundings.

In an earlier book[56] I reported curious instances of three distinguished flowering trees of the tropics whose blossoms emit unpleasant smells before pollination but are scentless afterwards. These trees are the Australian firewheel tree (*Stenocarpus sinuatus*), the princely *Metternichia principis* of Brazil, and *Clavija grandis* of Colombia.

No review of unpleasant odors in the forest would be complete without reference to a Malayan fruit called durian,[57] which is much loved by Malays but found objectionable by most travelers because of its smell. (See Chapter Six.)

Fortunately, the unpleasant smells of the forest are outnumbered by the fragrances which linger much longer in memory.

3. *The Self-Sacrificers*

The annual plants in our gardens come into flower, set seed, and die. One supreme effort and all is over—their life cycle has been completed, their purpose fulfilled. Biennials do this over a period of two years. Many larger plants, including a few palms, have the same sort of life cycle—grow, fruit, die—but over a longer period. An outstanding example is the century-plant,[58] which, after a long earthbound existence with only a stiff rosette of pointed leaves, suddenly throws a 20-foot flowering scape into the air. In some of the century-plant's relatives, thousands of bulbils form in the flower spike, all ready to grow. These drop off and take root all around "mama," but the parent plant dies. Flowering and fruiting may be delayed ten, twenty, or even thirty years (never a hundred years as the name implies), then flowering comes in a rush and in a few weeks the plant's life cycle is finished.

Plants which flower, fruit, and then die are called monocarps, from two Greek words signifying one-fruiting. And in all the tree world, outside of a few palms, there is only one genus of monocarps; this is a neotropical group in the citrus family named *Spathelia*. All of them—about ten species —are tall, thin, palmlike plants, without branches. The most famous, because seen by so many travelers in Jamaica, is the mountain-pride,[59] a tree often 30 to 50 feet high, though rarely more than 3 inches in diameter at the base.[60] The trees are in colonies in the mountains and their fishing-pole trunks are crowned by handsome pinnate, fernlike leaves. In spite of their early decease, the trees are often planted for their decorative appearance. Ordinarily a mountain-pride is eight to ten years old before it prepares to bloom. Then, out of the leafy crown bursts a great spreading cluster of beautiful red flowers—the panicle frequently 5 feet high and 8 feet across. Many seeds are produced, so that plenty of new trees are coming up all around. About six months elapse between flowering and the ripening of the seed. Then the tree dies and a new generation takes over.[61]

Scientists believe that *Spathelia* originated in the West Indies and that back in the days of the dinosaurs, when the Caribbean islands were connected by land bridges to South America, some *Spathelia* seeds got carried over to that continent. They grew up in different environments there, developing new characteristics, so that when a botanical explorer found one of these in Amazonas several million years later he thought it was a new genus and called it *Sohnreyia*.[62] When another explorer found one of the trees on the border between Guiana and Venezuela, he too decided it was a new genus and named it *Diomma*.[63] Today both of these names and the names of additional new species are included in *Spathelia*,[64] for, in trees with the monocarp habit of dying after fruiting, there is close alliance.

4. *The Tree World's Only Natural Mule*

Although the word "mule" usually refers to the sterile cross of the horse and the ass, it has also been used for hundreds of years to denote crosses in the plant world, the combining of two individuals (or more, through succeeding generations) in order to develop a progeny possessing the better qualities of the parents. Such crosses usually bear seed which may come true.

More strictly speaking, a plant "mule" would be a cross between two genera. As the relationship between plants becomes more distinct, the chances of producing vigorous offspring become more and more tenuous. Thus it is likely that combinations between genera within a family—the most distant crosses actually possible—will produce weak offspring whose powers of reproduction, like that of the mule in the animal world, are nil.[65]

Natural hybrids between tree species occur in the wild fairly frequently, the oaks offering numerous examples. As an accidental hybrid between two species in a garden, *Magnolia soulangeana* is noteworthy; it developed in a French château garden in the 1820s.

Until recently, however, a natural cross between two genera in the wild had been considered impossible. But in New Zealand such a natural hybrid did develop between two genera of trees in the myrtle family, and to it has been ascribed the name *Eugeniamyrtus smithii*.[66] According to Victor C. Davies, veteran nurseryman of New Plymouth, New Zealand, this hybrid originated in the garden of a Mr. Smith at Lower Hutt, Wellington, in the 1940s. Mr. Davies wrote:

> We obtained scions and rooted them, and in due course put it on the market, and each year sell quite a number. It appears to be a definite cross between *Myrtus bullata* and *Eugenia myrtifolia*. (I am using all the old names, as it is difficult to get used to the new names of these plants.) It flowers freely, and very much resembles *Eugenia myrtifolia*, but up to the present I have not seen any fruit.

Many artificial mules have been created by hybridizers, particularly among woody plants. Paterson[67] wrote of these bigeneric crosses:

> If one were asked to choose three of these plant mules for garden worth the choice would surely include *Cupressocyparis leylandii* which, with *Chamaecyparis nootkatensis*, incorporates all the advantages of its other parent, *Cupressus macrocarpa*, into a splendid hedge plant. *Osmarea burkwoodii* (*Osmanthus* x *Phillyrea*), an excellent evergreen flowering shrub, would also be considered. My third choice would be the remarkable cross between *Fatsia japonica* and *Hedera, Fatshedera lizei*, a valuable room plant which will survive considerable frost and ill treatment. It also has another advantage, a common name to remind you of the Latin—fat-headed Lizzie.

5. Dwindling Importance of the Male

The factory worker who spotted the sign: "Look alive, man; you can be replaced by a button!" has nothing on men in general. Despite bland assurances that obliteration of the male is not likely to spread to the animal kingdom, danger flags are flying. The tree world has started getting along without them. What may be next? At least two kinds of trees have demonstrated their ability in this connection.

In tropical western Africa grows a tree called *Pachira oleaginea*. Its big white "shaving-brush" flowers, which open at night, are probably fertilized by bats with pollen from flowers on the same tree. Fruits six inches long and three inches in diameter mature in two months, split open, and dump about twenty chestnut-like seeds on the ground. These usually germinate in a week.

So far, all is perfectly regular. The difficulties begin when the new seed starts sprouting. Careful study has shown[68] that although only one embryo was fertilized by the pollen, several additional embryos appear in the same seed. These fatherless scions develop faster than the sexually produced embryo, frequently outstripping it. Because they are vegetatively part of the mother tree and had no father, all are exactly alike in form. These are the seedlings which get planted to produce the succeeding generation of trees.

If this effacing of the male were an isolated case and could be confined to western Africa, human males might not need to feel concern. But now they must contend with a Malaysian fruit tree. The mangosteen[69] is a luscious fruit. Discussing its cultivation in Puerto Rico, Harold F. Winters[70] wrote:

> The seeds of the mangosteen are produced parthenocarpically, that is, without pollination of the flower. Genetically, the seedlings are exactly like the parent. In fact only one variety of mangosteen is known.

Obviously the situation, as far as males are concerned, is serious. Who was it who twitted: "What a fine world this would be, if the men were all transported far beyond the Northern Sea"?

How would you like to be a male flower on a mangosteen tree with absolutely nothing to do?

EIGHTEEN

The Two-Headed Monsters

A man of great stature, that had on every hand six fingers, and on
every foot six toes.   —II SAMUEL 21:20

The hydra-headed monsters of the tree world are all palms. They range as
two-headed freaks from the black hills of Haiti and the yellow pampas of
the Argentine to a five-headed horror in the jungles of Puerto Rico. They
are fit subjects for anybody's museum because in the world of palms
"there ain't no such thing!"

In the past fifty years great strides have been made by scientists in their
understanding of the palm family, and the number of described kinds
now exceeds one thousand. These plants have a code of behavior, and the
trees paraded in this chapter have violated the code. Palms are popularly
supposed:

(1) To have either fan or feather leaves—no other kind.[1]

(2) To propagate from seed only, with each seed producing only one
plant.[2]

(3) To be evergreen.

(4) To be nonpoisonous.[3]

(5) To grow primarily in the tropics.

(6) Never to allow winds to blow them over.[4]

(7) Always to grow straight up,[5] to have a single stem, and never to
have branches.[6]

As explained by the reference notes, there are plenty of exceptions to
these generalized statements. However, if you discover a palm with

branches, something definitely has gone wrong and further investigation is warranted.

Occasionally accidents happen, and then the nonbranching palms may branch. This event is extremely rare, because ordinarily when the bud at the tip of a palm shoot is broken or cut off the palm dies. This is the textbook dictum.

The branched palms illustrated in this chapter are therefore unique specimens. According to Dr. H. E. Moore,[7] no one knows exactly what happened to bring about such phenomena. Presumably when the tree was broken off, the apical bud was disturbed but not killed. Then from the wreckage of the tree arose an abnormal and unpredictable branching. The pictured examples are only a few of the known instances of this phenomenon.

The African oil palm[8] which produces the palm oil used in soap manufacture, can be added to the list of palms that may branch. Unwin[9] says:

> There is one forked palm on the right-hand side of the line about 7 miles from Ibadan [Nigeria], just beyond Moor plantation. This is a very rare occurrence, and I have only seen one in twelve years of traveling in Nigeria.

A few broad-leaved trees like the mango[10] and the rose-apple[11] produce polyembryonic seeds; this is the phenomenon of a single seed that produces two or more plants—twins, triplets, quads, or any other number. This quirk of nature is not repeated in the palm family—or almost never. The coconut with two sprouts pictured here is really the only one of its kind.

ABOVE: A four-headed Sabal palm in Florida. It was obviously broken and restarted more than once in its career. (Photo: Elbert Schory.)

ABOVE: A branched palm (*Washingtonia filifera*) in Oakland, California. (Photo: Ralph D. Cornell.)

LEFT: Twin coconuts (*Cocos nucifera*). Two sprouts from one nut is a hitherto unheard-of phenomenon. Photographed by the author at Stuart, Florida.

LEFT: Ambatch trees (*Aeschynomene elaphroxylon*) growing on a floating island in Lake Victoria, Africa. The wood is so light it is used to make pith helmets. (Photo: M. S. Philip.) RIGHT: Leaves, bright flower, and seed pod of the ambatch. (Photo: W. Carmichael.)

A man carries a balsa log 15 feet long and almost 20 inches in diameter at a sawmill in Ecuador. (Photo: International Balsa Co.)

NINETEEN

The Lightest Wood

A tree planted by the waters, and that spreadeth out her roots by the river, and shall not see when heat cometh, but her leaf shall be green; and shall not be careful in the year of drought.
—JEREMIAH 17:8

Trot out all contenders for the world's champion featherweight timber. Quickly eliminated from the contest are: lignum vitae,[1] because a cubic foot of it weighs 88½ pounds; the anjan tree[2] of India, a cubic foot of which weighs 82 pounds; ebony,[3] which weighs 73 pounds per cubic foot; and mahogany,[4] weighing 45 pounds per cubic foot. These might be heavyweight contenders,[5] but coming up now is the featherweight championship, which means that all entries must be lighter than cork,[6] which weighs 13 pounds per cubic foot.

At the moment it appears that balsa[7] is going to win. It weighs only 7 pounds per cubic foot—about half as much as cork. Are there other prospects? Yes, several woods are lighter than balsa, but for commercial use they lack something—mostly availability.

Balsa is a Spanish word meaning raft, applied to this tree because the trunks are often so used. It comes from a South American weed tree that grows so fast and so continuously that it never leaves annual rings. Its composition is a solid mass of cellulose, the big cells filled with sap so that a green log is heavy and must be dragged out of the woods by oxen. It is so spongy that it will decay if it is left lying on the ground more than a day or two. It is so soft that very sharp tools are required to cut it into

173

lumber. (Did you ever try slicing an angel-food cake with a dull knife?) But stand the lumber on end for air drying, or rush it into a kiln, and that sap evaporates quickly, leaving a wood that, pound for pound, is tougher than oak. No wonder that it is a strong contender for feather-weight-title honors.

The amazing lightness of dry balsa makes it of particular value where unusual strength is required without much extra weight. This is accomplished by laminating balsa with other woods, or veneering them on a balsa base. In airplane construction balsa boards or beams are half as heavy as spruce and will support fifty per cent more weight. Similarly, in steamship construction, partitions built of veneered balsa not only provide insulation where needed but save hundreds of tons in a ship's gross weight. Because of balsa's cellular constitution, it provides excellent insulation. In a test, frozen butter, packed in a balsa box, was shipped from Los Angeles to New York. It was still frozen on arrival, eight days later, though the average exterior temperature had been 82 degrees Fahrenheit. Balsa absorbs vibration and is often placed under heavy machinery to keep buildings from shaking. Balsa walls and ceilings absorb sound waves that might otherwise be a local nuisance.[8]

There are other woods lighter than balsa,[9] but they lack its uniformity, toughness, and accessibility. Only one of these is a conversation stopper—ambatch,[10] from which came the pith helmet you wore on safari when you killed the lion.

Ambatch, sometimes called pith-tree, is a weedy shrub or tree to 30 feet, growing in water on the margins of lakes, swamps, and rivers. Its stem is short, swollen, 10 to 12 inches in diameter at the base, quickly tapered until it is almost a cone, and covered with spines. The bark is smooth and green. The branches are covered with upcurved brown prickles ⅓ inch long. In appearance the tree is much like an acacia but differs in its handsome orange-yellow flowers which are pealike and very large, the corolla one and a half to two inches long. Eggeling[11] wrote of it:

> The wood has no commercial value, but the uses to which it is put by natives are of interest. On Lake Albert and on Lake Victoria it is used for floats for fishing-nets and lines. On Lake Nakivali and at Katunguru on the Kazinga Channel, the Banyankole fishermen fix a torpedo-shaped lump of Ambatch wood to the shafts of their fish spears. "This does not materially impede the spear's passage through the water, but causes it to bob up to the surface again in the event of a miss."[12]
> On the Nile, large blocks of the wood are attached by rope to the spears used for harpooning hippopotamuses and serve as buoys.
> Schweinfurth[13] gives an excellent description of the plant: "The Ambatch is distinguished for the unexampled lightness of its wood. . . . Only by taking

it into his hands could anyone believe that it were possible for one man to lift on his shoulders a raft made large enough to carry eight people on the water. The plant shoots up with great rapidity by the quiet places on the shore, and since it roots merely in the water, whole bushes are easily broken off by the force of wind or stream, and settle themselves afresh in other places. This is the true origin of the grass barriers so frequently mentioned as blocking the waters of the Upper Nile and in many cases making navigation utterly impossible."

Sir Harry Johnston[14] enlarges on this formation of sudd [floating vegetable matter]. He describes how the Ambatch trees "swell as they grow, and finally make quite a wall or breastwork of pithy wood, behind which masses of floating vegetation collect." He also states that "on many of the northern creeks of the Victoria Nyanza, protected from the waves of the open lake, this sudd or vegetable growth is gradually creating a soil and filling up the bays with what some day may be a land surface of peat, perhaps afterwards coal."

TWENTY

Trees That Twist

I may turn to the right hand, or to the left. —Genesis 24:49

Trees that are twisted appear to writhe in an anguished effort to escape from some unfriendly or intolerable factor in their environment. Actually they may have become twisted from any one of a score of other different causes; perhaps they spiraled because at some stage in their lives oblique growth was easier than straightaway.

Trees have been twisting for millions of years. In the past two centuries many scientists have puzzled, experimented, observed, and written about these swirlings from five different viewpoints:

1. Trees whose twisted exteriors were brought on by some kind of unnatural environmental stress or unbalanced supplies of growth material.

2. Trees whose twisted exteriors have resulted from hereditary factors or growth peculiarities. Sometimes these are passed on to succeeding generations and run true for a species. Again they may be sports that are subsequently propagated vegetatively (cuttings, grafts, etc.) in order to preserve this peculiarity.

3. Trees whose trunks have been twisted or gnarled by virus diseases.

4. Trees that are twisted on the inside instead of on the outside, affecting the grain of the wood and producing many strange and beautiful patterns. Usually this interior twisting is not apparent from the tree's exterior, except to an expert; and usually there is no connection between this interior twisting and any swirl that may appear on the outside.

5. Trees crushed to the ground or virtually torn out by their roots by

176

hurricanes or other natural violence, leaving the tree to twist its way back toward the sun and survival.

1. Twisting as the Result of Stresses

Stresses obviously are of many kinds and, once started, they may continue, they may cease, or they may reverse. Most trees in infancy have a photo-tropic tendency to spiral that seems to disappear as the growing points mature. During this initial interval an imbalance of auxin (growth materials) against gravity or light may encourage or originate a swirl. A tree on a river bank might be expected to twist from too much moisture on one side. A tree with a lopsided crown might easily be twisted by a prevailing wind. Trees on mountain tops are usually much twisted, though not always by wind; heredity or unsuitable climatic conditions can have the same effect.

The slash pine,[1] a low-elevation tree, twists very badly when planted at high elevations in South Africa under conditions quite unsuitable for its growth.[2] Scots pine[3] is found all over Europe and Asia with many races that range from gnarled dwarf trees to fine straight monarchs of 100 feet or more. Rather drastic results were obtained in the early 1800s from planting Scots pine seed at elevations not suited to the particular strain.

Soil deficiencies and rocky terrain often are responsible for twisting. So are excessive heat and dryness.

Reasoning that heat and drought, the chief natural causes of seedling damage and mortality, might be expected to cause stems to twist, scientists at the University of Georgia[4] successfully and consistently synthesized left- and right-hand spirals in trunks of young slash pines. Stresses caused by both drought and heat resulted in such consistent spiral twisting that the amount of twisting was eventually used to measure the degree of environmental stress. Other environmental stresses such as light intensity, ionizing radiation, competition, and day length did not produce spiral stems.[5]

In very dry localities in India[6] the sandan[7] grows as a small tree, with a tendency to produce a corkscrew-shaped stem. Elsewhere its twisting has been attributed to the mineral constituents of the wood cells.[8]

Some scientists believe that the twisting tendency may be inherited at the species level, and most agree that a potentiality for twisted stems is molded and developed by the interaction of trees with their environment. Trees most likely to twist often grow in rigorous climates, as at timber lines, in rocky cliffs, or on desert flats. In such places environmental conditions fluctuate rapidly with wide extremes of moisture and temperature.

177

The direction of the swirl taken by a tree when it starts to grow spirally has been the subject of much investigation. One enthusiastic observer[9] examined and kept records on several thousand twisted trees for six years, then could not use his data because the same trees behaved differently in varied locations or changed environment. He was wrong in his conclusion that right- and left-hand twists were equally frequent, for copious records exist to the contrary.

University of Georgia scientists found that the direction of the spiral did vary with the nature of the environmental stresses under observation: right-hand spirals exceeded left-hand three to one following heat stresses, and left-hand spirals predominated three to one following drought stresses. Combinations of heat and drought stresses produced approximately equal numbers of left- and right-hand spirals.[10] No one has yet explained the mechanics of twisting or how a plant retains a spiral pattern of growth.

A research scientist[11] in India showed that trees tend to twist to the right or left according to species. In certain species of pine in Europe and India, he pointed out, almost one hundred per cent of the trees over extensive areas may exhibit a definite left-hand twist. A changeover in the individual tree from a left-hand twist in youth to a right-hand twist later in life, recorded in the United States[12] for red spruce trees, he calls a "common occurrence" in India. Confusion enters here, however, because the writers are referring sometimes to exterior twist and sometimes to a twist in the wood grain.

Another Indian scientist[13] went to great lengths in the laboratory to prove that stem twisting results from circumnutation—the inequalities of growth on opposite sides of the stem. He demonstrated that stems are sensitive to electricity, heat, light, gravity, contact (with another object), and other stimuli. He found that the interaction of these factors determines the origin and continuation of twist, and even reversal of its direction.

It often appears that the choice of left- or right-hand swirling is largely accidental with trees (although not with vines, which twist one way or the other according to species, as discussed later). Occasionally, twin or double trees are found with one trunk spiraling to the left, the other to the right, as if they were balancing each other. The popular notion that most trees north of the equator spiral to the right, and those south of it to the left, is as false as the one-time theory that

When the tree was young a large owl sat in the top, watching the moon in its slow course across the sky. The twisting motion of the owl caused the spiral. We all know that most owls are right-handed which would explain the right spirals in this latitude.[14]

178

LEFT, TOP: A Jeffrey pine (*Pinus jeffreyi*) in Yosemite National Park, twisted by the prevailing winds of an exposed mountain top. (Photo: Wolfe.) LEFT, CENTER: A flat-topped Camperdown elm (*Ulmus glabra camperdownii*) in Dundee, Scotland, horribly twisted from the ground to the tips of the branches, which are weeping. (Photo: A. Muirhead Duncan.) LEFT, BOTTOM: This portly maiden doing a left-handed curtsy at Windsor, England, is an oak, about eight hundred years old. (Photo: J. E. Downward.) BELOW, RIGHT: A queen palm, often called *Cocos plumosus* (*Arecastrum romanzoffianum*) at Cypress Gardens, Florida. It was blown over in a hurricane but refused to die. (Photo: Cypress Gardens.)

LEFT: An ancient hemlock in North Carolina spiraling to the left. RIGHT: This double black locust in North Carolina twists one trunk to the right, one to the left.

LEFT: A very old European chestnut (*Castanea sativa*) at Kew, England. (Photo: Arnold Arboretum.) RIGHT: Two screw-pines (*Pandanus utilis*) growing side by side in a Florida garden, one twisting to the right, the other to the left. This is probably not a double tree but the result of two seeds germinated out of the same pod. (Photo: Ricou.)

LEFT: The crooked willow, frequently cultivated in gardens. (Photo: H. Smith.) RIGHT: The crooked hazelnut, which displays its quirks best in winter. In summer it is a leafy bower, and in the fall it is covered with tassels of golden flowers. (Photo: Arnold Arboretum.)

LEFT: The writhing trunk of an English yew tree (*Taxus baccata*). This is a two-hundred-year-old specimen at Williamsburg, Virginia. (Photo: Arnold Arboretum.) RIGHT: *Eucalyptus caesia* rarely goes into such distortions, but this fifteen-year-old tree in Victoria, Australia, put a left-handed twist into every branch. (Photo: Ernest E. Lord.)

When in Singapore, which lies about one degree north latitude, R. E. Holttum[15] found that the location of a tree on one or the other side of the equator makes no difference in the direction of twist. He pointed out that in the genus *Dioscorea* (the true yams), the whole genus may be divided into two distinct halves by the direction of twining; members of one subgenus always twist to the right, whether north or south of the equator, while members of the other subgenus invariably twist to the left.

But the yams are vines, not trees, and no connection has been found between the twining of a vine and the twisting of a tree. Nor is there any relationship between the spiral twisting of trunks and the spiral arrangement of leaves on certain trees, as the screw pine (*Pandanus*), which gets its common name from the placement of its branches and leaves.

2. Trees Twisted by Heredity

These are the trees that seem to enjoy life more than their fellows. They have no cares, they are uninfluenced by food, wind, soil conditions, or climatic squeezes. Their branches undulate gaily as if inviting the notice of those who pass their way.

Many of these kinky models are cultivated by nurserymen because, as yard specimens, they make ideal conversation pieces, and home owners are always looking for "something different." Among those best known in fine gardens of the United States are the crooked hazelnut[16] and the crooked willow,[17] but there are many others. The crooked features are usually perpetuated by propagating the plants from cuttings that have kinks.

An English gardener-humorist[18] established what he called his "lunatic asylum" in one corner of his yard. In it were plants that twisted, wept, had the wrong color in flowers, or were otherwise unacceptable in proper garden circles. His twisted hazel never produced a bit of straight wood; even the large crumpled leaves were twisted and slightly rolled, as if attacked by leaf-rolling caterpillars.

Considerable evidence has accumulated to prove that many kinds of tree twisting are hereditary. In the redwood forests of California, where saplings arise from the roots of fallen or cut trees, the new growth is always the same as that of the original tree: if it was twisted, all the new growth is twisted.[19] The same condition exists with old juniper trees at timber line: young trees sprouting from the base are all twisted in the same direction as the parent. Climatic conditions have nothing to do with this.

Coconut palms[20] rarely grow straight; they nearly always lean (though never with a prevailing wind), often far out over a lake or stream—even the ocean, for they are indifferent to salt. Unbalanced nutritional sources may cause their twist. The coconut palm in Indonesia with the corkscrew trunk (see photograph on page 185) might have developed this growth phenomenon from a greater hormone production of one leaf over that of its neighbor on the left or right. Or the twisting might have been hereditary. Once started, it can be exaggerated, reduced, eliminated, or reversed. Derx[21] pointed out that, although the spiral at first was very loose, the twists became more pronounced and closer together as the tree grew. He reported that the leaves too showed a distinct twist. The tree (in 1948) was bearing nuts, and tests were planned to determine whether the twisting habit would continue through the seeds into the next generation.

A palmetto[22] with a knot in its neck grows near the highway at Jensen Beach, Florida. The trunk makes a nearly horizontal semicircle just below the crown.

A crooked ornamental tree occasionally seen in Florida gardens is the Mexican ebony,[23] which does not need to be trained to have kinky branches; it was born that way. Its zigzag growth, starting off in a new direction at every node, is enough to attract attention, but the tree's pure white bark adds an extra feature.

Only hereditary urges could be suggested as the cause of perpetual twisting of certain *Lannea* trees in west tropical Africa. Of the fifteen species known, three[24] have bark that invariably twists to the right.

3. Trees Twisted by Disease

Discussion of tree twisting involves at least brief reference to torques caused by disease. Some instances are known to be caused by virus diseases, but nobody yet knows to what extent viruses are involved in other examples of twisting because the manifestations of such diseases are exceedingly varied.

Almost nothing positive has come to light on virus diseases in trees.[25] Most of the research done so far has been with fruit trees—particularly apples, cherries, and citrus—but the data are hopelessly confusing; research continues because the diseases cause heavy economic losses. Different kinds of apple trees, inoculated with identical virus material, react differently. Apple tree virus transmitted to other hosts, such as cherries, produces symptoms entirely different from those produced in apple, and the reverse is also true.

Donald Cation[26] has devoted his life to studying tree viruses. He cites instances of tortuous or delayed cambial growth, but observes that, although certain viruses can be demonstrated in these trees, there is no

183

ABOVE: *Magnolia denudata*, a Chinese tree with the ancestral urge to change direction at every node. RIGHT: An ancient medlar (*Mespilus germanica*), the same crooked-growing tree that its ancestors have been for thousands of years. (Photos: J. E. Downward.) BELOW: Australian pines (*Casuarina cunninghamiana*). Thousands of these have been planted along a Florida state road, and all of them twist to the right.

LEFT: An alligator juniper (*Juniperus deppeana* var. *pachyphloea*) in Arizona, which decided to imitate a barber pole by climbing another tree. (Photo: U.S. Forest Service.) BELOW, LEFT: A coconut palm (*Cocos nucifera*) in Indonesia. Its swirl is continued in the individual leaves far aloft. BELOW, RIGHT: A white-bark pine (*? Pinus bungeana*) in Montana. After the old tree died, a new shoot followed a vine around the dead tree until at about six feet off the ground it grew out as a tree in its own right. (Photo: U. S. Forest Service.)

LEFT: A walnut stump that has burls as well as highly figured wood. An expert can tell what figures he can get from a burl like this, and how to saw the stump for the finest grains. RIGHT: A maple tree that is a mass of burls, some in clusters, with indentations where curly maple pieces can be cut. (Photos: Norman H. Beer.)

LEFT: A Gravenstein apple-tree trunk, gnarled and twisted by a disease called "flat limb." (Photo: Victoria Department of Agriculture.) RIGHT: The tulipwood (*Harpullia pendula*) of Queensland rain forests. It is often irregular, grooved, or angular in cross section. (Photo: Francis, *Australian Rain Forest Trees.*)

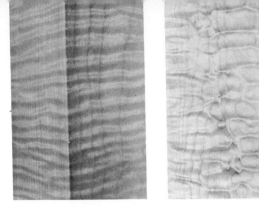

ABOVE, LEFT: A split block of mahogany (*Swietenia mahagoni*) showing inter-locking grain. (Photo: Ricou.) ABOVE, CENTER: The fiddleback figure that is obtained in maple if it is sawed correctly. ABOVE, RIGHT: The quilt figure in maple. (Photos: Harold O. Beals.)

LEFT: The "corduroy tree" (*Cryptocarya corrugata*) of the Queensland, Australia, rain forest. Its washboard-like sapwood is concealed by the heavy bark. (Photo: Queensland Department of Primary Industries, Brisbane.)

BELOW: Two illustrations of "indented ring" in southern pine (*Pinus palustris*). The cross section at left shows the injured cambium with places where it has failed to grow. The picture on the right shows how the log can be sawed to get the best figured wood. (Photos: Harold O. Beals.)

evidence that they cause the malformations because other trees with the same viruses fail to show this condition. Confusion continues. All that scientists know for sure is that sometimes virus diseases may twist the trunks of trees.

4. Trees That Are Twisted Inside

Spiral grain of the wood in tree stems is a normal phenomenon that has no place in this book. But because trees, like people, frequently hide inner turmoil under a placid exterior, and because the wood grain frequently goes haywire inside the tree and creates a host of fantastic disorders, a brief review of these abnormalities does belong here.

Studies[27] of spiraling in the wood of 2372 red spruce trees in the Adirondacks revealed the following facts:

1. Spiral may differ in degree or direction in various parts of the tree bole between bottom and top; this is the habit rather than the exception.

2. Spiral may differ in degree or direction in various parts of the bole between the center and the circumference; this is recorded in the bark as well as in the wood.

3. Young trees spiral mainly to the left, older trees to the right. The time of this reversal is closely associated with the change in the rate of growth (when tree reaches forest canopy and begins to get full sun). "Distortion occurs while the cells are in plastic condition, and light is doubtless the factor which determines the direction of torsion."[28] (*Sic!*)

Examination[29] of 140 Douglas fir[30] trees from ten localities in British Columbia and Washington showed that 64 per cent of them had, during youth, a left-hand spiral which gradually changed to right-hand at maturity, but 19 per cent maintained the left-hand twist of youth to maturity. Any change in direction of twist is measured by cutting (along the radius) a cross section of the tree; a special forester's tool records the angle of pitch of the grain at any growth ring.

When the spiraling of the wood grain goes wild, developing fantastic patterns, the trouble is in the cambium layer—the living, growing tissue that stands between the bark and last year's layer of wood. The cambium may spiral as naturally as a mountain climber who finds it easier to sidle along a slope than to go straight up. If progress of the spiral is delayed or blocked, or if the cambium is injured by worms or woodpeckers, browsing animals, disease, physical damage, or any other destructive force, growth is to some extent interrupted, disrupted, or delayed. In the confusion, the growth cells may go wild. Fancy patterns in the wood grain are the result.

When a disturbance of the cambium is severely localized, the condition at the point of injury may become so aggravated that a burl develops.

188

(The *erl* sound in English words must portray an around-and-around motion: swirl, twirl, whirl, birl, furl, purl, curl, etc.) The wood grain in a burl goes berserk and the tree bulges out instead of up, developing a fat half-rounded swelling on the trunk or branch that resembles a goiter. Growth peculiarities in this instance produce the utmost confusion, and the wood, with its amazing figures, is highly prized for veneer and turned articles.[31] Burls can occur on almost any kind of wood that develops cambium trouble.

Sometimes irregularities develop vertically in the cambium so that a tree grows normally in some areas but fails to grow in adjacent parts. This imbalance produces fluting that makes the trunk look like a group of organ pipes (see Chapter One). This sort of abnormality also plays queer tricks on the wood grain. In Connecticut, the red pine[32] often develops fluted stems, and the Yale School of Forestry is studying aspects of this puzzling phenomenon.

Similar factors are involved when some deterrent (a disease?) stops cambium growth in a very small area during a single season. In succeeding growing seasons less wood is added to the indented part than to parts that are normal, so that the indention goes a little deeper each year. This is very similar to the conditions which develop bird's-eye patterns except that in what is called "indented ring" the indentation is elliptical or lenticular, whereas in bird's-eye it is circular. Sometimes these elliptical indentations are called "bear scratches." They are commonly found in Sitka spruce[33] and Douglas fir.[34] The wood rays (see cross-section photographs, page 187) are usually glutted with food material which was stored in them and not used because of the restricted growth of the cambium. Occasionally this condition can be detected from the outside of the bark if the "bear scratches" are deep enough, but usually the turmoil within is obscured by a smooth and unruffled bark.[35]

Some undulations of wood fibers are difficult to explain. Slight spiraling is the rule rather than the exception in most trees. In certain domestic species, such as sycamore[36] and black gum,[37] and in many tropical trees, reversal of spiral takes place at fairly frequent and even intervals. In such instances, in successive layers of wood along a radius of the trunk or log, the spiral is first right-hand, then left-hand, then right-hand again to proximate degree, and so on, each layer including a number of growth increments. In other words, the fibers spiral in a given direction for a number of years, then the direction of pitch is reversed for a comparable period, after which the alignment returns approximately to the original slope. The cause of this is not known. Wood of this type in which the fiber alignment reverses at quite frequent intervals is designated as interlocked-grain wood.[38] Quarter-sawing of such a log (along the radius) gives a ribbon-striped figure.

This repeated reversal of the direction of wood grain is somewhat different from the once-in-a-lifetime shift of certain trees from left to right, though the causes of the reversal may prove to be the same.

Undulations in the direction or nature of fiber arrangement may produce wavy, curly, blister, quilted, and fiddleback patterns. The beauty of these various figures in wood depends largely on the skill of the sawyer.

Still another form of a whirling, disturbed interior that is hidden beneath smooth bark is manifested in several kinds of rain-forest trees in northern Queensland, where they are known collectively as corduroy trees.[39] Only two of them became large enough to be of commercial importance, the washing-board tree and the native tamarind. Their wood is close-textured and moderately hard, and weighs about fifty pounds per cubic foot. Both timbers are used for dressed household flooring and inside framing. Strangely enough, the unusual corrugations of the sapwood have no detrimental effect on the wood grain inside. Some she-oaks,[40] having very large rays, also show corrugated surfaces in the sapwood and inside the bark.[41]

The smooth outside bark of these corduroy trees hides the turmoil within, just as a person often hides distress under a serene exterior.

5. Trees Twisted by Storms

Determination to survive can be seen in trees of forests and dooryards over all the world. Faced by difficulties of violent proportions, they always struggle to keep alive.

All over Florida, palm trees smashed flat by hurricanes have refused to give up. Many have turned their crowns upward to the sun and continued growing, even though in contorted form.

In the northern states, snow and ice have crushed many trees to earth, particularly saplings, but almost invariably the trees manage to survive, lifting their heads proudly.

In Harvard Forest at Petersham, Massachusetts, a shelterwood strip of white pines[42] about 18 years old was hit by an unusually heavy, wet snowfall on April 12, 1933. The trees were 6 to 10 feet tall, and so thickly set that their number was estimated at 30,000 per acre. The snow bent the trees over almost to the ground and held them that way for weeks, long enough for their tips to turn upward, reaching for the sun. Subsequent piling of snow and ice made great bows in their trunks. Through the years, as the trees continued this curving growth, their trunks came to resemble easy chairs. The stand is thinner now, but many trees with rocking-chair lines persist.[43]

TWENTY-ONE

Subterranean Trees

There is nothing covered, that shall not be revealed.
—Matthew 10:26

Subterranean trees are trees that live below the ground. The reader has already met *Welwitschia*,[1] whose one-foot trunk merges imperceptibly with the root below the earth's surface. He has read about *Nypa* palms that do their branching in the soil.[2] He will read farther along in this book[3] about a tree that grew in a river bed and got covered with silt during a flood, yet grew above the silt, refusing to die. Later came another flood and more silt, but each time the tree stretched itself up and up, above the silt, and kept on growing, until it became one of the tallest of trees.

On the west coast of Holland there are poplar trees[4] 50 to 100 feet tall that have been totally submerged by sand dunes, yet keep on living. Only their uppermost twigs can be seen above the sand, leafing out and growing as if nothing had happened. These are subterranean trees.

In northeastern Brazil there is a rather large area of desert, centering around the province of Goiaz. Here grows a tree of the custard-apple family (*Annonaceae*) that develops a big underground trunk of soft wood, sometimes 4 feet in diameter. During the frequent drought periods, which may last for years, the leaves and branches above the surface of the ground become withered and completely dry. With seasonal rains, the trunk sprouts new branches, puts on bright green leaves, and produces flowers that are followed by typical custard-apple fruits, highly aromatic. Soon the drought returns. The leaves fall, the twigs dry up and break off, and for another eight months or so nothing is visible above the surface of the ground, except the stump—waiting for another rain.[5]

PART V

Trees Shackled to Fame by Size, Antiquity, or Superstition

TWENTY-TWO

The Oldest and Biggest Trees

The trees went forth on a time to anoint a king over them.
—JUDGES 9:8

Tree enthusiasts never tire of talking about the tallest trees, the biggest trees, the oldest trees. Conversation thrives because the stories never agree. John Bunyan stalks through the timber, and utterly fantastic yarns are born about the trees just over yonder hill. Who shall say which reports are exaggerated and which are true? Many competent observers have been badly misled, and guesswork easily takes over when measuring sticks fall short. The reader can only sort the results and evaluate them.

The tallest trees that have ever grown on the earth were not California redwoods or giant eucalypts from Australia; they were monkey-thorn trees[1] that used to grow along the banks of the Magalakwini river, a tributary of the Limpopo in northwest Transvaal, Africa. H. A. Lueckhoff[2] of Pretoria wrote:

Acacia galpinii generally grows along water courses and is known to reach very large size. The trees in question were, however, quite exceptional. The information which we have on these trees is contained in an article in the Johannesburg Afrikaans paper *Die Vaderland*, dated 3 December 1932, and written by Eugene N. Marais. Marais was a well known South African naturalist. . . .

These observations were made in 1907 when he visited this remote area to study the trees. He found that a number of the large Acacias had died or been blown over and burnt by fire. In the case of one tree the trunk had been completely reduced to ash and a perfectly circular crater of ash, 108 feet in circumference, was left where the trunk had entered the ground. In other words the tree had had a girth of approximately 108 feet. The ash pit was plumbed to a depth of 40 feet after which further measurement was not possible. Obviously the fire had burnt the underground stem until it had been smothered in its own ash and could not continue down any farther. Further observations by Marais on the sandbanks along the river satisfied him that the stems of these giant old trees had, during the course of ages, been silted up with sand brought down by the river to a depth of well over 100 feet. . . .

The largest standing tree at that time was carefully measured by a land surveyor. It had a height of 210 feet and a girth, 3 feet above the ground, of 78 feet, with a crown spread of approximately 180 feet. On the basis of his observation on the depth of sand, the burnt out tree, taper etc., Marais concluded that were it possible to excavate the sand away from this tree, it would have had a basal girth of approximately 146 feet and a height in the neighbourhood of 400 feet! At that time the remains of considerably larger trees, which had been destroyed by hurricane or fire, were still visible.

Unfortunately these old trees have all been destroyed by fire and storm and have completely disappeared. This was confirmed by an officer of this Department who visited the area about 20 years ago.

This *Acacia*, usually called *apiesdoring* by South Africans, still grows in the Transvaal but maximum heights are 80 feet, according to Palmer and Pitman.[3] It is a magnificent spreading giant with luxuriant light-green foliage, parrot's beak thorns on its trunk and branches, and flower spikes which produce maroon buds and golden blossoms at the same time. The same authors report that "a big tree in full bloom is said to be 'too bright to look at.' " Palgrave[4] reports a maximum trunk diameter of 4 feet.[5]

Sequoia[6] in California and *Eucalyptus*[7] in Australia have been altitude rivals for many years, primarily because many of the early reports on the Australian trees were greatly exaggerated.[8] The American Forestry Association publishes a *Social Register of Big Trees*[9] which lists as present champion of all redwood trees in the United States a specimen 300 feet high in Big Tree Park on Redwood Highway, California, but adds: "The tallest tree on record is a redwood in Humboldt County, California, extending skyward to 368 feet, 7 inches. This . . . was discovered and measured by the forest engineering class of Humboldt State College, Arcata, California in 1956."

The *National Geographic*[10] featured the discovery of "the world's tallest tree," but the forest monarch described is inches short of the above record (which is not mentioned in the magazine). According to the *National Geographic*, the three tallest redwoods, all in the Redwood Creek Grove in Humboldt County, measure 367.8, 367.4, and 364.3 feet high.

Here is the American Forestry Association's record of the "champion" trees in the United States with heights exceeding 200 feet.

	Circumference at 4½ feet	Height	Spread	Location
Redwood (Sequoia sempervirens)	65'9"*	300'	—	Big Tree Park
Giant sequoia (Sequoiadendron giganteum)	101'6"**	272'	90'	Sequoia National Park
Noble fir (Abies procera)	28'4"	278'	47'	Columbia National Forest, Washington
Douglas fir (Pseudotsuga menziesii)	53'4"	221'	61'	Olympic National Park
Western white pine (Pinus monticola)	21'3"	219'	36'	Near Elk River, Idaho
Lawson cypress (Chamaecyparis lawsoniana)	27'2"	200'	—	Squaw Creek, Coos County, Oregon

* At 6 feet
** At base

The *National Geographic* adds that a Douglas fir at Ryderwood, Washington, measures 324 feet, and that a giant sequoia in California, known as the McKinley tree, measures 291 feet.

Walter Fry,[11] of Sequoia National Park wrote of some Big Trees, or giant sequoias, that were bigger than these record figures:

When it is considered that lightning, fire, or uprooting has in the past destroyed the largest specimens of the Big Trees while they were still in the prime of life, it is difficult to estimate the size which the giants may attain. . . .

There are many prostrate trees [in Sequoia National Park] which have been burned out by repeated fires; and it is by visiting these hollow logs and by entering their black tunnels that one may best obtain an idea of the immensity of the trees. . . . There is the first discovered hollow log of the "Father of the Forest" in the Calaveras North Grove, a tree which in its prime is accredited with a height of about 400 feet and a base circumference of 110 feet. . . .

As to the height of the Big Tree, the tallest I have measured on the ground was 347 feet long. This prostrate tree was in the Redwood Mountain Grove. Two fallen trees in the Giant Forest were, respectively, 318 and 329 feet.

A tree which is 300 feet high, which is 30 feet in diameter, and which weighs 2,000 tons, is more than a big tree. It is a Big Tree.

195

Australia's tallest tree is a eucalyptus, commonly referred to as pepper-mint-gum, mountain-ash, giant stringybark, swamp-gum, or Australian oak. Black[12] wrote:

Some of the Gippsland eucalypts rank among the loftiest trees in the world, but the heights recorded in Baron von Mueller's day and accepted by him, appear to have been much exaggerated. These heights were from 400 to 500 feet for the loftiest trees. In 1888 rewards totaling £120 were offered to anyone who could point out a tree of 400 feet. The highest tree which could then be found proved, when scientific measurements were taken, to be a specimen of *Eucalyptus regnans* 326 feet, 1 inch high, growing on Mount Baw Baw, Gippsland.

On the contrary, a modern forestry handbook published by the Australian government[13] says:

Under typical conditions heights range from 175 to 250 feet, but measurements of over 350 feet have been recorded. Whilst very large diameters do occur, typical measurements are 6 to 9 feet.

The *National Geographic* in its article on tall trees reports a mountain-ash in Tasmania's Styx River valley measuring 322 feet.

De la Ruë[14] reports a *Eucalyptus* near Melbourne 300 feet high and 26 feet in diameter at the base, and adds that among big trees in the tropics the accepted records go to an *Agathis* 230 feet high in the Celebes, a *Eucalyptus* in New Britain, 233 feet, and a *Koompassia* in Borneo, 275 feet. Broadly speaking, the tallest tree that is commonly found in tropical forests is the kapok or silk-cotton, *Ceiba pentandra*, often about 200 feet.

The variety of "guess-timates" of tree sizes is reflected in this extract from a Longview, Washington, newspaper:[15]

The timber they're cutting today would be toothpick stuff to those Paul Bunyan loggers in the old days. . . .

But, there's still some big ones being cut or still standing in the evergreen forests of the Pacific Northwest. If you don't agree, it's time to get into the argument.

The verbal scrap over the biggest tree in the tall timber country has been going on for years. It harkens back to the days when steam donkeys were an innovation to the logging game and some of the smaller operators still used oxen and lots of skid grease to get the timber to the river.

They argued in the bunkhouses back in those days and the debates still spring up wherever woodsmen get together, with the boys spinning yarns about the timbers that made mighty Paul grunt when he helped his blue ox, Babe, get the load started for white water.

Up in British Columbia they tell about a Douglas fir felled in 1895 that was 417 feet tall, 300 feet to the first limb and 25 feet through at the butt.

The towering giant was felled near North Vancouver, B.C., in the days when the forests reached down close to the city. But, as the years have

LEFT: California big-trees (*Sequoiadendron giganteum*)—not as tall as the redwoods, but older and larger in circumference. (Photo: USDA.) RIGHT: An Australian giant, *Agathis palmerstonii*, usually called kauri pine. This tree measures 90 feet to the first limb and at breast height is 25½ feet in circumference. (Photo: Australian Photo Service.)

LEFT: Mountain ash (*Eucalyptus regnans*) of Australia. This was once thought to be taller than the California redwoods, but measurement has proved otherwise. (Photo: H. T. Reeves.) RIGHT: Redwoods (*Sequoia sempervirens*), the tallest trees in the modern world. (Photo: USDA.)

ABOVE, LEFT: A bristlecone pine (*Pinus aristata*) near timberline in Colorado. Trees of this kind are now acknowledged to be the oldest. (Photo: *American Forests*.) ABOVE, RIGHT: Cycads (*Lepidozamia peroffskyana*) in Australia. (Photo: Harry Oakman.) CENTER, RIGHT: Old English yews (*Taxus baccata*) achieve enormous girth by producing multiple trunks around the original stem. This monster, with a 33-foot circumference at 4½ feet above the ground, is in Hertfordshire, England. (Photo: Miles Hadfield.) BOTTOM, RIGHT: A great ahuehuete (*Taxodium mucronatum*) or Mexican cypress at Tule, near Oahaca. The trunk's circumference is 162 feet. (Photo: H. W. Rickett.)

198

passed, many timbermen have contended that the tree was not a Douglas fir, as originally claimed, but actually was a redwood similar to those that grow in northern California.

Thick trunks are no indication of age. The baobab[16] in Africa often achieves a diameter of 30 feet at the base, and the distinguished botanist Alexander von Humboldt was deceived into believing that it was "the oldest organic monument of our planet." Adanson, whose name the genus bears, traveled in Senegal in 1794 and found a tree 30 feet in diameter which he calculated to be 5150 years old. Livingstone spoke of the hollowed-out trunk of a baobab within which 20 to 30 men could lie down with ease.[17] A fungus causes the trunks of many baobabs to become hollow, and such trees often are utilized as human habitations. D. B. Fanshawe, a forester[18] in Northern Rhodesia, reported that at Katima in the Caprivi Strip (which connected Southern Rhodesia with South-West Africa), there is "a baobab with a built-in toilet complete with waterflush."

Ernest E. Lord of Melbourne wrote in a letter that in a remote northwestern community of Australia, a 2000-year-old Queensland boabab[19] had a hollow base with 20 square feet of floor space within. It was used as the town jail.

Other trees of great girth often have a reputation of being exceedingly old. Willis[20] says the famous dragon-tree[21] at Teneriffe in the Canary Islands, which was blown down in a storm in 1868, was 70 feet high, 45 feet in girth, "and was supposed to be 6,000 years old." Several very large dragon-trees still stand in the Canaries, but residents now are content to refer to them merely as "very old"; no record of their real age exists.

The olive[22] "is a tree of slow growth, very tenacious of life and of great longevity—so great indeed that it is thought probable that the trees at present existing in the Vale of Gethsemane are those which existed at the commencement of the Christian era.[23]

The cypress tree[24] of Mexico achieves great age. The Montezuma tree in Chapultepec park in Mexico City is 200 feet high and 45 feet in circumference. The giant tree at El Tule is "more than 160 feet in circumference";[25] its age is estimated variously from 2000 to 4000 years. H. F. Macmillan[26] tells of other ancient trees:

A cypress tree (*Cupressus*) at Chapultepec in Mexico is believed to be 6,000 years old. . . . A Bo or Peepul-tree (*Ficus religiosa*) at Anuradhapura, Ceylon, is supposed to be the oldest historical tree known. It was brought as a young plant from India in 288 b.c. and is still flourishing, or at least a portion of it is.

Scientists who have spent a lot of time counting annual rings have concluded that the oldest redwoods are about 2200 years, and the oldest big-trees from 3200 to 3500 years old. John Muir wrote that he had counted 4000 rings on a *Sequoia* back in 1880, but there is no way to verify his count, for the stump was never found.

The Ghana observer, Taylor[27] points out that in the tropics, particularly in high forest and with humid conditions, the growth rings in trees cannot be relied on as being annual; consequently they are of no real value in estimating age. (Climatic conditions in the tropics make a resting period unnecessary.) Carbon-14 tests such as have been used to determine the age of *Welwitschia* in South-West Africa[28] may prove more practical.

The scientists who study the relationships between climate and the growth rings of trees are responsible for discovering that the bristlecone pine[29] is the oldest living tree. Dr. Edmund Schulman of the University of Arizona, found Methuselah, 4600 years old, in Inyo National Forest in the White Mountains of Central California, two miles up, in rugged and forbidding land. He described and pictured his success in the March 1958 issue of *National Geographic*. Schulman found 17 trees more than 4000 years old.

The bristlecone pine grows all over the high mountains of Colorado, Arizona, and New Mexico, but it appears to achieve its greatest longevity in the White Mountains of California, where rainfall is 10 inches a year and the "soil" is mostly rocks. In a sense, it is a tree that lives on borrowed time because the tree as a whole does not live the full span of several thousand years. In fact, most of the tree dies; a single branch takes over the business of living, fed by a narrow strip of bark. Before the main part of this branch gives out, a branch of it takes over. It is a sort of tree relay race against time. Consequently its profound age is not any more remarkable than that of some of the ancients cited in this book in which the entire tree, not just a part of it, has persisted for thousands of years.

Bunyanesque confusion also surrounds a group of palmlike plants on Tambourine Mountain, 50 miles southwest of Brisbane, Australia. Scientists call them cycads,[30] natives call them *burrawongs*. These down-under plants of the genus *Lepidozamia*[31] are stalwart trees, mostly 12 to 15 feet high, although "Great-Grandfather Peter" (destroyed by vandals about 30 years ago) reached 25 feet. A newspaper report[32] of the wanton slaughter of this and other cycads in the neighborhood started the ridiculous story that here "was the oldest living thing in the world."

Charles Joseph Chamberlain of the University of Chicago made himself the world's foremost authority on cycads and wrote several books about his lifetime findings.[33] Yet Chamberlain was caught in the middle of an amazing contradiction. Jackson quotes him as saying in 1912 that the Australian cycads were "the most ancient living flora in the world." Then he quotes him as saying in 1936 that an intimate examination of the oldest cycad (Great-Grandfather Peter) showed it "to have lived 15,000 years." Jackson says that Dr. A. D. Herbert, lecturer in botany at the University of Queensland, went to Tambourine Mountain with two hundred volunteers, and replanted the upper part of the tree that had been chopped down, believing that it contained enough nourishment to support itself ten or twelve years, during which time they hoped it would reroot. Dr. Herbert is quoted as confirming the statement that the tree was the oldest living thing in the world.

The only trouble with the statement attributed to Chamberlain and "confirmed" by Herbert in the newspaper account is that it is not true. It is, rather, a fantastic exaggeration. In his book *The Living Cycads*, Chamberlain says that if the Australian trees have the same growth rate as the *Dioon* (a Mexican genus of cycad), he doubted if there would be any living plants more than 500 years old. Other than this, Chamberlain made no reference to the age of these plants. Either he was pulling the leg of the Australian newspaper reporter, or he was misquoted for the sake of a big story.

L. S. Johnson, the chief Australian authority on cycads, wrote:[34]

Popular and press reports attribute great individual ages (to 10,000 years or more) to large species of this plant. . . . Plants have attained a height of 2 meters (80 inches) in less than a century under poor conditions in the Sydney Botanic Garden. Since the plants grow only by apical increase of a single stem, even the tallest individuals . . . would be less than 500 years old.

Elsewhere Johnson says that massive trees of *Macrozamia moorei* have developed in less than a century.

TWENTY-THREE

Prehistoric Trees

As the days of a tree are the days of my people. —ISAIAH 65:22

Two kinds of trees whose ancestors grew before the Rocky Mountains were formed are cultivated as ornamentals in the United States and other countries. The better-known of these is the ginkgo, or maidenhair-tree,[1] commonly so called because of the resemblance of its two-lobed leaves to the fanlike leaflets of some maidenhair ferns. It is a survivor of a once-great vegetation, a relic of the past, or, as Charles Darwin expressed it, a living fossil. This very same species was thriving 125,000,000 years ago when dinosaurs were still roaming the earth.[2]

The maidenhair-tree is prized as an ornamental, particularly for street planting, because of its upright habit, its hardiness as far north as New York, its freedom from insect pests, ease of pruning, and adaptability to congested or sooty urban situations where many other trees fail. In appearance it is unusually dignified, with neat fanlike deciduous leaves that grow in clusters from short spurlike shoots on the branches.

In its method of reproduction the maidenhair, or ginkgo, is unique among trees. Its sexual activities are paralleled only among ferns and lower plants in which fertilization is effected by swimming male cells. In all other trees the male cells are nonmotile. Sexes in the ginkgo are on different trees, and pollination is effected by moving male cells. As females are undesirable in general planting because of the offensive odor of the ripening fruits, nursery propagation is usually achieved by grafting male budwood onto the easily grown seedlings.

ABOVE: Maidenhair trees (*Ginkgo biloba*). (Photo: U.S. Department of Agriculture.) BELOW, RIGHT: Close-up of leaves of the maidenhair tree.

LEFT: A dawn redwood (*Metasequoia glyptostroboides*), ten years old. (Photo: William R. Carpenter.)

The maidenhair-tree first came to the attention of western botanists in 1712, but it was not actually reintroduced into the United States until 70 years later. The oldest specimen in this country is in the Woodlawn Cemetery, West Philadelphia—an old monarch that was planted in 1784. Found wild only in China, the maidenhair today is grown in mild Temperate Zone areas all over the world.

During the Miocene age, ginkgo trees flourished in what was then the subtropical climate of central Washington, where their petrified stumps can be seen in Ginkgo Forest State Park, at Vantage, near Ellenburg.

The other prehistoric tree, the dawn redwood,[3] is not so well known because it has been in the United States only since the 1940s. Although the tree had previously been known as a fossil, it suddenly came to life in 1941 when four living specimens were found by Professor T. Kan in Szechuan Province, China. "The *Metasequoia* story, however, had its beginning nearly a hundred years ago," wrote Dr. Francis de Vos.[4] He added:

In mid-1800 a fossil plant that was to be later named *Sequoia langsdorffi* was discovered in deposits laid down during the Eocene, a geological period dating back 70 million years. During this period the plant was wide spread in the middle latitudes of North America and Asia. Similar fossil plants were discovered and were also assigned as species of the genus *Sequoia* because they were thought to represent ancestral forms, or to be closely related to the Redwood, *Sequoia sempervirens*. . . . A Japanese botanist named Miki, in 1941, established the new genus *Metasequoia*. This was four years before it was definitely known that living plants of this species existed in China.

Metasequoia was found to occur naturally in Hupeh and Szechuan provinces in Western China at approximately 30 degrees north latitude. Its range is limited to an area of approximately 300 square miles. It occurs at altitudes of from 2,100 to 4,000 feet and in sandy, slightly acid soils. It apparently grows best along streams and in seepage areas which probably accounts for its native name Shui-sha meaning water fir or spruce. The largest tree measured was about 105 feet in height and 7 feet in diameter.

It is to the credit of the late Dr. E. D. Merrill of the Arnold Arboretum that the *Metasequoia* is now so widely found in cultivation. In 1947 the Arnold Arboretum provided funds for a collecting trip to procure seeds from China.

These seeds were distributed through the United States Department of Agriculture to experimental growers from Florida to Connecticut and westward to Colorado, and many of the trees are now growing in this wide area.

Actual tests proved that the seedlings had different rates of growth and varied in habit from globose to narrowly pryramidal. The pick of the lot appears to be a fast-growing, narrow-pyramidal seedling at the United States National Arboretum in Washington that was named National; this reached 10 feet in the first five years.

Metasequoia trees are deciduous. Their leaves are bright green in summer and turn an attractive coppery red in the fall before they drop.

TWENTY-FOUR

The Man-Eating Tree

If it had not been the Lord who was on our side . . . then they had swallowed us up quick. —PSALMS 124:2,3

The alleged discovery of a man-eating tree that killed and swallowed its prey made a big stir in the Sunday newspapers half a century ago. This fantastic story had been rehashed in various publications for 150 years.[1] It was a good yarn so long as Madagascar, the Philippines, and other remote areas remained unexplored; nobody could prove the narrator a liar. Moreover, the fiction did have some basis of fact. Certain plants do swallow and digest insects and other small animals. The biggest of these flycatchers are the pitcher-plants[2] of Borneo, whose cup-shaped leaves contain liquids to which victims are attracted, only to drown and be digested. But the largest pitchers are only 24 inches long and the plants which bear them are vines, not trees.

Most famous of the "man-eaters" was the so-called upas tree.[3] This name as used in print was also a fiction because it was applied usually to a giant tree of the nettle family[4] that grows from India and Ceylon eastward through Burma and Malaysia as far as the Philippine Islands. But if the storyteller got pinned down, the identity of the upas tree shifted to one of the strychnine trees,[5] of a totally different family (the *Loganiaceae*).

Chief reason for this confusion was the trickiness of natives who used the juice of these and other plants as an instrument of death. They tried desperately to keep their poison formulas secret. Burkill[6] wrote:

206

As soon as Europeans reached Malaysia they were bound to become acquainted with poison arrows and darts, but it was a long time before the poisons were traced to the plants which yield them. Friar Odoric, who lived about 1286–1331, was the first to give the West a description of them. Thousands of Portuguese, Dutch, and English died of poison-arrow shots, while exploring Malaysia, but 400 years passed before the source of the poison was determined. In the mid-seventeenth [sic] century, a Dutch government was established at Macassar, and the botanist Rumphius (G. E. Rumpf) importuned the governor for information on the source of the poisons. He was forced to wait 15 years for the information he sought, and then it was deliberately falsified and garbled. To frustrate further inquiry, the botanist was told in some detail that it was dangerous to go near the tree. Rumphius faithfully recorded all this information[7] and strengthened the foundation of the upas tree story. He wrote:

"Under the tree itself no plant, shrub or grass grows—not only within its periphery but even not within a stone's throw of it; the soil is sterile, dark, and as if burned. Such poisonousness does the tree exhibit that from the infected air birds perching on the branches are stupefied and fall dead, and their feathers strew the soil."

[Then, ready to believe anything, Rumphius goes on:]

"So caustic were the branches sent to me in a stout bamboo vessel that when the hand was placed on the vessel, a tingling was produced such as one feels on coming out of the cold into the warmth."

[Rumphius then reverts to the information given him as follows:]

"Everything perishes which is affected by its exhalation, so that all animals avoid it, and birds seek not to fly over it. No man dare approach it unless his arms, legs, and head be protected by clothes."

This same false information was obtained and published by other scientists[8] who visited Malaya. Out of it grew wild tales of human sacrifices to appease the tree, with young girls thrown to the monster, or persons grabbed by writhing branches, and a lot of similar nonsense. The first feature story embodying these fantastic reports was written for an English magazine in 1783 by a Dutch physician named Foersch. Foersch's great sin was that he asserted himself a witness to the fantastic events he recorded. It is known that there was a third-class surgeon named Foersch in the Dutch army service at that time. It was not until 1805 that Leschenault de la Tour, the French king's botanist in Pondicherry, proceeded to Java to see the tree and watch the preparation of the poison. It was Leschenault who resolved the confusion between *Antiaris* and the strychnine tree.[9]

Without question, the latex of the former and the seeds of the latter are extremely poisonous, and have been used by natives as arrow poisons for thousands of years.

Rumors of a man-eating tree in the interior of Brazil have been

"Escaped from the embrace of the man-eating tree." (*American Weekly*, January 4, 1925. Courtesy Field Museum of Natural History.)

mentioned by newspapers there from time to time. During the Chaco war between Paraguay and Bolivia, corpses were found frequently under a strange tree—human skeletons wrapped in leaves of enormous size. Blossfeld[10] lived for a time in Mato Grosso and made a point of investigating the story. He found that the strange tree in question was *Philodendron bipinnatifidum*, which does have leaves 3 feet or more long. According to the rumor, the men were attracted to the tree by its highly aromatic flowers; these acted as a narcotic, drawing men from afar and overcoming them so that the leaves might wrap around the body and absorb the blood. In truth, the flowers are aromatic, but what would attract a man lost in the spiny, shadeless desert of the Chaco would be the shade such a plant would afford and the sweet pulp of its fruits which, like the related ceriman,[11] are edible. However, there is neither narcotic nor poison in the flowers or fruit. The corpses were those of men who, wounded, or dying of thirst, sought the plant. The leaves, bending naturally to the earth, covered them, but not to suck blood. Blossfeld says the story still persists in Brazil; it is too good a newspaper tale to be thoughtlessly discarded.

LEFT: A "deadly" upas tree (*Antiaris toxicaria*) growing in Singapore. (Photo: L. M. Burkill.) RIGHT: A pitcher plant (*Nepenthes*) in Borneo. The pitchers are modified leaves containing liquid in which insects drown. The insects are later digested and absorbed by the plant. (Photo: Paul and Dorothy Allen.)

LEFT: The Burmese lacquer tree (*Melanorrhoea*). It has pretty yellow flowers, but its volatile sap is poisonous to exposed skin. (Photo: Tem Smitinand.) RIGHT: A coral-plant (*Jatropha multifida*) ornamenting a Florida garden. Its latex and fruit are poisonous. (Photo: *St. Petersburg Times*.)

Crataeva religiosa, one of the trees sacred to Hindus. The flowers reveal that it belongs to the family of "cat whiskers," as the capers are sometimes called. (Photo: K. M. Vaid.)

LEFT: Flowers of the pin-cushion tree (*Nauclea esculenta*). These are revered by worshipers of Vishnu. The tree belongs to the coffee family. (Photo: Ricou.) RIGHT: *Ficus religiosa,* venerated by both Hindus and Buddhists. It is called bo-tree in Ceylon and peepul in India.

TWENTY-FIVE

Trees Feared and Revered

Hurt not . . . the trees.   —REVELATION 7:3

Fear and love are close neighbors among the trees!

The sap of the so-called man-eating tree[1] is deadly poisonous, but it is only one of thousands of trees whose juices will kill. Their physiological properties have been used by natives of many lands in primitive medicine and in preparing poisoned arrows and darts.

Scores of trees contain narcotic or hypnotic agents, and these are used by natives of many lands when they want fish to eat. The leaves or bark are mascerated and thrown into a quiet pool in a stream. The fish are stunned by the poison and come floating belly up, ready to be caught by hand. Those not caught, soon recover, and the narcotic involved does not affect the wholesomeness of the fish as food.

Children often get into trouble by eating harmful flowers, adults most often by eating a toxic fruit or seed, by coming into contact with a caustic sap, or by being too close to trees whose pollen can cause severe skin rash or respiratory disorders. The cashew-nut[2] and many of its relatives are offenders. The shell of the cashew-nut itself is very poisonous until roasted, and the fumes that rise from roasting it are highly irritating, even deadly. The mango[3] is a delicious fruit, but many people react violently to the skin, the sap of the tree, or emanations from the bloom. Poison ivy[4] belongs to this same family. Some of its tree relatives are so virulent that they should be approached only with great caution. An example is the Burmese lacquer tree.[5] It is one of five kinds of trees that

211

are feared and shunned by Malayan foresters because their pollen or volatile sap causes such a severe rash among timber-fellers that pain, fever, and even death may ensue.[6]

Many forest trees are avoided because they sting viciously. This is particularly true of nettles like the giant stinging-tree[7] in the rain forests of northern Queensland. F. M. Bailey[8] reported finding specimens with trunks 10 feet in diameter. Bushmen avoid these trees as they would a plague, for the young leaves particularly, and also the branchlets, are covered with stinging silicone hairs that inject formic acid into the skin of anyone who touches them. The result is intensely painful. Dried leaves of the tree cause violent sneezing.

Dr. David Fairchild[9] reported realistically on his experiences with *Laportea* in the Philippines.

> A stinging nettle, what of it? Who has not been stung by one some time or other? They make you uncomfortable for a time and then the pain passes. This was my feeling when I was warned not to touch the leaves of *Laportea luzonensis*, a relative of our "singing nettle." To prove I did not fear it I carefully touched one of the glandular poison hairs with my forefinger. The pain that shot up my finger was intense. I expected, of course, that it would subside in a few minutes, but there was pain in that finger for days, and a feeling of paralysis in the tip. This *Laportea* is a handsome plant; the leaves are a gorgeous green, with purple midribs, and the fruits are a most intense blue. I wanted a color photograph of it, and if it had been a rattlesnake we could not have handled it more carefully as we took its picture.
>
> Mr. Sulit informed me that the species I had tested was as nothing in virulence to "the other one," *L. subclausa*. . . .
>
> A species of this nettle tree which occurs in Australia stings so badly that the naturalist, le Souef, reports that he felt the effects of its stinging hairs for months. Horses suffer severely from it, he says, but cattle do not; indicating, possibly, the existence of some powerful protein poison, the action of which may be explained, perhaps, when chemists know the molecular constitution of nerve substance.

The mingling of fact and fiction regarding deadly trees is not confined to any special part of the world. In most undeveloped countries it is usually difficult to determine to what extent the reports of poison are influenced by superstition and deceit. Some yarns about trees are nothing short of ridiculous.

In Southern Rhodesia there is a tree known to the Barotse tribe as muti-usinazita,[10] "the tree without a name," because the natives are forbidden, on pain of death, to name it or even to point at it. Perhaps the tribe holds the tree sacred because their kings are traditionally crowned beneath it.

In parts of west Africa, planting a cola tree[11] is an impious act and it is believed that the person who commits it will die when the tree flowers. Where superstition forbids planting the seed, trees are obtained by transplanting seedlings produced by nature. In other areas, pruning a cola tree is an impious act. Elsewhere the owners of cola trees slash the bark and beat the tree with a club to accelerate fruit bearing.[12]

In Peru a poison tree,[13] according to Poeppig,[14] is notorious among the Indians for its baleful qualities. They even fear to sleep beneath it lest they become afflicted with gangrenous sores which are attributed to the sap.

Natives of Lower California claim that their arrow-tree (*hierbe de flecha*)[15] is dangerous, and warn travelers that if they fall asleep under it they will wake up blind. The leaves of the tree are used to stupefy fish.

In Ghana the natives call a certain tree "close your eyes" (*kataw'ani* in the Twi language).[16] It "is supposed to be narcotic to those who sit or sleep under it, and is therefore regarded with suspicion."[17]

The frosting on the cake comes from northern Nigeria where a *Crotalaria* tree[18] is used as "a sort of love potion, to induce the voluntary return of a runaway wife if she can be got to drink or eat of it unknowingly." The account continues:

Particularly fortunate as a love-philtre is a grub sometimes found inside the stem; this with proper ceremony and selected additions is made into a salve to rub on the eyes, which will render the subject attractive to all women.[19]

Also in west Africa grows a bean tree of the genus *Loesnera*.[20] It is held in such high superstitious regard that severe penalties are inflicted on anyone who cuts a tree. Most potent charms are made from it, and best of all, it carries on conversations! (See Chapter Twenty-eight.)

Another five-foot bookshelf would be required to describe all the trees that have exercised fearful, dangerous, mystic, mythological, or superstitious influences on man. In the jet age man has come to respect, rather than fear, the trees that are dangerous to his welfare. And he has extended his respect to trees that, rather than being dangerous, are inspiring and uplifting.

Christian countries attach special significance to palm branches and to the cedars-of-Lebanon, not overlooking the fig, fir, olive, juniper, pomegranate, willow, and myrtle, which are among the trees mentioned in the Bible. And our mythology would be lost without the apple, laurel, holly, and others.

Similarly, people in other lands venerate trees that are identified with establishment of their religions. *Ficus religiosa*, usually called bo tree, and *Crateva religiosa*—note the specific epithet for both trees—are sacred to Hindus.

Were it not for Chinese temple plantings, the maidenhair-tree[21] would not be available today for cultivation in western countries. It has never been found wild, and is otherwise known only from fossil specimens.

In front of Buddhist temples and shrines, portia trees[22] and relatives of ebony and persimmon[23] are often planted. The portias have yellow mallow-like flowers that turn purple as they fade. Both kinds are handsome trees, easily deserving of the reverence accorded them by worshipers.

PART VI

The Rugged Individualists

TWENTY-SIX

Trees That Tell Time and Predict the Weather

Ye can discern the face of the sky. —MATTHEW 16:3

Watching the leaves of a favorite tree may be an outdated method of predicting the weather, but every American farmer knows it is going to rain when maple leaves curl and turn bottom up in a freshening wind. A woodsman says he can tell by the thickness of lichens on his nut trees just how tough the winter is going to be. The maple-sugar farmer can tell what month of the year it is just by looking at his trees, and the turpentine gatherer tells time by his pines. A black gum signals the oncoming winter before the katydid wakes up.

People who live with trees learn really to know their habits and their moods. Cowan[1] observed in India that the leaves of the rain-tree[2] have the remarkable power of changing their position in accordance with atmospheric conditions. He wrote: "In full sunshine they are horizontally spread, allowing no single beam of light to penetrate the dense crown; but at night, in dull weather, or during rain, the pairs of leaflets fold together, the leaf stalks droop and each pinna swivels on its thickened base so that the leaves all lie sideways."[3] The tamarind[4] folds its leaflets at night and in overcast weather, with the result that in Burma the people of a village choose a big tamarind as the abode of the rain god.[5]

In west tropical Africa, trees prove to be unusual timekeepers, and they are recognized as dependable prognosticators, even as alarm clocks. Irvine[6] cites four examples:

Griffonia[7] has 2-inch, inflated pods which explode "with a loud noise," which "is the signal to the farmers of the Accra Plains that the time has come to plant their crops."

Claoxylon[8] is a 60-foot tree. "When the fruits are ripe" it is time for the Christmas–New Year festival.

The poplar[9] of Liberia is a 100-foot tree. "In Apollonia the appearance of the young red leaves is an indication that the fishing season has arrived."

Trichilia[10] is a 60-foot tree that flowers in February and again in August. "The flowering of this tree indicates the . . . time of second planting of corn, just before the second rains come."

Dalziel[11] reported that the native pear tree[12] in the eastern province of Nigeria is a clock, for "the planting of field crops commences when the tree shows buds," and that in Sierra Leone the full ripening of the fruit of *Alchornea cordifolia* "is regarded as a sign that the rainy season is over."

In the Fiji Islands the flowering of the coral-tree[13] is taken as a signal that it is time to start planting the yams."[14]

Yet all these timing devices fade into insignificance when compared to the exquisite precision achieved by the shrubby simpoh,[15] a large evergreen shrub in Malaya (often to 20 feet) with almost the aspect of a rank tropical weed. "But the more we become acquainted with it," wrote Corner,[16] "the greater is our admiration," adding:

> It is a plant of enormous vigor . . . and once it has begun to flower at the age of three or four, it blooms every day of its life which may be fifty, if not a hundred, years. . . . It is possessed also of a marvelous precision. . . .
>
> The flower buds open one at a time, in succession, from base to apex of the inflorescence and there is an interval of 2 to 6, but generally 3 or 4, days between the opening of successive flowers. The bud begins to swell visibly and to turn yellow at the end on the morning before the day on which it opens; about 3 A.M. on the next day, the petals separate and the flowers become bell-shaped; and by an hour before sunrise it is fully open. The petals drop off about 4 o'clock in the afternoon and the same night the sepals begin to fold back on the young fruit but they are not tightly shut until the following afternoon. . . .
>
> The fruits take EXACTLY five weeks to set: on the 36th day after the petals fall, the fruit opens at 3 A.M. (it splits into 7 or 8 rays, pink with white borders) and the pink star is expanded long before sunrise. . . .
>
> The time of opening of the flowers and fruits, about 3 A.M., is that period in the twenty-four hours when the temperature is becoming steadiest and lowest, when the humidity of the air is greatest so that dew is settling, and when the sky is darkest: it is the most inactive time of a day for a green plant. One or other, or all of these conditions, must be involved in the opening of the flowers and fruits, but how they affect the plant and what its means of control, are problems beyond our understanding.

The gigantic saman tree (*Samanea saman*) in Tobago that supported the tree house in Walt Disney's motion picture *Swiss Family Robinson*. (Photo: Copyright © 1960 Walt Disney Productions. World rights reserved.)

TWENTY-SEVEN

Trees That Make Rain

And I will rain upon him . . . an overflowing rain.—Ezekiel 38:22

Trees that produce rain whenever moisture is needed should be a welcome addition to modern gardens. Such trees do exist! Just how practical they would prove in everyman's garden is another question.

Many authentic instances have been reported of trees producing rain. Frequently it has been the result of accumulated water-spitting insects on the branches. Again, trees have produced moisture in quantity with no insects present. These true reports—some easily explained, others mysterious—have been so confused with mythological rain-trees that the search for truth follows treacherous paths.

The most famous of historical rain-trees was being advertised two thousand years ago as the source of the local water supply on Hierro, most westerly of the Canary Island. The English botanist Hutchinson[1] writes:

The Canary archipelago was probably known to the earliest voyagers, the Phoenicians and the Carthaginians, many hundreds of years before the Christian era, [but] we know for certain it was visited by Roman navigators during the reign of Juba II, King of Mauritania, about 25 B.C. The Romans regarded the islands as being the western boundary of the world, and Pliny has given us Juba's account of them, in which he mentions a tree from which water was obtained. The particular tree of Hierro is supposed to have been of the laurel family.[2] It grew in a hollow on a hill, and whilst in the heat of the day it drooped, in the night time it condensed enough water from the clouds to supply the whole island. Beneath this precious tree a stone well was built to conserve the water. The Spanish name for it was *El Garve.*

So famous was this tree at the beginning of the seventeenth century that pictures of it were used as frontispieces in contemporaneous herbals.

The trouble with this yarn is that it had some basis in fact. The extent of the moist evergreen forest in the Canaries is determined largely by the cloud belt which hovers over the mountains and supplies moisture to the vegetation by condensation on the foliage; preservation of that forest covering is therefore vital to the water supply of the islands. Las Mercedes wood on Tenerife is a good example of such protection; outside of the forested areas, the Canary Islands are largely desert. Similarly the tall timber along the coastal ranges of Washington and Oregon is largely responsible for the high humidity, or "instant rainfall," in that area. Taking away the trees that create rainy conditions has established many a desert.

Condensation of moisture from the air often causes foliage to drip, making the ground wet under a tree. Palmer and Pitman[3] explain:

> In warm humid areas trees sometimes appear to "rain" through their leaves. This happens only when the roots take up more moisture than the tree can dispose of by normal transpiration. The water must find an outlet, and the surplus passes through special openings—hydatodes—usually on the margins of the leaves. In dry areas this never occurs in trees, for the moisture is given off through normal transpiration. It is possible that some of South Africa's rain trees in the north and north-east in particular give off water by this method.

Dalziel[4] says of the African breadfruit[5] that "the soil under the tree is moist throughout the dry season from condensation, as in the case of *Myrianthus arboreus.*"

Fairchild wrote:[6] "The nearest I ever came to seeing a tree rain was at Orotava. The dark volcanic strand there was planted to tamarind trees[7] and in the evenings their twigs—pendent branches—were always dripping a salty water. It was the condensed fog from the sea."

Blossfeld[8] says that in Brazil the Australian pine, or horsetail tree,[9] condenses air humidity on its twigs, and adds that in the São Paulo district the soil around this tree is always moist. For this reason, vanilla growers use this particular tree to shade their plantings.

Palmer and Pitman compound the mystery of rain-trees by reporting:

> From time to time other species in South Africa have been known to rain, and the reasons for this have not always been understood. For instance, a fine sweet-thorn, *Acacia karroo,* in the grounds of the Division of Botany in Pretoria, exuded a gentle, misty moisture for several weeks on end. This was perfectly tasteless, like water, and was apparently not caused by insects. Certainly entomologists could find no sign of any. The cause remains a mystery, and the tree has never rained again.

Dalziel quotes Lane-Poole as saying that *Bridelia ferruginea*, of the poinsettia family, "has the property of dripping water all through the dry season."

Perhaps the most controversial and therefore best known of rain trees is the South American saman,[10] prized the world over for its umbrageous shade. The "tree house" in Walt Disney's 1960 movie of *Swiss Family Robinson* was built in a gigantic saman tree on the island of Tobago, in one corner of the local cricket grounds. This tree measures 250 feet from side to side and is 200 feet high.

The argument over the tree's connection with rain stems from the fact that it probably produces moisture partly by condensation but sometimes as the result of insect infestation. Macmillan[11] reflects the former view:

> The small pinnate leaves, which form a canopy of shade in the daytime, close up at night, so that during a period of drought a patch of green grass may be seen beneath, while the surrounding ground is parched and brown. This led to the supposition that the tree mysteriously produced rain at night; hence the name Rain-tree.

Ernst[12] wrote of this tree:

> In the month of April the young leaves are still delicate and transparent. During the whole day a fine spray of rain is to be noticed under the tree, even in the driest air, so that the strongly tinted iron-clay soil is distinctly moist. The phenomenon diminishes with the development of the leaves, and ceases when they are fully grown.

He attributes the rain to secretion from glands on the footstalk of the leaf, on which drops of liquid are found; these are rapidly renewed when removed with blotting paper.

Others who have experienced moisture under a saman echo the explanation given by Spruce:[13]

> The Tamia-caspi, or rain-tree of the eastern Peruvian Andes, is not a myth but a fact, although not exactly in the way popular rumor has lately presented it. I first witnessed the phenomenon in September, 1855, when residing at Tarapolo . . . a few days eastward of Moyobamba. A little after 7 o'clock we came under a lowish, spreading tree, from which, with a perfectly clear sky overhead, a smart rain was falling. A glance upward showed a multitude of cicadas, sucking the juices of the tender young branches and leaves, and squirting forth slender streams of limpid fluid. My two Peruvians were already familiar with the phenomenon, and they knew very well that almost any tree, when in a state to afford food to the nearly omnivorous cicada, might become a Tamia-caspi, or rain-tree. This particular tree was evidently, from its foliage, an *Acacia*. Among the trees on which I have seen cicadas feed, is one closely allied to the Acacias, the beautiful *Pithecellobium saman*. Another leguminous tree visited by cicadas is *Andira inermis*, and there are many more.

The same story in less scientific garb was told a century earlier by Cockburn:[14]

Near the mountains of Vera Paz [Guatemala] we came out on a large plain, where were numbers of fine deer, and in the middle stood a tree of unusual size, spreading its branches over a vast compass of ground. We had perceived, at some distance off, the ground about it to be wet, at which we began to be somewhat surprised, as well knowing there had been no rain fallen for near six months past. At last, to our great amazement, we saw water dropping, or, as it were, distilling fast from the end of every leaf.

Cooke[15] reprints a newspaper story of 1877, quoting the United States consul at Moyobamba, in northern Peru, where

the tree is stated to absorb and condense the humidity of the atmosphere with astonishing energy, and it is said that the water may frequently be seen to ooze from the trunk and fall in rain from its branches, in such quantity that the ground beneath is converted into a perfect swamp. The tree is said to possess this property in the highest degree during the summer season principally, when the rivers are low, and water is scarce, whence it was suggested that the tree should be planted in the arid regions of Peru, for the benefit of the farmers there.

Henry Hurd Rusby[16] wrote in 1926 of a rain tree in Bolivia:

One of the strangest phenomena observed by the members of the Mulford Exploration party of 1921 was that of a rather copious rainfall from the branches of a tree at mid-day in perfectly clear weather and in brilliant sunshine. The tree stood on a dry bank, in an open place by the side of the road, and with few other trees about it. The rainfall was continuous and steady, and its pattering was like that of a mild shower on one of our summer days. It was sufficient to wet one's clothing in a few moments, if standing beneath the tree.

The size of the tree was about that of a large wild-cherry tree. There being no convenient way of climbing it, it was felled, when the cause of the shower was found to be a profusion of caterpillars' nests, of all sizes up to a foot or more in length, which occupied the forks of the branches and branchlets. They closely resembled the nests of our common tent caterpillar, except that they were surcharged with water, in which abundant larvae led an aquatic existence. The water was evidently drawn from the bark of the tree where covered by nests. No openings in the bark could be detected with the naked eye, and the party had no time for an investigation of the mechanism of the procedure. The tree was in flower-bud at the time, and the specimens secured proved it to be *Lonchocarpus pluvialis*.

Audas[17] in Australia says that the rivulet, rain, or weeping tree[18] there is so called because a species of froghopper lives on the sap of the softer parts of the tree and these are attacked by ants in search of moisture, causing a dropping of fluid from the tree.

Baron,[19] after exploring Madagascar, wrote:

The rain-tree of the Canary Islands as shown by Duret, *Histoire Admirabile*, 1605.

The rain-tree as shown in Bauhin and Cherler, *Historia Plantarum Generalis*, 1619.

Leptolaena pauciflora is a hard-wooded tree from the trunk and branches of which, at certain seasons of the year, there is a ceaseless dropping of water, sufficient indeed to keep the ground quite damp. This is caused by a number of hemipterous insects crowding together in a slimy liquid.

Sibree[20] wrote:

It is well known by those who live in Madagascar that there are, at certain seasons of the year, a number of insects found on trees which produce a constant dropping of water. Happening one day to be standing under a peach-tree in our garden from which water was dropping, I found that there were clusters of insects on some of the smaller branches. In each cluster there were about twenty to thirty insects, and these were partly covered with froth, from which the water came. The insects producing this appeared . . . to be . . . the larval form of a species of beetle. The sap of the tree is extracted in such quantities as to maintain their bodies in a state of saturated humidity. The activity of the larvae seems to increase as the heat of the day progresses, and to diminish again towards evening. But the object of this abstraction of fluid from the tree, and the purpose it serves, is still a subject needing investigation. I have observed these insects on other trees—mangoes, acacia, *zàhana*, and others; they appear indeed to be very common, and the ground underneath the branches where they cluster is covered with small patches soaked with water.

Palmer and Pitman describe the activities of a froghopper or spittle-bug in South Africa:

The immature insects or larvae pierce the wood of the branches with their needle-fine, beak-like mouthpieces, sucking up the sap at tremendous speed and ejecting it as froth which covers them, and collecting, drips from the tree like water.

The explorer David Livingstone was fascinated by these little insects but he was wrong in believing that they drew their water from the atmosphere. He noticed the phenomenon chiefly on fig trees in Africa.

It is not necessary to travel around the world to learn about rain-trees. Witness this report[21] from Dallas, Texas, about a redbud tree[22] that went on a crying jag:

> The W. S. Werners had a new way figured out how to beat the heat today. They just stood under their "crying" redbud tree. From the branches of the tree spurt tiny jets of a clear liquid. Werner said that from a distance in late afternoon it "looks like a fine mist."
>
> Closer observations revealed the branches producing droplets which the Dallas man described as "large tears." The Werners first noticed the tree's built-in sprinkling system two weeks ago. A nurseryman said the trunk may have loaded up on water during the heavy spring rains.
>
> Lately, Werner said, the tree has been on one long crying jag. "This morning it was going real good," he said.
>
> Real cool, agreed the neighbors.

TWENTY-EIGHT

Trees That Make Noises

When thou hearest the sound of going in the tops of the mulberry trees. —I CHRONICLES 14:15

The cathedral of the forest casts a spell of its own. Walk through it with your ears open on a dry and windy autumn day, and you will hear the swish and rustle of leaves all about you. Your ears will pick up a sighing and soughing as the air strums the needles of the pines to produce aeolian music. If the trees are monarchs of the past, you will hear some creaks and groans, and now and then a squeal as boughs rub together to tear the bark, or a loud crack as a dead branch falls.

These are the commonplace noises of the trees, only a part of the racket trees can make. Such rudimentary vibrations, along with the whistle and bluster of the wind, may drown other sounds of the forest. Outside factors distract, and the rush of modern living may draw attention elsewhere so that one simply neglects to listen. Suppose, then, that on a quiet day, and for a few tranquil moments, you stand motionless among the trees with Whittier and invoke the spirit of the forest.

> Drop Thy still dews of quietness,
> Till all our strivings cease;
> Take from us now the strain and stress,
> And let our ordered lives confess
> The beauty of Thy peace.

Immediately you begin to hear sounds of the forest that are reserved for those who really listen. Frederick W. Coe wrote:[1]

Bark peeling from a tree would ordinarily not be thought of as a noisy process, but in a grove of the Pacific madrones[2] in mid-July, on a hot, dry day, there is a constant whisper of sound and a fine confetti of small pieces of bark float [sic] down from the trunk and all the branches exposed to direct sunlight. . . . Only a tissue paper layer of bark peels, but this comes from the whole tree and forms a light carpet on the forest floor.

After seeing bark peel in this manner, I wondered if the sycamore[3] trees are even noisier in their peeling. The large eucalyptus trees nearby with strips of bark twenty-five feet long hanging from the clean, white trunks also will be "listened" for on some hot, dry day.

The writer's assumption was correct: eucalyptus trees do make noises. Dr. Hewitt[4] wrote from Australia: "Yes, when the bark of Eucalypts . . . drops away, it does make noises like tearing paper or linen. Often this sound is caused by large strips peeling downward under their own weight."

Not all tree noises are so readily explained. Humboldt[5] refers to a terrible crash heard on quiet nights in the Amazon region. Other explorers who have heard similar noises have credited them to the cannonball-tree,[6] but without any apparent reason. The botanist Spruce[7] investigated the origin of this noise, which he too had heard and compared to the firing of a big cannon. The phenomenon must not be rare, because Blossfeld[8] reported (1964) that he himself had heard it while on the Inca River in the upper Amazon region. He attributed the crash to the violent bursting of tissues in extremely fast-growing tree trunks, when heat and moisture stimulate the sapwood to a rate of growth that cannot be accommodated by the tissues. This makes the sapwood split internally. Blossfeld said he had observed such inside splits in pieces of firewood loaded on steamships on the Amazon.

Another kind of tree noise is reported by Blossfeld:

An old-time resident of Hong Kong, who visited me here in São Paulo, told of travelling up the Yang Tse Kiang River to a region where bamboo is grown in large areas to supply most of China with building lumber. He obtained living quarters at an inn that stood in the middle of a grove of giant bamboo. Before dawn he was awakened by an awful squeaking, whining, and faint screaming coming from the bamboo grove. Alarmed, he called his companion, who explained to him that the noises were produced by the the growth of the shoots of young Giant Bamboo, as they pierced their way through the bracts and sheaths clothing the base of each shoot. On warm, moist mornings, bamboo grows at an astonishing speed, and friction produces these terrifying noises.

Frequently heard are the trees that whisper, though their voices are occasionally raised in pitch. A tropical Asian tree that has become naturalized in the West Indies and Florida bears the twitting name of woman's

tongue.[9] It provides magnificent shade, and might be more widely cultivated were it not for a host of foot-long pods that hang all winter, after
the greenery is gone, and shake their loose seeds madly with every passing
gust.

In west tropical Africa, the conversational tree[10] is held in superstitious
regard, and there is a severe penalty for cutting it. Dalziel[11] says that it is
still regarded as a counselor, and that people pay large sums to witch
doctors to sit by it and recount their troubles, as they pluck a few leaves.

Something akin to this persists in Liberia, where a bean tree[12] is considered a powerful juju. Dalziel[13] tells that a native's friend whose name is
spoken is expected to come or hear a message if snuff made from the dried
leaves is blown from the hand in his direction.

Extensive references[14] are made in silvicultural literature to the magic
camphor language spoken when crystals are to be collected from the
Bornean camphor tree.[15] This strangest of tongues, which originated in
Johore, is used when camphor beads are being collected from this tree, but
at no other time. The natives believe that if they speak in any other
language no camphor will be obtained. Their product is ten times[16] as
valuable as that of the Chinese camphor tree.[17] The tree grows abundantly
within its natural range, but only occasionally produces camphor crystals.
It is not a true camphor, but its product is similar and it serves in some
of the same uses.

> The Malayans and other Johore natives believe that each species of tree has
> a spirit or divinity that presides over its affairs. The spirit of the camphor-
> tree is known by the name of Bisan—literally "a woman." Her resting-place
> is near the trees; and when at night a peculiar noise is heard in the woods,
> resembling that of a cicada, the Bisan is believed to be singing and camphor
> will surely be found in the neighborhood.
>
> But the spirit of the camphor-trees seems to be jealous of the precious
> gum and must be propitiated, and if she knows that hunters are in quest of it
> she will endeavor to turn their steps aside. The natives think that she is
> acquainted with both the Malay and Jakun languages, and that if the
> camphor-hunters spoke either of those she would know that they had come
> for camphor and would defeat their purpose. So it is necessary to speak in a
> tongue that she does not understand. For this purpose the "camphor lan-
> guage" has been invented. It consists of a mixture of Jakun and Malay words,
> but these are curiously altered or reversed; and the natives believe that the
> divinity of the camphor-tree is completely confused when she hears this
> jargon.[18]

According to the account given by the Jakuns,[19] the camphor occurs in
cracks in the interior of the tree, which has to be split into pieces and the
wood carefully scraped to get the gum. This is washed free from fragments

226

of wood and sap, and sold to the Chinese, who use it in embalming. Very few of these trees contain camphor. The hunters first test the tree by making a deep cut in the bark; if there is a faint odor of camphor they cut down the tree and thoroughly examine it, but not otherwise.

If at this point the reader's credulity is being a little strained, he should take down an encyclopedia and read what his own ancestors accomplished in their dealings with the rowan, ash, oak, witch-hazel, and a few other trees, not too many years ago.

Out in the far reaches of the Pacific is a big island called Bougainville. In World War II a lot of soldiers became aware of its existence. In swampy places on that island grows the crying tree.[20] The natives, it is reported, say that the flowers make a peculiar crying sound when they are opening.[21]

In central Africa grows one of the most beautiful shade trees in the world; it is called the hissing tree.[22] Palgrave[23] wrote of it:

> *Parinari mobola* is quite widely known as "The Hissing Tree." This intriguing name has arisen as the result of a belief that as the tree is chopped it hisses. The natives declare that as the axe blade bites into the trunk this hissing sound is clearly audible. We have set out deliberately to prove or disprove this theory, and have never heard any unusual sound on chopping the tree. It is just possible that such a sound is given out only at certain times of the year, for instance, perhaps as the sap is rising in spring, but we are far more inclined to believe that this is simply a myth which has arisen round this tree as a result of native legend and superstition.

The fact that one observer has not heard the tree hiss may prove only that he was not there at the right time. Unfortunately the hissing myth gets no support from one forester[24] who remarks that *Parinari* trees are so valuable as fruit trees, chiefly for beer brewing, that the legend may have been invented to keep people from cutting them down.

Turning from superstition to the more familiar ground of reality, we find noisy seed-pods on many trees in the pea family (*Leguminosae*). As these pods shrink in drying, they twist away from their seams and split with an explosive sound. Dalziel[25] wrote that the very hard and woody pods of *Afzelia africana* "burst violently" to discharge the seeds; and he described the fruits of *Berlinia* as "usually leathery or half-woody, flat and often resembling the sole of a shoe, bursting violently."

Another close observer of the traits of tropical trees, G. L. Guy,[26] wrote that the seed-pods of *Baikiaea plurijuga*, three *Brachystegia* species, and *Isoberlinia* all explode with some violence, so that on a hot October day a *Baikiaea* forest resounds with fusillades like pistol shots.

Unwin[27] says that the African oil bean[28] has pods 12 inches long which explode with "a loud report not unlike the sound of a 12-bore gun."

The pods of several of the so-called orchid-trees[29] of tropical regions pop open audibly on the drying branches. In woodlands throughout eastern North America, last year's fruits of witch-hazel (*Hamamelis virginiana*) expel their seeds explosively in autumn while the current season's slender-petaled blossoms are opening on bare branches.

Pine cones used for Christmas decoration will sometimes shoot their seeds across a room as indoor heat dries and forces the woody scales apart. This is especially true of the Swiss stone pine (*Pinus pinea*). Of other popping pines, Frederick W. Coe[30] has written:

> The Monterey Pine (*Pinus radiata*) is widely planted in the San Francisco Bay region and a mature grove is found near the Letterman Army Hospital on the Presidio. One hot September day at noon I was walking through this grove and noticed a popping, crackling noise coming from high in these pines. After careful study with the help of binoculars, I found this was coming from cones which were opening their scales and shedding seeds. Once in awhile a few seeds would come spiralling down. This pine belongs to the closed cone group but apparently sun heat is enough to open them in some cases, while the Lodgepole Pine (*P. contorta* and var. *Murrayana*) and Bishop Pine (*P. muricata*) need intense heat from fires to fully open the cones and shed their seeds.

A sound like the popping of corn was noted at another time by Mr. Coe. This came from the opening of pods on acacia trees naturalized in Marin County, California. It was a hot June day with low humidity.

Perhaps the most famous, because one of the most violent, of these seed-poppers is a neotropical evergreen tree, variously known as sandbox or shotgun tree.[31] When ripe, its pods catapult the seeds as much as 200 feet. Mary Barrett[32] calls it "quite a dangerous tree; it stabs, poisons, and shoots."

The common name sandbox tree goes back to the days when goose·quills were used as pens. It was the custom to keep a little box of fine sand on the writing desk, partly to dust on newly written papers to expedite drying of the ink, but more particularly to serve as a receptacle for the quill; the sand kept it clean. The seed pods of *Hura* are the size and shape of an extra-large tangerine, with ribs all around. If the top is sawed off the green fruit and the seeds are dumped out, the shell dries brown and unbroken. It makes a very pretty desk ornament with its squat shape and heavy ribbing. For many years such shells were exported from the West Indies to Europe and America to serve as pen stands.

Another common name for *Hura* is monkey dinner-bell, which arises from the habit of the fruit, when ripe, of exploding with considerable noise. The vicinity is showered with sharp-pointed segments of shell and many flat brown seeds that look a bit like thin lima beans. These are poisonous to human beings and to most animals.

The Brazilian tree from which natural rubber is derived[33] has a 3-inch, 3-lobed fruit capsule, the rind thin and the inner wall bony. When ripe, it explodes violently, and Ridley[34] says the seeds may be blown as far as 40 yards from the tree.

This pop-snap-crackle process of seeds goes on in your own back yard, on the castor-oil plant[35] and many small herbs. But these do not make such a loud racket.

The connection between trees and sound vibrations gets a reverse twist in Perth, West Australia. *The Tree Society's Newsletter* reports:[36]

Plants thrive on music, says Mrs. J. R. Brown of Ardrosse, on the Yorke Peninsula. She has been playing violin music to her plants since November, and claims to have seen a remarkable increase in growth and colour, even after ten days.

For half an hour each morning she has played violin concertos to the flowers, vegetables, and weeds in her garden. The growth of weeds and vegetables has not been as good as in the flowers. . . .

She said that sound waves stimulated something in the plant that formed a carbon layer to increase the plant's bloom. Flowers seemed to like the violin. Vegetables liked a lower-pitched sound.

H. G. Schaffer[37] says the government of Madras State in India is making field tests to determine whether music encourages plant growth. Loudspeakers are broadcasting music over the rice fields, and careful records are being kept to compare the yields with control fields that get no music. This experiment followed a report by Dr. T. C. N. Singh, head of the botany department at Annamalai University, South India, that bombarding plant cells with rhythmic sound vibrations stimulates plant growth.

ABOVE, LEFT: Seed pods of the commercial rubber tree (*Hevea brasiliensis*), which explode when ripe, throwing seeds a hundred feet. (Photo: Pan American Union.) ABOVE, RIGHT: This "camote" or swelling on the root of a Mexican tree (*Ceiba parvifolia*) is an underground water reservoir. (Photo: M. F. Moseley, Jr.) RIGHT: Seed pods of *Berlinia grandiflora* in Ghana, often 12 inches long. They split open with a loud bang when ripe.

BELOW, LEFT: The carambola (*Averrhoa carambola*). Its leaves are usually horizontal, but they droop if touched in the daytime; at night they move without outside stimulus. BELOW, RIGHT: Fruits of the sandbox tree (*Hura crepitans*). The tree is so named because the fruits were once used as pen stands. (Photo: Julia Morton.)

TWENTY-NINE

Trees That Supply Water,
Milk, and Salt

I will give to eat of the tree of life.   —REVELATION 2:7

Unfortunately, if a reader gets caught in the woods without a meal ticket, he will probably not have this book in his knapsack. Nonetheless, I am impelled to include a few trees that could save his life or at least add flavor to what food he could find in the wilds. In different parts of the world there are trees, if you know them, which can provide water, milk, and salt.

To a traveler in distress, water is usually the most urgent need. Anywhere in the tropics, the ubiquitous coconut palm[1] is man's best friend, for it supplies both food and drink. In Australia or on the islands of the South Pacific, the Australian pine[2] and the flower stalks of various palm trees offer fluids to relieve thirst. The tropical survival expert Richard A. Howard[3] wrote:

Drinking of the sap or juice of trees was reported in several stories. Casuarina, the Australian pine, is mentioned in one story as supplying a potable liquid when a large branch was cut and the sap allowed to run from the branch. The reference adds that the tree was called the "bleeding tree" by the local natives and unfortunately it was protected by a native tabu against injury.

Sap was obtained from various palm trees by cutting the flower stalk and collecting the drink in canteens or sections of bamboo. The buri, nipa, coconut, and sugar palms were mentioned in various accounts as being used in this fashion. . . .

In Africa several trees provide drinkable liquid. Dalziel[4] says of the corkwood or umbrella-tree:[5] "The young branches contain a potable water, and are broken off by hunters and by monkeys to suck. The cut stem exudes water for a considerable time, and similarly the roots, the yield being supplemented by renewing the cut surface and beating the divided limb after some hours."

An Australian tree that stores water is the Queensland bottle-tree (*Brachychiton rupestris*).

The flower buds of the African tulip-tree[6] are so full of water that the common name of fountain-tree is applied in some localities. The trunk of the traveler's-tree[7] will yield enough moisture to assuage thirst. Several African trees are used as water reservoirs. Story[8] wrote that the wood-oil-nut tree[9] "sometimes collects and holds rain water in hollows in its trunk," and that the older caper-trees,[10] which are often hollow, form natural reservoirs for rain water, and these are tapped by the bushmen.

From another part of Africa, G. L. Guy[11] wrote:

> The baobab[12] is used as a water reservoir in the Sudan and very probably elsewhere. The savages there hollow out the stems and fill them with water in the rainy season for later consumption. They hammer wooden spikes into the stems to make ladders for easy access to the water. . . .
>
> I use the word "savages" deliberately; one of my happier memories of the Sudan is being waited on at table by a stark naked savage of over 6 feet 8 inches in height—his sole garb was woodash, a topknot and a spear. Just as interesting as some of the Paris cafés!

Another tree that produces large underground "bulbs" on its roots to serve as water reservoirs during dry periods is the umbú (*Spondias tuberosa*) in northeastern Brazil.[13] This should not be confused with the Argentine "ombu" (*Phytolacca dioica*.)

In writing of Florida plants for survival, Julia Morton[14] suggests many additional ones to provide various items of food and drink.

This discussion of trees that act as water reservoirs has been predicated on the belief that the trees were doing this for the benefit of mankind; upon more mature reflection, this seems highly unlikely. Many trees store water against long periods of drought, desiccating winds, and parching sun. A reservoir in the tree's tissues provides an emergency ration of water that may have to last for months, even years.

An astonishing modification of this reservoir system is found on the roots of a Mexican tree commonly called *el pochote*.[15] This species occurs in Puebla, Oaxaca, Morelos, and Guerrero in thorn forests where a short rainy season is followed by a long, extreme drought. The tree grows on dry slopes, its roots have no contact with deep soil water, and its flowers and fruits are produced during a period when the soil obviously lacks an adequate supply of available water.

Muller[16] discovered large, subspherical, soft organs on the roots of five trees. These structures, which may reach 12 inches in diameter, are called locally "camotes." They arise as small fleshy swellings on young roots and remain attached for many years. The rough, corky exterior surrounds a soft, fibrous, spongy interior. Early in the dry season, these camotes contain large quantities of water; late in the dry season they have been depleted of water. Obviously the water supply for the tree is accumulated in this underground reservoir during the rainy season and for use later. Detailed studies of this phenomenon have been made by M. F. Moseley, Jr.[17]

The milk-tree,[18] which grows from Venezuela north to Costa Rica, was brought to public attention a century ago by Alexander von Humboldt.[19] He wrote:

For many weeks we have heard a great deal of a tree whose juice is a nourishing milk. The tree itself is called the Cow Tree and we were assured that the Negroes on the farm, who are in the habit of drinking large quantities of this vegetable milk, consider it as highly nutritive; an assertion which startled us the more, as almost all lactescent vegetable fluids are acrid, bitter, and more or less poisonous. Experience, however, proved to us during our residence at Bárbula that the virtues of the Cow Tree, or Palo de Vaca, have not been exaggerated. This fine tree bears the general aspect of the Star-apple tree (*Chrysophyllum cainito*); its oblong, pointed, coriaceous, and alternate leaves are about 10" long and marked with lateral nerves, which are parallel and project beneath. The flower we had no opportunity of seeing; the fruit is somewhat fleshy and contains one or two kernels. Incisions made in the trunk of the tree are followed by a profuse flow of gluey and thickish milk, destitute of acridity and exhaling a very agreeable balsamic odor. It was offered to us in calabashes, and though we drank large quantities of it, both at night before going to bed and again early in the morning, we experienced no uncomfortable effects. The viscidity of this milk alone renders it rather unpleasant to those who are unaccustomed to it.

The Negroes and free people who work in the plantations use it by soaking in it bread made from maize, manioc, aropa, and cassava; and the superintendent of the farm assured us that the slaves become visibly fatter during the season when the Palo de Vaca yields most milk. When exposed to the air this fluid displays on its surface, probably by the absorption of the atmospheric oxygen, membranes of a highly animal nature, yellowish and thready, like those of cheese; which, when separated from the more watery liquid, are nearly as elastic as those of caoutchouc, but in process of time exhibit the same tendency to putrefaction as gelatine. The people give the name of cheese to the curd which thus separates when brought into contact with the air and say that a space of five or six days suffices to turn it sour, as I found to be the case in some small quantities that I brought to Valencia. The milk itself, kept in a corked bottle, had deposited a small portion of coagulum and, far from becoming fetid, continued to exhale balsamic scent. When mingled with cold water the fresh fluid coagulated with difficulty, but contact with nitric acid produced the separation of the viscous membranes.

Analysis of the latex of this cow-tree showed its composition to be 57 per cent water, 37 per cent wax, and about 5 per cent gum and sugar.[20] Record and Hess[21] suggest that the latex is apparently harmless when drunk in small quantities, but it is better suited to making chewing gum.

Paul Fountain,[22] a later explorer than Humboldt, was enthusiastic about this snack bar of the forest. He described the sap as a milk "having all the properties of the finest cow's milk." Further:

> It is highly nutritious, and will mix with water, hot or cold, and never curdles in coffee, cocoa, or tea. It keeps good for a week, even in this climate, and has much the taste of cow's milk in which cinnamon has been steeped. It is rather thicker than ordinary milk, having the feel in the mouth of liquid gum. If left standing for a time a thick, unctuous cream arises, which, when dry, has the consistence of wax. I have drunk large quantities of it, both as it came from the tree, and also mixed with tea, cocoa, and whisky, with all of which it combines better than cow's milk; and I can say that it is not only exceedingly sustaining, but has not the slightest deleterious quality. When I could get it I always chose it in preference to cow's milk. It is obtained either by wounding the bark of the trunk, or breaking the smaller branches. It runs freely, and several quarts can be obtained from a single tree in the course of a few hours.

In many countries where salt beds do not occur, the natives turn to certain plants as a source of this seasoning. Morton mentions three plants of Florida that can be used in this way: the common palmetto,[23] one of the mangroves,[24] and one of the bananas.[25] Dalziel says that a vegetable salt is prepared from the ashes of the toothbrush tree[26] in the Lake Chad region of central Africa. The roots, and possibly also the stems, of this soft-wooded tree "are widely used by Mohammedans, in imitation of the Prophet, to clean the teeth or to relieve toothache." Another African plant, *Hygrophila spinosa*, is also burned to obtain salt from the ashes.

THIRTY

Trees That Flap Their Leaves

The sound of a shaken leaf shall chase them. —LEVITICUS 26:36

A few trees, along with some lesser plants, have the power to move their leaves. In its different manifestations this power seems to be a defense mechanism, provided by nature to help certain trees survive difficulties of their environment.

The movements are of two kinds. The first, noted elsewhere in this book, involves a variety of broad-leaved Australian trees. They resist dehydration by twisting their leaves in such a way that the edge of each leaf, instead of the flat surface, faces the boiling sun and follows it across the sky. Obviously such twisting is in the petiole (stem) of the leaf, rather than in its surface.

The second kind of movement is incited by either of two causes: (1) a more or less violent physical attack on the plant, or (2) reduction in the amount of sunlight (the advent of nightfall or its equivalent in heavy storm clouds).

To facilitate the reader's understanding of these phenomena, it is easier to start explanations with examples of the last and then proceed backward. Every householder has noticed at dusk that the clover[1] on his lawn raises its leaves and folds them together like a pair of hands. This tiny plant has the physical power to raise the leaflets against gravity and force them into a vertical position. Presumably this maneuver, as in the case of the Australian trees, is a defense measure to prevent evaporation of moisture from the leaf surface.

235

Exactly the same phenomenon takes place among many tropical trees, notably the saman,[2] which by day is a tower of green shade against a hot sun in the New World tropics, but by night is completely open to the sky as the tree folds its leaves upward against gravity, into tight vertical planes. This procedure illustrates what some careless writers of the past have called "the sleep of plants," which is misleading because instead of relaxing (as in the case of human sleep) the plant is exerting physical power to maintain its leaves in a vertical position. The plant cannot relax until the sun returns and the leaves can drop back into their normal horizontal position. Cooke[3] wrote that the expression "sleep of plants" must be accepted as a poetic simile because there is no analogy between it and the sleep of animals.

The movement of leaves resulting from a physical attack on the plant is similar, but reversed. The sensitive plant,[4] a tropical weed often appearing in greenhouses and warm gardens, collapses its leaves if even lightly touched by passing hand or obstacle. This involves the same flapping maneuver that the saman tree uses, except that here the collapsing mechanism operates first and drops the leaves into a vertical or folded state; then, after an interval (if the sun is shining), the plant pushes the leaves back up against gravity to their normal status. Perhaps the sensitive plant, bumped by a cow's nose, no longer looks "good enough to eat" and by feigning a "wilted" condition saves its own life.

In the tropics are many "sensitive" trees and shrubs, and the up-and-down, up-and-down movements of their leaves may be diurnal, or continuous twenty-four hours a day, or voluntary, or involuntary.

The camrunga tree[5] of India, cultivated in Florida as a salad-fruit tree under the common name carambola, is remarkably sensitive. Hogg[6] wrote:

The leaves are pinnated, or feathered, with alternate leaflets, and an odd one at the end. Their common position in the daytime is horizontal. On being touched they move downwards, frequently in so great a degree that the two opposite leaves almost touch one another by their undersides, and the leaflets sometimes either come into contact, or even pass each other. The whole of the leaflets of one leaf move by striking the branch with the fingernail, or each leaflet can be moved singly by making an impression which shall not extend beyond it. Thus the leaflets of one side of the leaf may be made to move one after another, whilst the opposite ones continue as they were, or they may be made to move alternately in any order by merely touching the leaflet intended to be put in motion.

After sunset the leaves go to sleep, first moving down so as to touch one another by their undersides; they, therefore, perform a greater motion at night of themselves than they can be made to do during the day by external impressions. The rays of the sun may be concentrated by a lens upon the leaflets without producing any motion; but when directed upon the leafstalk the response is almost instantaneous. The leaves move rapidly under the influence of an electric shock.

Two thousand years ago Pliny observed this condition of temporary repose in plants and regarded it as closely allied to the sensitiveness of touch. Linnaeus and others wrote about such movements of leaves as take place periodically toward the close of day, consisting of movements upward or downward into such a position that the blade of the leaf shall be vertical or nearly so. Darwin[7] wrote:

> The leaves of many plants place themselves at night in widely different positions from what they hold during the day, but with the one point in common, that their upper surfaces avoid facing the zenith, often with the additional fact that they come into close contact with opposite leaves or leaflets. This clearly indicates, it seems to us, that the object gained is the protection of the upper surfaces from being chilled at night by radiation. There is nothing improbable in the upper surface needing protection more than the lower, as the two differ in function and structure.

The bilimbi,[8] a 50-foot Indian tree, and some of its movements, were known nearly two hundred years ago.[9] Darwin reported that the leaves not only move spontaneously during the day, but:

> They move also in response to a touch, being what is termed "sensitive," and finally they subside into a condition of sleep at night. It is said to be a remarkable sight to observe the leaflets of this tree sinking rapidly one after the other, and then slowly rising. At night the leaflets hang down vertically, and are then motionless.
>
> By regulating the light in a conservatory, the behaviour of a plant under variations of light was observed. A leaflet was seen to rise in diffused light for twenty-five minutes, and then a blind was removed so that a strong light fell upon it, and within a minute the leaflet began to fall. The descent was accomplished by six descending steps, that is, by falls succeeded by a slight rising, so as to cause a kind of oscillation, each fall being greater than the rise. The plant was again shaded, and a long slow rise commenced, which continued until the sunlight was again admitted.
>
> It is unnecessary to enter into all the minute details of this experiment, the object being to show that a rise and fall of the leaflets took place as a consequence of the increase or diminution of direct sunlight.

Darwin insisted that this movement in these plants is continuous, to a greater or lesser extent, by night as well as by day except when pressure prevents motion. He explained:

> Any one who had never observed continuously a sleeping plant would naturally suppose that the leaves moved only in the evening when going to

sleep, and in the morning when awaking; but he would be quite mistaken, for we have found no exception to the rule that leaves which sleep continue to move during the whole twenty-four hours; they move, however, more quickly when going to sleep, and when awaking, than at other times. That they are not stationary during the day has been demonstrated.

THIRTY-ONE

Trees That Display Affection

Then shall all the trees of the wood rejoice.   —PSALMS 96:12

Many things are hard to believe, even if true. More and better understanding must precede conviction. This is particularly true in approaching a thesis that trees in the forest can display affection for each other. You find this difficult to accept? The Queen was having the same trouble with Alice:

> "I can't believe *that!*" said Alice.
> "Can't you?" the Queen said in a pitying tone. "Try again: draw a long breath, and shut your eyes."
> Alice laughed. "There's no use trying," she said. "One *can't* believe impossible things."
> "I daresay you haven't had much practice," said the Queen. "When I was your age, I always did it for half an hour a day. Why, sometimes I've believed as many as six impossible things before breakfast."[1]

So if you are a devout disbeliever, you can scarcely relish a chapter assembled for the pleasure of those who like to listen for whispering voices on moonlight nights, who believe in fairies, and who know there are affections deep enough to encompass all things and all people.

The task here is to explain how two trees become so much in love with each other that they decide to join forces against the world and grow as one.

> "Curiouser and curiouser," cried Alice.[2]

This is not an isolated instance; the photographs on pages 241-42 offer plenty of examples. It does not appear to be a case of two trees living as cheaply as one. It could not be a result of lack of room in the forest. Unquestionably these are instances of two trees sensing each other's need of companionship and support. They knew they were competent to go on alone like ordinary trees, but they rebelled at that label of "ordinary," and decided to be extraordinary. They agreed to join forces and become Siamese twins in the twilight of their glorious careers. Said one tree to the other:

> Grow old along with me!
> The best is yet to be,
> The last of life, for which the first was made.
> Our times are in his hand
> Who saith, "A whole I planned,
> Youth shows but half; trust God: see all, nor be afraid!"[3]

And so they put their arms around each other and grew as one big tree. Vicissitudes of the past were no longer important. Wounds of yesteryear healed over and scars were hidden by the growth of healthy new bark. The trunk of the combined tree grew bigger above the union and the very divergence of the supporting trunks gave the united tree greater resilience, more latent strength against the storm.

Some might say that the junction where the trunks grew together isn't pretty. But answer this question: Was the face of a friend ever anything but beautiful and grand? And so we know that friendship and affection do dwell in the forest and do bring close together two kindred souls that feel the need of each other.

The scoffers may ridicule, but what can they prove? They have no sensible explanation of their own. They tell you that trees do not feel, but they are wrong! They say they are just poor dumb things. But if that were true, how would the trees know when to bloom, and when to seed, and how to distribute their seeds in a hostile world? The scoffers know as little about trees as they do about fairies.

What happens when one of the twin trees dies?

> Life! We've been long together,
> Through pleasant and through cloudy weather;
> 'Tis hard to part when friends are dear,
> Perhaps 'twill cost a sigh, a tear;
>
> Then steal away, give little warning;
>   Choose thine own time;
> Say not "Good-night"; but in some brighter clime
>   Bid me "Good-morning."[4]

Another explanation suggested by some of these pictures of two trees growing as one is that the weaker just decided to attach itself to the

RIGHT: "What vicissitudes we've known together!" chant these bristlecone pines (*Pinus aristata*) on a windswept mountain top in Oregon. BELOW, LEFT: These pine trees started out together, but could not get along. Later, however, the smaller one threw her arms around the other, and the two became one tree. (Photos: American Forestry Association.) BELOW, RIGHT: "May I have this dance with you?" said one elm to another, a long time ago. (Photo: Robert A. Lehman, American Forestry Association.)

LEFT: "Life will be easier if I can just lean on you," said the little pine to the bigger. And so they grew on together. (Photo: American Forestry Association.) RIGHT: This scribbly gum (*Eucalyptus haemastoma*) grows near Brisbane, Australia. Can we perceive frequent interruptions in the bonds of affection? (Photo: Brisbane Department of Works.)

LEFT: Two elm trees in England that decided to join together and raise a new generation. (Photo: H. Smith.) RIGHT: Two great elms have joined hands to live and die together on a roadside in New York. (Photo: Robert A. Lehman, American Forestry Association.)

stronger with a leechlike hold. This conduct has its human counterparts; there are plenty of individuals who prefer to lean on somebody else instead of charting their own course through life.

Trees with double trunks are frequent in cut-over lands in the United States, particularly among the oaks, probably the result of stump sprouting, but such doubles do not always fuse. Dean Hume[5] says that the holly trees at Mount Vernon offer grand examples, because four out of thirteen are double trees—that is, two trees planted in the same hole. They have grown together from ground level upward to heights of 1½ to 5 feet and now appear at casual glance to have single trunks.

In Brazil there is a different kind of affectionate tree. *Ceiba rivieri* hasn't much backbone, so from its slender trunk it puts out adventitious (misplaced) roots that surround a host tree and hold the *Ceiba* upright. This is similar to the clasping roots of the strangling figs[6] except that the *Ceiba* does not strangle its host, but merely clings to it. It raises its crown above the host and decorates its irregular top with ruddy red flowers in July. The tree grows in the mountains about Rio de Janeiro.[7] The climbing screw pine supports itself on other trees in the same way. (See Chapter Fifteen.)

THIRTY-TWO

The Tree That Gets Stark Naked

They were . . . naked . . . and were not ashamed.—GENESIS 2:25

Many trees have much bigger leaves when they are young than when they reach maturity. This switch is often a confusing factor in tree identification. Some genera such as *Eucalyptus* change not only the size of their leaves but their shape, and even their arrangement on the stems. No experienced forester ever tries to identify a *Eucalyptus* tree by the leaves on young growth.

This variation in leaf form reaches perhaps its most exaggerated aspects in west tropical Africa, in a genus of trees in the *Buddleja* family called *Anthocleista*. This scientific name literally means "flower-shut-up" because the corolla is closed off by the crown in its throat. The native names for the dozen or more species which are found in Nigeria, Ivory Coast, Ghana, and on to the Cameroons, can mostly be translated "cabbage tree," perhaps because the big floppy leaves of some kinds, when young, suggest the outer leaves of the common cabbage.[1] However, in the tropics a good many different trees are called cabbage trees if their leaves are clustered in bunches at the branch tips. Other common names for *Anthocleista* are fever tree[2] and murderer's mat.[3]

Essentially they are weed trees, springing up quickly in cut-over land, and they have a pachycaulous or spongy trunk that never branches but shoots straight for the sky. Pairs of opposite leaves sprout directly from the trunk, each pair at right angles to the one below or above it.

The size of these leaves is astonishing. On young plants up to 10 feet high, the leaves may be 7½ feet long. The petioles (leaf-stalks) of these enormous leaves are almost like branches. They are fastened together at the base by a sort of collar around the tree, a heavy leaf on one side counterbalanced by an equally heavy leaf on the other.[4] The collar consists of two sheaths that fit around the trunk of the tree and grow together. This arrangement is needed to support the weight of the enormous juvenile leaves.

This broad double sheath, tightly wrapped around the tree's trunk, is set off by four stiff, sharp auricles, two on either side of the junction of the leaf bases, and just below the auricles is a double, forking thorn. One pair of leaves extends east and west from the trunk, the next pair above it stretches north and south, and so on up the soft trunk. A crown of these enormous leaves at the top of a slender young stem is a striking sight in forest undergrowth.[5]

For a long time these big leaves stand at an acute upward angle. Gradually, as they grow longer and heavier, they sag until their stalks stand out almost horizontally. After a while the leaves appear to grow weary of the strain. The collars, or double sheaths, loosen their clasp on the trunk, they begin to shrivel, and the trunk's integument peels away.

An examination of the photographs (page 246) reveals that the leaves and the trunk's covering are all of one piece. The dying leaves pull and tug and tear at their anchorage until something has to give, and then they fall. The soft tissue remaining on the stem disintegrates, and the naked trunk stands forth.

When the leaves fall clear and are held up for inspection, they prove to be longer than the height of the man who lifts them. The next question is: What does the tree look like after all the leaves, sheaths, auricles, bark, and other parts are gone? It resembles a thorny pillar that has been skeletonized by worms or insects. It is completely barkless. Someone has suggested that it looks like a pecky-cypress telephone pole. The cracks and fissures that line its surface are not deep. Unlike the grooves and hollows that form in some other trees under different circumstances, catching water and becoming mosquito-breeding traps, these are only surface deep. The trunk's exterior at this stage is a sort of network of fibers rather than a gouged-out plane. Etched on the trunk are the cicatrices of the fallen leaves, moon-shaped scars in a regular alternating pattern of exceptional design. The vicious thorns are set to the four points of the compass, unaffected by the leaf droppings. Nearly all *Anthocleista* trees have these thorns.

From this point the plant leaves the juvenile stage of its existence behind, and starts to mature as a tree. First of all it generates a new bark,

TOP, LEFT: A young *Anthocleista* tree about 2 inches in diameter. TOP, CENTER: Full view of the young tree, 10 feet high. The big leaves are forming rapidly. TOP, RIGHT: The tree has grown to about 4 inches in diameter, with leaves so heavy that the petioles (which look like branches) are becoming more horizontal. (Several petioles in front have been cut off.) BOTTOM, LEFT: Now the leaves are getting tired. As they fall, their weight tugs the sheaths from the trunk. BOTTOM, CENTER: The stripped tree in close-up, barkless, cracked, and corrugated, with the crescent-shaped cicatrices of the fallen leaves. BOTTOM, RIGHT: The trunk has begun to generate bark to cover its nakedness. (Photos: Francis Hallé.)

though this does not fully succeed in obscuring the scars and corrugations of its earlier life. They are still visible through the new covering. (Many trees generate new bark in this manner, a common example being the cork oak.[6]) *Anthocleista* trees ultimately become forest monarchs, frequently 60 to 80 feet tall, and their girth may be 4 feet or more.

The soft wood has no commercial value. It is easy to work, but it has no resistance to decay. Tribesmen in Nigeria often use it as a quiver to hold arrows because a small log is easily hollowed.[7] The trunk in the juvenile stage is so spongy and full of moisture that it is very heavy; when dry it can be used for firewood. However, a Mendi superstition warns that if it is burned, people sitting around the fire will get sick.[8]

When *Anthocleista* trees mature, they no longer produce the enormous leaves that marked their childhood. Generally the mature leaves are only 6 to 18 inches long.

THIRTY-THREE

The Tree That Does Arithmetic

Add ye year to year. —Isaiah 29:1

Trees that tell time (described in Chapter Twenty-six) still do not attain the tree world's ultimate in mathematical precision. In west tropical Africa (Ghana, Sierra Leone, Ivory Coast) there is a tree that can multiply and add. Its whole life is wrapped up in an algebraic equation.

This is not intended as a joke. The photograph and drawing on pages 249 and 250 were made by Francis Hallé, a botanist stationed in Ivory Coast,[1] to simplify the understanding of this remarkable tree.

The tree has no common name in English and its scientific name is a jawbreaker—*Schumanniophyton problematicum*.[2] However, the specific epithet at least recognizes the tree's mathematical bent. It is in the coffee family,[3] grows from 20 to 40 feet high, and has exceptionally large leaves that are attached in groups of three at the end of each branch.

The tree's manner of growth expresses a formula that reads thus:

$$N = (Y \times 12) + 4$$

This tells how many leaves the tree has. The exact number is represented in the formula by the letter N. The letter Y represents the age of the tree in years, and if the formula is completed for any given tree, the exact number of leaves on that tree is determined.

The explanation of this phenomenon is easily understood by reference to Mr. Hallé's schematic drawing of one[4] of the *Schumanniophyton* trees opposite. It is only a *schema*, because at each node of the trunk there

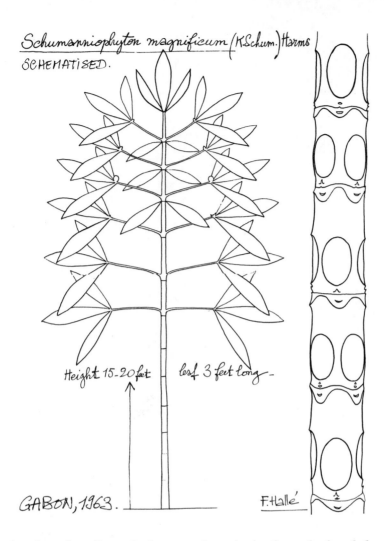

Schumanniophyton magnificum (K.Schum.) Harms
SCHEMATISED.

Height 15-20 feet

leaf 3 feet long

GABON, 1963.

F. Hallé

are *four* branches (instead of two as shown). At the end of each branch are three leaves, each of which is 3 feet long. Thus at each node the four branches carry a total of twelve leaves; such a set of branches develops each year as the tree reaches toward its maximum of 15 to 20 feet. The addition of an extra 4 at the end of the formula is necessary because there are four leaves in the crown of the tree. (See photograph, page 250.) Next year these will become the annual four-branch growth, and a new set of four crown leaves will be added.

Two kinds of *Schumanniophyton* trees are considered here. *S. magnificum* is used in the drawing because it has such handsome big leaves. The leaves of *S. problematicum* are only half as big, but the tree itself gets much taller. The algebraic formula applies alike to both trees.

ABOVE: The keppel tree (*Stelechocarpus burahol*), which . produces its sweet, juicy fruit on the trunk and larger branches. This one is in eastern Indonesia. (Photo: Bogor Botanic Garden.)

BELOW: The dense, dark green foliage of the miraculous African fruit tree (*Synsepalum dulcificum*), photographed in Florida. (Photo: Julia Morton.)

BELOW: The west African tree that does arithmetic, *Schumanniophyton problematicum*. (Photo: Francis Hallé.)

ABOVE: The olive-size fruit of *Synsepalum dulcificum*. When eaten, its pulp masks the taste buds so that other things eaten afterward taste sweeter than sugar. (Photo: International Minerals and Chemical Corporation.)

THIRTY-FOUR

Trees to Make Life Sweeter

*Blessed are they that do his commandments, that they may have
the right to the tree of life, and may enter in through the gates
into the city.* —REVELATION 22:14

As the end of the parade of strange trees draws near, two are selected for
the role of making life sweeter.

One of these is the miraculous-fruit[1] from west tropical Africa. It is a
shrub or treelet to 15 feet that produces quantities of olive-shaped fruits
which have an unexplained and almost unparalleled effect on man's tasting
equipment.[2] The pulp of the fruit, when eaten, masks or paralyzes the
sour taste buds of the tongue in such a way that everything eaten thereafter becomes deliciously sweet, even lime juice. Chemists[3] have found
this miraculous-fruit-induced sweetness "more desirable than any of the
known natural or synthetic sweeteners."

When the fruit is eaten, the curious, lingering aftereffect persists for an
hour or more, depending on the amount consumed.

The miraculous-fruit is at first green, turning dusky red when ripe. It is
less than an inch long, about the size of a small damson plum. When
Fairchild[4] learned that the fruits were good to eat, he helped himself
liberally without paying much attention to the story of their miraculous
power. The thin, soft, slightly saccharine pulp failed to thrill him, for he
reported the fruit "not good enough to become excited over, though not
at all bad." Later he found the beer he was drinking too sweet. He tried
a lemon, and when it too was excessively sweet, he rushed out and stripped

251

nearby trees of fruit to get the seeds for introduction into the United States. That was in 1919, and, although nearly fifty years have elapsed, very few miraculous-fruit trees are to be found growing in Florida or Puerto Rico.

Natives of the area from Ghana to the Congo, where the tree is indigenous, use the miraculous-fruits to sweeten their palm wine; or perhaps eating the fruit paralyzes their taste buds so they cannot savor the poor quality of their wine.

The other tree that can make life sweeter grows in Indonesia, where its common name is keppel.[5] Just as an excess of garlic makes a person reek from every pore, the consumption of keppel apples causes all bodily excrements, including perspiration, to smell like violets. The tree was formerly planted about the palace harems in Java, but denied to the common people, who were told that if they ate its fruits bad luck would follow. In a harem lacking modern sanitary conveniences, the aroma of violets could be of great advantage.

Fairchild[6] reported finding the tree in Jakarta and said the taste of the fruit reminded him of the pawpaws[7] he had eaten in woods in Kansas as a boy. The trees were scattered through the spacious grounds of the deserted and ruined Water Palace, and Fairchild thrilled to see their pink and wine-red new foliage, but they were not in fruit.

The keppel tree bears its fruits in bunches on the trunk like the cacao[8] or chocolate tree. Fairchild did find some of the fruits in a market and in comparing them with the pawpaw found them juicier and sweeter, with a delicious aroma. "I think one might become extremely fond of them," he wrote. The keppel belongs to the custard-apple family, along with the cherimoya, soursop, sugar-apple, and pawpaw.

Unfortunately for those who crave the scent of violets in their harems, realization of the dream must be delayed, as the keppel is not in cultivation in the United States. However, its possibilities have not been overlooked by fruit fanciers in Florida.[9]

Epilogue

Dr. Karl Menninger
The Menninger Foundation
Topeka, Kansas

Dear Brother Karl:

Fifty years of your life have been invested in efforts to understand troubled people. On this stroll through an assembly of fantastic trees, you could scarcely help smiling as you noted the counterparts of personalities twisted by environment. When we were boys our father used to take us through those woods on Martin's Hill that today are part of your hospital grounds and tried to arouse in us a little interest in the trees. He saw their struggle for existence, and he taught us to recognize the hickories because they were toughest and the hazels because they were noisiest and the box-elders because they were quick-growing and the black walnuts because their wood was the richest and their nuts the sweetest. I remember him helping you dig a walnut tree and bring it home, and the two of you planted it in our yard where it thrived. It was always "Karl's tree."

And here we are, fifty years later, talking about trees again! The examples cited in this museum of trees are mostly from the tropics; first, because ten times as many kinds of trees grow there as in the Temperate Zone, and second, because exaggerated conditions of heat, moisture, or drought which prevail there play important parts in producing behavior patterns

LEFT: This tropical African *Balanites wilsoniana* guards its fruit crop against marauders. Like people, trees develop their own defenses. (Photo: Francis Hallé.)
RIGHT: Within the past century a flow of lava passed this spot in Hawaii, congealing around a giant tree. Eventually the burned wood rotted away, leaving a lava tree. The rest of the lava turned to dust and blew away, and new vegetation has replaced the ashes and memories of horror. (Photo: Ray J. Baker.)

This eucalyptus tree in England fell full-length on the ground in its prime, but survived by sending up vertical sprouts which established their own root systems. (Photo: H. Smith.)

that are strikingly different from those with which most of the readers of this book are familiar.

One example might be cited from tropical forestry which does not obtain in the Temperate Zone. Farmers clearing medium-sized trees from dry upland areas in the tropics find the job much tougher than clearing trees twice the size from rain-forest lands. The reason is that upland savanna trees are so used to being seared by brush fires in the dry season (which is also the flowering and fruiting period), that they have learned to reproduce their species alternately by suckers from the roots as soon as the fire passes; hence chopping and burning these trees does not destroy them; twice as many come up from the roots. On the other hand, the big trees of the rain forest have lost the power of reproduction by root suckers, and if they are cut and burned the forest never comes back. Extremes of drought (plus fire) and excessive moisture have created here two different behavior patterns.

The desiccating effect of the sun's rays in hot countries has compelled many trees to invent protective devices that assist in the collection or retention of moisture. Again certain trees growing in swamps or areas of excessive rainfall have devised ways to prevent their being waterlogged or washed away. These measures to adapt to environment result in many trees' developing special peculiarities.

Wind pressure plays an important part in the tree world, just as pressures do in the human world; wind buffeting is a sort of physical jostling. Some rocks resist root growth and cause choking. Competition with other plants for a share of the sunlight and rain is sometimes intense. Battling against destructive animals, parasites, fungi, and diseases can be as violent among trees as in the human jungle. All these pressures shape trees strangely. Vigor and might prevail over most of their enemies, though the scars of battle remain even after victory. The vicissitudes of the struggle, however, affect the way the trees grow, the way they adjust themselves to their surroundings, the way they erect defenses, the way they reproduce their kind, and even their outward appearance.

Sometimes a monument remains in mute testimony to a mortal struggle in which the tree did not defeat its enemy. In Hawaii "lava trees" sometimes commemorate such past heroics. The flow of molten lava covers vast areas, consuming small stuff in its fury and impregnating giant trees in its path. Later, when the lava has cooled and disintegrated and the ashes have blown away, the giant trees remain as solid lava statues, soon surrounded by new vegetation which has never felt the ravages of fire.

All our lives you and I have watched this struggle between trees and their environment. Because trees are the only replaceable natural resource,

255

we have both spent parts of our lives in the development and study of trees, the roles they play in human affairs, their promise for the future. We have personally watched the adaptive methods of many trees to survive difficulties they meet. You have grown scores of ornamental and fruiting trees on your own place and I imagine they have provided many a lesson in behavior, environment, breeding, natural antagonisms, and peaceful compromises. More than once you have thought of those trees as you have struggled to plumb the depths of human maladjustments and to understand the determination of both man and tree to live in spite of all obstacles.

All life is a struggle. The urge to live is as indomitable in trees as in people; *per aspera* we reach *ad astra*. In spite of fire, drought, sorrow, loss, hunger, storm, flood, wind, and sometimes perhaps the burden of too-good fortune, trees—like human beings—do (sometimes) survive, and set for mankind an example of patience, persistence, endurance, and above all adaptation.

He who reads this book must be tree conscious. As he learns more about the wonderful world of trees and the fight they put up to live, perhaps he will understand better how currents and pressures can turn even our human world upside down.

Affectionately and arboreally,
Your brother,
Ed

June 1, 1966

Bibliography

(*Principal publications referred to.*)

Audas, J.W.: *Native Trees of Australia*. Whitcombe and Tombs, Melbourne, 1952.

Bates, H.W.: *A Naturalist on the River Amazons*. Reprint, University of California Press, Berkeley, 1962.

Black, J.M.: *Flora of South Australia*. 2d ed., Government Printer, Adelaide, 1948. (*Supplement*, 1962).

Botting, Douglas: *Island of the Dragon's Blood*. Wilfred Funk, Inc., New York, 1958; Hodder and Stoughton Ltd., London.

Burkill, I.H.: *A Dictionary of the Economic Products of the Malay Peninsula*. Government Printer, Singapore, 1935.

Cooke, M.C.: *Freaks and Marvels of Plant Life*. Society for Promoting Christian Knowledge, London, n.d.

Corner, E.J.H.: *The Life of Plants*. Weidenfeld and Nicolson, London, 1964.
————: *Wayside Trees of Malaya*. Government Printer, Singapore, 1958.

Cowen, D.V.: *Flowering Trees and Shrubs in India*. Thacker, Spink, and Co., Ltd., Bombay, 4th ed. 1965.

Dalziel, J.M.: *Useful Plants of West Tropical Africa*. Crown Agents for the Colonies, London, 1948.

Daubenmire, R.F.: *Plants and Environment*. John Wiley and Sons, Inc., New York, 2d ed. 1959.

Degener, Otto: *Plants Hawaii National Park*. Author, Waialua, Oahu, Hawaii, 1930.

De la Rüe, E. Albert: *The Tropics*. Alfred A. Knopf, New York, 1957.

Fairchild, David: *Exploring for Plants*. Macmillan, New York, 1930.

Francis, W.D.: *Australian Rain Forest Trees*. Forestry and Timber Bureau, Canberra, 1951.

257

Hutchinson, John: *A Botanist in Southern Africa*. Gawthorn, London, 1946.
Irvine, F.R.: *Woody Plants of Ghana*. Oxford University Press, New York, 1961.
Lindley, John, and Moore, Thomas: *A Treasury of Botany*. Longmans, Green and Company, London, 1884.
Lord, Ernest E.: *Shrubs and Trees for Australian Gardens*. Lothian Publishing Co., Melbourne, 4th ed. 1964.
Macmillan, H.F.: *Tropical Planting and Gardening*. Macmillan, London, 5th ed. 1948.
Menninger, Edwin A.: *Flowering Trees of the World*. Hearthside Press, New York, 1962.
Merrill, E.D.: *Plant Life of the Pacific World*. Macmillan, New York, 1945.
Morton, Julia F.: *Wild Plants for Survival in South Florida*. Hurricane House Publishers, Inc., Coconut Grove, Florida, 1962.
Palgrave, Keith C.: *Trees of Central Africa*. National Publications Trust, Salisbury, Southern Rhodesia, 1956.
Palmer, Eve, and Pitman, Norah: *Trees of South Africa*. A. A. Balkema, Cape Town, 1961.
Philipson, W.R.: *The Immaculate Forest*. Philosophical Library, New York, 1952.
Puri, G.S.: *Indian Forest Ecology*. Oxford Book and Stationery Co., New Delhi, 1960.
Record, Samuel J., and Hess, Robert W.: *Timbers of the New World*. Yale University Press, New Haven, 1943.
Ridley, Henry N.: *The Dispersal of Seeds throughout the World*. L. Reeve and Co., Ashford, Kent, England, n.d.
Schweinfurth, Georg August: *The Heart of Africa*. New York, 1874.
Spruce, Richard: *Notes of a Botanist on the Amazon and Andes*. Macmillan, London, 1908.
Taylor, C.J.: *Synecology and Silviculture in Ghana*. Thomas Nelson Sons, Edinburgh, 1960.
Troup, Robert Scott: *Silviculture of Indian Trees*. The Clarendon Press, Oxford, 1921.
Unwin, A. Harold: *West African Forests and Forestry*. E.P. Dutton and Co., New York, 1920.
Van Steenis, C.G.G.J.: *Flora Malesiana*. Noordhoff, Groningen, Holland, 1959—.
Wallace, Alfred Russel: *A Narrative of Travels on the Amazon and Rio Negro*. Macmillan, London, 1853. 2d ed., Ward, Lock and Company, London, 1889.
———: *Palm Trees of the Amazon and Their Uses*. London, 1853.
Willis, J.C.: *A Dictionary of the Flowering Plants and Ferns*. Cambridge University Press, 6th ed., revised, 1955.

Notes

(Works not cited fully here are listed in the Bibliography, page 257.)

Prologue
(pages *ix-xii*)

1. *Phytolacca dioica* L.
2. *Yucca brevifolia* Engelm.
3. *Coffea arabica* L.
4. *Brachystegia russelliae* I. M. Johnston.
5. *Garcinia livingstonei* T. Anders.
6. *Acacia albida* Delile. See Taylor, C.J.: *Op. cit.*
7. Ruiz, Hipolito: *Travels of Ruiz, Pavon and Dombey in Peru and Chile* (1777-1788). Translated by B. E. Dahlgren, Field Museum of Natural History, Chicago. Pub. 467, p. 27.
8. Dr. Hui-Lin Li, taxonomist of the Morris Arboretum and Associate Professor of Botany at University of Pennsylvania, Philadelphia, observed these growths on trees in Tokyo that had been badly trimmed, "where they nearly always developed on untrimmed branches or stumps of branches remaining on the trunk." He concluded that these growths are the result not only of old age "but also of wounds causing disruption of normal sap flow." *American Horticultural Magazine* 40:3 (July 1961).
9. *Wormia suffruticosa* Griff. and *Adinandra dumosa* Jack.
10. *Phyllocarpus septentrionalis* Donn.-Smith.
11. *Hymenolobium* sp. See Menninger, Edwin A.: *Op. cit.*
12. *Homalium grandiflorum* Benth. See Corner, E.J.H.: *Op. cit.*
13. *Artocarpus anisophyllus* Miq.

Chapter One: *Trunks Are Not All Alike*
(pages 7-17)

(1)

1. *Melaleuca quinquenervia* (Cav.) S. T. Blake.
2. *Psidium guajava* L.
3. Notably *Lagerstroemia subcostata* Koehne.

4. *Colubrina* sp.
5. *Platanus occidentalis* L. or *P. acerifolia* Willd.
6. *Albizzia tanganyicensis* E. G. Baker, and *Commiphora marlothii* Engl.
7. *Quercus suber* L.
8. *Hibiscus* sp.
9. *Adansonia digitata* L.
10. Dalziel, J.M.: *Op. cit.*
11. *Bombax ellipticum* HBK. This is often erroneously called *Pachira*, which is a different genus of trees.

(2)

12. Notably Taylor in Ghana, Corner in Malaya, Puri in India, and Francis in Australia. See Bibliography.
13. *Inocarpus edulis* Forst. [= I. *fagifer* (Parkinson) Fosberg.]
14. Record and Hess.: *Op. cit.*
15. Hohenkirk, L.S.: in *Journ. Bd. Agr. Brit. Guiana* **12**:3:185 (1920).
16. *Aspidosperma excelsum* Benth.
17. Lindley and Moore.: *Op. cit.*

(3)

18. *Sesamothamnus lugardii* N.E.Br.
19. *Adansonia digitata* L.

(4)

20. Corner, E.J.H.: *Op. cit.*
21. Ridley, Henry N.: *Op. cit. Flora of the Malay Peninsula.*
22. *Adina rubescens* Hemsl.
23. Foxworthy, F.W.: *Malayan Forest Records* No. 3, pp. 178-179 (1927).
24. Ridley, Henry N.: *Agric. Bull. Straits and F.M.S.I.*, p. 207 (1902).
25. *Aspidosperma aquaticum* Ducke.
26. Record and Hess.: *Op. cit.*

(5)

27. *Angophora lanceolata* Cav. (Myrtaceae).
28. Oakman, Harry: *Trees of Australia*. Jacaranda Press, Brisbane, 1962. Mr. Oakman was park superintendent in Brisbane for fifteen years, and is now aiding in park development in the new Australian capital, Canberra City.
29. *Phytolacca dioica* L.
30. *Populus deltoides* Marsh.
31. *Chamaecyparis lawsoniana* Parl.

(6)

32. *Betula papyrifera* Marsh.
33. *Eucalyptus grandis* Maiden.
34. *Pinus bungeana* Zucc.
35. Unwin, A. Harold.: *Op. cit.*
36. *Lophira alata* Banks ex Gaert.

(7)

37. Corner, E.J.H.: "The Durian Theory or the Origin of the Modern Tree." *Annals of Botany*, n.s. **13**:367-414. (1949). This thesis is elaborated in the same author's *The Life of Plants*, Weidendeld and Nicolson, London, 1964.
38. *Cussonia bancoensis* Aubrev. and Pellegr.

Chapter Two: Unique Branching
(pages 18-20)

1. *Araucaria excelsa* L.
2. Corner, E.J.H.: *Op. cit.*

Chapter Three: Roots That Go Wild
(pages 21-39)

1. Emeneau: *The Strangling Figs in Sanskrit Literature*. 1949. Also Viennot: "Le Culte de l'Arbre dans l'Inde Ancienne" in *Ann. Mus. Guimet* Vol. 59, pp. 1-290 (1954).
2. Willis, J.C.: *Op. cit.*
3. *Avicennia nitida* Jacq.

(1)

4. *Metrosideros excelsa* Sol. ex Gaertn. [= *M. tomentosa* A. Rich.]
5. Laing and Blackwell: *Plants of New Zealand*. Ed. 7. Whitcombe and Tombs, Ltd., Christchurch, 1964. Another authority agrees: Lord, Ernest E.: *Op. cit.*
6. *Dacrydium cupressinum* Lamb.
7. *Metrosideros robustum* A. Cunn.
8. Elliott, Douglas: in *Journal of Royal Horticultural Society*, London, August, 1958.

(2)

9. *Ficus benghalensis* L.
10. Willis, J.C.: *Op. cit.*
11. *Ficus elastica* Roxb.

(3)

12. *Ficus aurea* Nutt.

(4)

13. *Nuytsia floribunda* R. Br.
•14. *Gaiadendron* and *Nuytsia*, both showy-flowered trees, are described in Menninger: *Op. cit.*
15. *Loranthus terrestris* Hook.f. and *L. ligustrinus* Wall. in India and *L. buchneri* Engl. in Africa.
16. *Atkinsonia ligustrina* (A. Cunn. ex F. Muell.) F. Muell. For a description of its root parasitism see Menzies and McKee in *Proc. Linn. Soc. N.S.W.* 84:1:389 (1959).

17. Dr. John S. Beard is director of Queen's Park and Botanic Garden at Perth, West Australia.
18. *Australian Plants* is published quarterly by the Society for Growing Australian Plants, 250 Picnic Point Road, Picnic Point, N.S.W.
19. Herbert, D.A.: "The Western Australian Christmas Tree, Its Structure and Parasitism." *Journ. and Proc. Roy. Soc. W. Austr.* 5: 72-88.

(5)

20. *Pandanus* spp.
21. This is called *Iriartea* by some authors.
22. Bates, H.W.: *Op. cit.*
23. *Musanga smithii* R. Br.
24. Dalziel, J.M.: *Op. cit.* See also Chipp: *Kew Bulletin* 1913:96.
25. *Dillenia reticulata* King.
26. Corner, E.J.H.: *Op. cit.*
27. *Xylopia ferruginea* Baill.
28. De la Rüë, E. Albert: *Op. cit.*, p. 45.
29. *Uapaca guineensis* Muell. Arg.
30. Irvine, F.R.: *Op. cit.*
31. *Desbordesia oblonga* A. Chev. of the Irvingaceae, formerly placed in the Simarubaceae.
32. Walker, A., and Sillans, R.: *Les Plantes Utiles du Gabon*. Paul Lechevalier, Paris, 1961.
33. *Elaeocarpus littoralis* Teijsm. and Binn. ex Kurz.
34. In personal correspondence.

(6)

35. De la Rüe, E. Albert: *Op. cit.*
36. Petch, T.: "Buttressed Roots." *Ann. Bot. Gard.* Peradeniya. 11:277-85 (1930).
37. Francis, W.D.: "Development of Buttresses in Queensland Trees" in *Proc. Roy. Soc. Queensl.* (Australia) 36:21-37 (1924).
38. Taylor, C.J.: *Op. cit.*
39. Petch, T.: *Op. cit.* (see note 36).
40. Taylor, C.J.: *Op. cit.*

(7)

41. *Taxodium distichum* Rich.
42. Daubenmire, R.F.: *Op. cit.*
43. Chief of the mangrove trees in salt water are *Rhizophora mangle* L., *Avicennia nitida* Jacq., *Laguncularia racemosa* Gaertn.f., *Sonneratia* sp., and *Carapa granatum* (Koenig) Alston.
44. Chief of the mangrove trees in fresh water are *Elaeocarpus littoralis* Teisjm. and Binn. ex Kurz, *Xylopia ferruginea* Baill., *X. fusca* Maing. ex Hook.f., *Calophyllum* sp., the wild nutmeg in Malaya (*Myristica elliptica* Wall.), various species of *Lophopetalum* which are big timber trees of the Celastraceae, and some palms like *Raphia*.

45. *Arachis hypogaea* L. Other genera with underground fruiting habits are *Kerstingiella* and *Voandzeia*.
46. Corner, E.J.H.: *Op. cit.*

Chapter Four: *Even the Leaves Are Queer*
(pages 40-53)

(1)

1. Lindley and Moore: *Op. cit.* says the native name "tumbo" is applied generally to all plants that have a short, thick, woody trunk.
2. Is this the origin of the English word "jumbo"?
3. *Welwitschia mirabilis* Hook.f. [= **W**. *bainesii* Hook.f.]
4. In *Curtis's Botanical Magazine* 5368 (March 1, 1863).
5. *Trans. Linnean Society* **24**:1. 1863.
6. Thomas Baines, traveling the Damara country in 1862, made colorful sketches of the plant and sent them with some cones to Dr. Hooker at Kew.
7. *Acacia karroo* Hayne.

(2)

8. See Chapter Thirty-two.
9. Examples are *Cordia sebestena* and *Sterculia apetala*.
10. *Ficus krishnae* was described by de Candolle in 1901 as a separate species, but Dr. K. Biswas, superintendent of the Royal Botanic Garden, Calcutta, has shown it is merely a variety of *F. benghalensis*. See Benthall: *Trees of Calcutta*. Also *Current Science* III:9 (March 1935).
11. *Ravenala madagascariensis* J. F. Gmel.
12. *Sterculia apetala* Karst.
13. A mounted leaf even larger than this, contributed by the author, may be seen at the New York Botanical Garden.
14. The twenty-five species of *Anthocleista* are called cabbage trees because the leaves are in cabbage-like heads at the tips of the branches. See Chapter Eleven.
15. Rendle *et al.*: *Catalog of Plants Collected by Mr. and Mrs. P. A. Talbot in Oban District, Southern Nigeria*. British Museum, London, 1913.
16. Wallace, Alfred Russel: *Palm Trees*.
17. *Raphia taedigera* Mart.
18. *Maximiliana regia* Mart.
19. Cooke, M.C.: *Op. cit.*
20. *Corypha umbraculifera* L.

(3)

21. *Pseudopanax ferox* T. Kirk and *P. crassifolium* (Sol. ex A. Cunn.) Koch.
22. *Sophora tetraptera* J. Miller.
23. *Dacrydium kirkii* F. Muell. ex Parl.
24. *Elaeocarpus hookerianus* Raoul.

25. *Plagianthus betulinus* A. Cunn.
26. *Pennantia corymbosa* Forst.
27. Van Steenis, C.G.G.J.: *Op. cit.*
28. Lord, E.E.: *Op. cit.*
29. Corner, E.J.H.: *Op. cit.*
30. *Artocarpus elastica* Reinw.
31. Taylor, C.J.: *Op. cit.*

(4)

32. *Terminalia catappa* L.
33. For a list of these see Menninger, Edwin A.: *Op. cit.*
34. *Tournefortia gnaphalodes* R. Br.
35. *Conocarpus erectus* L.
36. *Argyroxiphium macrocephalum* A. Gray.
37. Degener, Otto: *Flora Hawaiiensis*, 1922—; also *Plants Hawaii National Park*, 1930. Author, Waialua, Oahu, Hawaii.
38. Baker, Ray Jerome: *Familiar Hawaiian Flowers.* Author, Honolulu, 1934.
39. *Leucadendron argenteum* R. Br.
40. *Chrysophyllum olivaeforme* L.

(5)

41. *Phylloxylon ensifolium* Baill. [= *Neobaronia phyllanthoides* Baker.]
42. Baron, ———: *Flora of Madagascar* **xix**: 255, 275. This *Flora* was continued by John Gilbert Baker, **xx**: 87-304, also 313-336, in *Journal of the Linnean Society*, London, 1883-1889.
43. *Phyllobotryum soyauxianum* Baill.
44. *Ginko biloba* L.
45. Li, Hui-Lin in *American Horticultural Magazine* 40:3 (July 1961).
46. Makino in *Journ. Jap. Bot.* 6 (1):5 (1929).
47. *Homalocladium platycladum* L. H. Bailey.
48. *Ruscus aculeatus* L.

Chapter Five: *The Flowers Are Twisted*
(pages 54-65)

1. Earth figs (*Ficus* sp.), as described in a previous chapter, do just this.

(1)

2. *Chiranthodendron pentadactylon* Larreategui [= *Cheirostemon platanoides* Humb. and Bonpl.; *Chiranthodendron platanoides* Baill.]
3. *Curtis's Botanical Magazine*, Plate 5135 (1859).
4. Standley and Steyermark: *Flora of Guatemala.* Chicago Natural History Museum, Chicago, 1955—.

(2)

5. *Strophanthus boivini* Baill.

(3)

6. Named in honor of F. P. Park, an African explorer.
7. For classification of the Brazilian species see *Archives of the Institute of Vegetable Biology*, IV (2937).
8. *Kigelia* and *Adansonia* also dangle their flowers at the ends of long ropes. See Index.
9. Fairchild, David: *Op. cit.*
10. *Tricuspidaria lanceolata* Miq.
11. See Menninger, Edwin A.: *Op. cit.*

(4)

12. Philipson, W.R.: *Op. cit.*
13. Wallace, Alfred Russel: *A Narrative of Travels on the Amazon and Rio Negro, Op. cit.* I:39.
14. *Artocarpus heterophyllus* Lam. [= *A. integrifolius* not L.f.]
15. Also cauliflorous are the African breadfruit (*Treculia africana* Decne.), *Cola nitida* A. Chev. and *C. chlamydantha* K. Schum., *Napoleona parviflora* Bak.f. and *Angylocalyx oligophyllus* Bak.f. Also in this book see *Parmentiera, Omphalocarpum, Couroupita*, etc., in Index.

(5)

16. *Theobroma cacao* L.
17. Allen, Paul: in *Bulletin of Fairchild Tropical Garden*, Miami, Florida ix:5 (Feb. 1954). Reprinted by permission.

(6)

18. *Myrciaria cauliflora* Berg.
19. This section is based on an article by the author in *National Horticultural Magazine*, July 1959. For an explanation of the distinguishing features of *Myrciaria cauliflora* Berg., *M. jaboticaba* Berg., and *M. trunciflora* Berg., see Hoehne, F.C.: *Indigenous Fruit Trees of Brazil*. Instituto de Botánica, São Paulo, 1960.

(7)

20. Hill, F.L.: "Plant Collecting in Australia." *Journ. of Royal Horticultural Society*, London. (July 1956).
21. Corner, E.J.H.: *Op. cit.*
22. *Pterocarpus indicus* Willd.
23. *Dyera costulata* Hook. f.
24. *Eugenia grandis* Wight [= *Syzygium grande* Wall.]
25. Richards, P.W.: *The Tropical Rain Forest*. Cambridge University Press, Cambridge, 1952.
26. Spruce, Richard: *Op. cit.*
27. Corner, E.J.H.: *Op. cit.*
28. Van Steenis, C.G.G.J.: "Gregarious Flowering of *Strobilanthes* in Malaysia." *Ann. Roy. Bot. Gard.*, Calcutta (1942).
29. Petch, T.: "Gregarious Flowering." *Ann. Roy. Bot. Gard.*, Peradeniya 9:101-17 (1924).

30. Holttum, R.E.: "The Flowering of Tembusu Trees in Singapore," 1928-1935." *Gardens Bulletin,* Singapore 9:73-8.
31. Vaughn and Wiehe: "Studies on the Vegetation of Mauritius." *Journ. Ecol.* **25**:289-342.
32. The common pond rush.

Chapter Six: *Strange Fruits and Nuts*
(pages 66-85)

(1)

1. Seychelles (pronounced *Say-shells*) is a group of 27 islands in the Indian Ocean 600 miles east of Madagascar. The nuts grow on only three of the islands.
2. *Lodoicea maldivica* Pers.
3. Bailey, L.H.: "Palmae Sechellarum." *Gentes Herbarum* **iv**:1.
4. Durocher-Yvon, F.: "Seychelles Botanical Treasure." *La Revue Agricola* (Mauritius). **xxvi**:2. pp. 69-87.
5. The specific name of the tree, *maldivica,* is derived from this misinformation.
6. Hooker, Sir Joseph, in *Curtis's Botanical Magazine* 2734-8.
7. Bailey, L.H.: *Op. cit.* (see note 3).

(2)

8. *Durio zibethinus* Murr. The Italian *zibetto* = civet.
9. See Menninger, Edwin A.: *Op. cit.*
10. Corner, E.J.H.: *Op. cit.*
11. Macmillan, H.F.: *Op. cit.*
12. Wallace, Alfred Russel: *The Malay Archipelago.* Harper and Brothers, New York, 1869.

(3)

13. *Guilielma gasipaes* L. H. Bailey.
14. *Hyphaene thebaica* Mart.
15. Lindley and Moore: *Op. cit.*
16. *Melocanna bambusoides* Trin.
17. Kurz, Sulpiz: *Forest Flora of British Burma.* Calcutta, 1877.
18. This gregarious flowering was noted in previous chapter.
19. Troup, Robert Scott: *Op. cit.*

(4)

20. Tamayo, Francisso: *Arboles en Flor de Venezuela.* Compania Shell, 1959.
21. *Heliocarpus americanus* L.
22. *Vernonia colorata* (Willd.) Drake, a tree relative of the fall-flowering perennial known as ironweed.
23. *Bixa orellana* L.
24. *Heisteria parvifolia* Smith.
25. Aubreville, A.: *La Flore Forestière de la Côte d'Ivoire.*

26. *Aptandra zenkeri* Engl.
27. Dalziel, J.M.: *Op. cit.*
28. Fairchild, David: *Op. cit.*
29. *Nymania capensis* Lindb.
30. Palmer and Pitman: *Op. cit.*
31. *Blighia sapida* Kon. The generic name honors Captain William Bligh of H.M.S. *Bounty* who in 1787 was appointed to convey the breadfruit and other trees from Tahiti to the West Indies.

(5)

32. Corner, E.J.H.: *Op. cit.*
33. *Oroxylon indicum* Vent.
34. *Pajanelia longifolia* K. Schum. [= *P. multijuga* DC.]
35. *Stereospermum fimbriatum* DC.
36. *Cassia abbreviata* Oliver var. *granitica*.
37. Palmer and Pitman: *Op. cit.*
38. *Parmentiera cereifera* Seem.
39. *Moringa oleifera* (L.) Lamarck.
40. *Heterophragma adenophyllum* Seem.

(6)

41. *Dimorphandra mora* Benth. and Hook.f. [= *Mora excelsa* Benth.]
42. *Sturtevant's Notes on Edible Plants* (U. P. Hedrick, ed.) New York Agric. Exper. Sta., Geneva, 1919.
43. Cooke, M.C.: *Op. cit.*
44. Brown, C.B.: *Camp Life in British Guiana*, p. 383 (1876).
45. *Entada phaseaoloides* Merr. [= *E. scandens* Benth.]
46. *Entada pursaetha* DC.
47. *Entada gigas* Fawcett and Rendle. Mackay bean.
48. *Omphalocarpum procerum* Beauv.
49. Kennedy, Jas. D.: *Forest Flora of Southern Nigeria*. Lagos, 1936.
50. Unwin, A. Harold: *Op. cit.*
51. *Omphalocarpum anocentrum* Pierre [= *O. elatum* Piers.]
52. *Kigelia pinnata* DC.
53. *Crescentia cujete* L.
54. *Couroupita guianensis* Aubl.
55. Very young calabash fruits are pickled and eaten in Jamaica.
56. Two other kinds of calabash trees are cultivated in Florida, one a native, the other from Mexico.
57. Standley, Paul C.: *Flora of Costa Rica*. Field Museum of Natural History, Chicago. Vol. 18, 1937-1938.
58. *Lagenaria siceraria* Standley.
59. Balfour, J.H., quoted in Lindley and Moore: *Op. cit.*
60. *Monodora myristica* Dun. See Menninger, Edwin A.: *Op. cit.*
61. Battiscombe, Edward: *Trees and Shrubs of Kenya Colony*. Government Printer, Nairobi.
62. Hiern, N. P.: *Catalog of the African Plants Collected by Dr. Friedrich Welwitsch in 1853-61*. London, 1894.

63. *Bertholettia excelsa* H. and B.
64. *Lecythis zabucajo* Aubl. and other species.
65. *Carica papaya* L.
66. *Artocarpus incisa* L.f.
67. *Artocarpus heterophyllus* Lam. [= *A. integrifolius* not L.]
68. Corner, E.J.H.: *Op. cit.*
69. *Treculia africana* Decne.
70. Dalziel, J.M.: *Op. cit.*

Chapter Seven: *Desert Preparation for an Astronaut*

(pages 87-102)

(1)

1. *Pachycormus discolor* (Benth.) Coville [= *Veatchia cedrosensis* A. Gray.]
2. Dr. J. A. Veatch, quoted by Edward Goldman: "Plant Records of an Expedition to Lower California." *U.S. Natl. Herb.* 16:14 (1916).
3. Howard E. Gates, Corona, Calif., in correspondence.
4. *Bursera microphylla* Gray.

(2)

5. *Idria columnaris* Kellogg. In Mexico it is called "cirio" or wax candle. The nickname "boojum tree" was given to it by a distinguished desert ecologist, Godfrey Sykes of the Desert Botanical Laboratory, Tucson, Arizona, in reference to the legendary creature in Lewis Carroll's *The Hunting of the Snark.*
6. Walker, Lewis Wayne: "Boogum—Desert Contortionist." *Natural History* 60:224-226 (May 1951).
7. Center, Arthur L.: "The Boojim Tree of Baja." *American Forests* 67:26-7 (June 1961).
8. Krutch, Joseph Wood: *The Forgotten Peninsula.* William Sloane Associates, New York, 1961. Quoted by permission.
9. Standley, Paul C.: *Trees and Shrubs of Mexico.* U.S. National Herbarium, Vol. 23. Washington 1920-1926. Repr. 1961 Smithsonian Institution, Washington.
10. Clavijero, Francisco: *Historia de la California.*
11. *Fouquieria* sp. For description of cultivated species see *Baileya* 10:139 (1961).
12. Krutch, Joseph Wood: *Op. cit.* (see note 8).

(3)

13. Choux, Pierre: *Les Didiereacées, Xerophytes de Madagascar.* Fascicule xvii of Memoires de l'Academie Malagache, Tananarive (1934). This 70-page book, with many photographs, is a detailed discussion of this group. Baillon's original description was in *Bull. Soc. Linn.* I:258 (1880). Engler and Prantl: *Nat. Pfl.* III:5:461-2 (1896) devotes 16 lines to the genus. Choux gives additional references.

14. *Carnegiea gigantea* Brit. and Rose [= *Cereus giganteus* Engl.]
15. *Pachycereus pringlei* Brit. and Rose.
16. For example, *Euphorbia enterophona* Drake.
17. *Euphorbia obovalifolia* A. Rich. [= *E. winkleri* Pax.]
18. *Euphorbia candelabrum* Tremant ex Kotschy.
19. *Euphorbia nyikae* Pax. ex Engl.

(4)

20. *Harpagophytum grandidiere* Baill.
21. See Menninger, Edwin A.: *Op. cit.*
22. MacOwan, Peter: *Agricultural Journal* (Cape of Good Hope) **13**:406 (1898).

(5)

23. *Fagara davyi* Verdoorn. Several species are recognized, though they are much confused. The genus is closely allied to the American prickly-ash (*Xanthoxylum americanum* Mill.) and to certain weed trees in Florida.
24. Lueckhoff, H.A., Forest Research Institute, Pretoria, South Africa, in personal correspondence.
25. Verdoorn, Frans: *Journal of Botany* **lvii**:205 (1919).
26. Palmer and Pitman: *Op. cit.*

(6)

27. Alexander, E.J.: *Succulent Plants of New and Old World Deserts.* New York Botanical Garden, 3d ed. 1950.
28. *Pachypodium namaquanum* Welw.
29. Findley, R. in *Journ. Roy. Hort. Soc.*, London (Feb. 1962).
30. C. K. Brain of the staff of the Queen Victoria Museum, Causeway, Salisbury, Southern Rhodesia.
31. Hutchinson, John: *Op. cit.*
32. *Pachypodium succulentum* (L.f.) DC.
33. Chittenden, F.J., ed., *Royal Horticultural Society's Dictionary of Gardening.* Oxford University Press, 1951.
34. Corner, E.J.H.: *Op. cit. The Life of Plants.*
35. This puts *Pachypodium* in the category of pachycaulous trees described in Chapter One. Although the trunks may be woody, they are milky and not very hard.
36. *Pachypodium saundersii* N.E.Br.
37. Welwitsch, Friedrich: *Trans. Linnean Soc.*, London **xxvii**:42 (1869). See also Hiern, N.P.: *Catalog of the African Plants Collected by Dr. Friedrich Welwitsch in 1853-61.* London, 1894.
38. *Pachypodium lealii* Welw.
39. *Pachypodium rutabergianum* Vatke.
40. *Pachypodium giganteum* Engl.

(7)

41. *Moringa ovalifolia* Dinter and Berger.
42. *Moringa oleifera* (L.) Lamarck.
43. Dinter, Kurt: *Neue Pflanzen Deutsch-Südwest Afrika* 45 (1914).

(8)

44. Botting, Douglas: *Island of the Dragon's Blood*. Reprinted by permission of the publishers: Wilfred Funk, Inc. New York, 1958; Hodder and Stoughton Ltd., London.
45. *Dendrosicyos socotrana* Balf.f.
46. Botting, Douglas: *Op. cit.* See note 44.
47. Balfour, Isaac Bayley: *Proc. Roy. Soc. Edinburgh* **xi**:513 (1882).
48. Lemée A.: *Dictionnaire . . . Phanerogames* **ii**:514 (1930).
49. Wellsted, J.R.: "Memoir on the Island of Socotra." *Journ. Roy. Geographic Soc. London* v:198 (1835).
50. Balfour, Isaac Bayley: "Botany of Socotra." *Trans. Roy. Soc. Edinburgh,* **xxxi** (1888).

(9)

51. *Adenium socotranum* Vierh.
52. See Menninger, Edwin A.: *Op. cit.*
53. Botting, Douglas: *Op. cit.* See note 44.
54. *Adenium boehmianum* Schinz.
55. *Dorstenia gigas* Schweinf.

(10)

56. *Adenia pechuelii* Engl. This belongs in the passion-flower family (Passifloraceae) and should not be confused with *Adenium* of the dogbane family (Apocynaceae).
57. Alexander, E.J.: *Op. cit.* (see note 27).
58. This was formerly called *Echinothamnus pechuelii.*
59. *Cissus macropus* Welw.
60. Chittenden, F.J.: *Op. cit.* (see note 33).
61. *Pachypodium saundersii* N.E.Br.
62. Palgrave, Keith C.: *Op. cit.*

Chapter Eight: *Obesity among Trees*

(pages 103-110)

(1)

1. Adapted from an article by the author in *Tropics* I:11 (June 1962).
2. *Adansonia digitata* L.
3. *Adansonia gregorii* F. Muell.
4. Palgrave, Keith C.: *Op. cit.*
5. *African Wild Life* iv:2:143, Johannesburg.
6. Anton-Smith, J., Mt. Makulu Research Station, Chilanga, Northern Rhodesia (Zambia).

(2)

7. See Chapter Seventeen on smelly trees.
8. *Phytolacca dioica* L.
9. Swindon, Walter L.: *American Weekly of Buenos Aires* 3:31:5 (Nov. 21, 1925).
10. Eckert, Allen W.: *American Forests*, Oct. 1961.

(3)

11. *Brachychiton rupestris* K. Schum. The epithet *rupestris* means growing in rocky places.
12. With all due respect to the trademark owner.
13. Audas, J.W.: *Op. cit.*
14. Lord, E.E.: *Op. cit.*
15. *Brachychiton populneum* R. Br.

(4)

16. *Ceiba pentandra* (L.) Gaertn.
17. The Java tree is usually called var. *indica,* and different names have been suggested for the kinds growing in Africa.
18. Dalziel, J.M.: *Op. cit.*
19. Fawcett and Rendle: *Flora of Jamaica.* British Museum, London, 1910-1936.
20. Standley, Paul C.: *Flora of Costa Rica.* Field Museum of Natural History, Chicago, Vol. 18, 1937-1938.
21. Dalziel, J.M.: *Op. cit.*
22. Kapok fiber is also derived to a limited extent from a related tree, *Bombax malabaricum* DC., from India.

(5)

23. *Colpothrinax wrightii* Griseb. and H. Wendl.
24. Moore, H.E., Jr.: "The Cuban Belly Palm." *Principes* iv:2 (April 1960).

Chapter Nine: *The Lily Hexapod*

(pages 111-121)

(1)

1. Lindley and Moore in *A Treasury of Botany* say that when the palmlike trunks are denuded of leaves (as by fire), the plants have been compared to and even mistaken for black men holding spears—hence their common colonial name.
2. Perhaps a corruption of *Yucca,* a related plant in the lily family.
3. Ben Jones: in *Gardeners Chronicle Gardening Illustrated,* July 14, 1962.
4. 636 Fifth Avenue, New York, N.Y.
5. Ewart, A.J.: *Flora of Victoria.* University of Melbourne, 1930.
6. Lewis, C.F.: "Observations on the Age of the Australian Grass Trees." *Victorian Naturalist* 72:124 (Dec. 1955).
7. Lord, E.E.: *Op. cit.*
8. Audas, J.W.: *Op. cit.*

(2)

9. *Dracaena cinnabari* Balf.f.
10. Botting, Douglas: *Op. cit.* (see note 44, Chapter Seven).
11. The cucumber, myrrh, frankincense, and *Adenium* trees are described elsewhere in this book.

12. Cinnabar is red mercuric sulphide. Both the genuine and synthetic are often called dragon's blood. Several organic resins bear this name, not only those from *Dracaena* trees but also from the fruit of climbing palms in the genera *Calamus* and *Daemonorops* from Malaya.
13. *Dracaena draco* L. This is cultivated in San Diego, California, parks, and elsewhere in the United States.
14. Willis, J.C.: *Op. cit.*
15. Lindley and Moore: *Op. cit.*

(3)

16. *Beaucarnea recurvata* Lemaire.
17. *Nolina bigelovii* Watson.
18. *Dasylirion acotriche* Zuccarini.

(5)

19. *Yucca brevifolia* Engl. [= *Clistoyucca arborescens* Trel.]
20. *Yucca gloriosa* L.
21. *Yucca australis* Trel.
22. *Yucca whipplei* Torr.

(6)

23. Strang, H.E.: *Vellozia* I:22.
24. Quoted from a review of Marianne North's book *Recollections of a Happy Life* in *Journ. Roy. Hort. Soc.* lxxxix:6 (June 1964).

Chapter Ten: *Gigantism*
(pages 122-127)

1. Huxley, Julian: *Exotic Plants of the World*. Hanover House, New York, 1957. Reprinted by permission.
2. Synge, Patrick M.: *Mountains of the Moon*. Lindsay Drummond, Ltd., London, 1938. Quoted by permission.
3. Perry, Roger: "Giant Mountain Plants of the Tropics." *Gardener's Chronicle*, July 4, 1964.
4. *Neurophyllodes arboreum* (A. Gray) Degener [= *Geranium arboreum* A. Gray.]
5. Degener, Otto: *Plants Hawaii National Park*. Reprinted by permission.
6. Chock, Alvin R.: in *Hawaiian Botanical Society Newsletter*, March 1963. Reprinted by permission. Chock is assistant botanist at the Bernice P. Bishop Museum in Honolulu.
7. Huxley, Julian: *Op. cit.* (see note 1).
8. Daubenmire, R.F.: *Op. cit.*

Chapter Eleven: *The Cabbage-Trees of St. Helena*
(pages 128-134)

1. The author acknowledges the collaboration of N. R. Kerr, headmaster of East Bergholt Modern School, East Bergholt, Colchester, Essex, Eng-

land, in the preparation of this chapter, and the descriptions are largely his. Formerly Superintendent of Education in St. Helena, he studied and wrote of the flora while there and is now preparing a more extended work. Several of the photographs were taken by Mr. Kerr. The author also acknowledges the assistance of Arthur Loveridge of Varneys, St. Helena, and of G. C. Lawrence, government information officer at The Castle, St. Helena, in obtaining additional facts and photographs. These are possibly the only photographs in the world of these strange trees.

2. In the tropics the name "cabbage trees" is applied to many different trees whose leaves are born in clusters at the branch tips.

3. Hutchinson, John: *Op. cit.*

4. *Araucaria excelsa* R. Br.

5. *Phormium tenax* Forst.

6. *Rubus pinnatus* Willd.

7. See Chapter Ten on Gigantism.

8. *Melanodendron integrifolium* DC.

9. *Senecio leucadendron* Benth. and Hook.f.

10. *Petrobium arboreum* R.Br.

11. *Hedyotis arborea* Roxb. This is not one of the cabbage trees but belongs in the coffee family.

12. Melliss, J.C.: *St. Helena.* 1875. This rare book is in the Harvard College library.

13. The Indian botanist Dr. William Roxburgh stayed for a year (1813-14) in St. Helena and drew up an alphabetical list of plants on the island. This was published as an appendix to *Tracts Relative to the Island of St. Helena* (1816) by General Alexander Beatson, one-time governor.

14. Roxburgh called this *Solidago spuria.* Melliss called it *Aster gummiferus.*

15. William Burchell, who spent the years 1805 to 1810 collecting plants in St. Helena. His specimens are at Kew.

16. Burchell called this the bastard cabbage tree.

17. Originally called *Petrobium arboreum* R.Br., now transferred to *Laxmannia arborea* Forster.

18. *Senecio prenanthiflorus* Benth. and Hook.f. This is also called red cabbage and sparwood by some authors.

19. *Psiadia rotundifolis* Hook.f.

20. *Gardener's Chronicle* **III**:iii:180 (1888).

21. Melliss called this *Aster burchellii.*

Chapter Twelve: *Birds, Elephants, and Turtles*

(pages 135-137)

1. Ridley, H.N.: *Op. cit.*

2. *Schinus terebinthifolius* Raddi.

3. *Juniperus silicicola* Bailey.

4. Kerner, A.: *Natural History of Plants.* Blackie and Son, London, 1902.

5. Roessler, E.S.: "Viability of Weed Seeds after Ingestion by California Linnets." *Condor* **38**:62 (1936).

6. *Lycopersicon esculentum* var. *minor* L.
7. Rick, C.M., and Bowman, R.I.: "Galapagos Tomatoes and Tortoises." *Evolution* **15**:407-417 (Dec. 1961).
8. Dr. Herbert G. Baker, director of Botanical Garden, University of California, Berkeley.
9. *Adansonia digitata* L.
10. *Kigelia africana* Benth.
11. *Ricinodendron rautanenii* Schinz.
12. G. L. Guy, director of National Museum, Bulawayo, Rhodesia.
13. *Ochroma lagopus.* See Chapter Nineteen.
14. Dr. Charles J. Taylor in correspondence. He is author of *Synecology and Silviculture in Ghana.*
15. *Musanga* sp. See Taylor: *Op. cit.*, p. 255.
16. Boughey, A.S.: in *Ohio Journ. of Science* **63**:5 (Sept. 1963).
17. *Acacia giraffae* Burch.
18. C. T. White, former government botanist at the Brisbane Botanic Garden.
19. *Elaeocarpus grandis* F. Muell.

Chapter Thirteen: *The Wasp Trees*
(pages 139-140)

1. *Ficus* species. The edible fig is only one of some 2000 kinds of *Ficus* trees, shrubs, or vines.
2. *Hevea brasiliensis* Muell. Arg.
3. Corner, E.J.H.: *Op. cit.*
4. Moraceae, commonly called the mulberry family.

Chapter Fourteen: *Tree Flowers Pollinated by Bats*
(pages 141-142)

1. Cockrum, E. Lendell, and Hayward, Bruce J.: "Hummingbird Bats." *Natural History* **lxxi**:8 (Oct. 1962).
2. Harris, B.J., and Baker, H.G.: "Pollination of Flowers by Bats in Ghana." *The Nigerian Field* **xxiv**:4 (Oct. 1959). Also by the same authors see: "Bat-Pollination of the Silk-Cotton Tree in Ghana." *Journal of the West African Science Assn.* **V**:1:1-9 (Feb. 1959). "Pollination of *Kigelia africana* Benth." *Journ. West African Science Assn.* **iv**:1 (Feb. 1958). "The Pollination of *Parkia* by Bats and Its Attendant Evolutionary Problems." Evolution **xi**:4 (Dec. 1957).
3. See note 1.

Chapter Fifteen: *The Rat "Tree"*
(pages 144-145)

1. *Freycinetia arborea* Gaud. The Hawaiians call it *ieie*. It belongs to the Pandanaceae or screw pine family.
2. Degener, Otto: *Plants Hawaii National Park*. Reprinted by permission.

Chapter Sixteen: *Ant Trees*
(pages 146-154)

1. No space can be devoted here to the part which ants play in the pollination of certain flowers, or the ways in which some flowers prevent ants from stealing pollen, or the part ants play in seed dispersal.
2. Charles Darwin, in his editorial remarks on Spruce's monograph on ant trees. See Note 3.
3. Spruce, Richard: *Op. cit.* Vol. II, pp. 384-412.
4. Blow guns. See Wallace, Alfred Russel: *A Narrative of Travels . . ., Op. cit.* Chap. XII, First ed.
5. Willis, J.C.: *Op. cit.*
6. *Acacia propanolobium* Harms ex Sjostedt.
7. Dale, Ivan R., and Greenway, P.J.: *Kenya Trees and Shrubs.* Buchanan's Kenya Estates, Ltd., Nairobi, 1961.
8. Corner, E.J.H.: *Op. cit.*
9. *Macaranga triloba* Muell. Arg.; *M. cornuta* Muell. Arg.; *M. griffithiana* Muell. Arg.; *M. kingii* Hook.f. *M. hypoleuca* Muell. Arg.—white mahang; *M. hosei* King—King's mahang; *M. maingayi* Hook.f.—Maingay's mahang; *M. punticulata* Gage.
10. Baker, J.A.: "Notes on the Biology of *Macaranga* spp." in *Garden Bulletin, Straits Settlements* viii:1:63 (Oct. 10, 1934).
11. Spruce, Richard: *Op. cit.*
12. Merrill, E.D.: *Op. cit.*
13. For more facts on ant trees see I. W. Bailey's *Contributions to Plant Anatomy*; also I. Van der Pijl: "Some Remarks on Myrmecophytes" in *Phytomorphology* 5:2,3 (Oct. 1955). Both these sources give long lists of additional references.

Chapter Seventeen: *Sexual Curiosities*
(pages 155-168)

1. Excluding a few palms.
2. Excluding many instances of vegetative offshoots, root suckers, etc.

(1)

3. *Cycas circinalis* L. This is more correctly called "false sago."
4. *Cycas revoluta* Thunb. Although called "sago palm," it is not a palm. The real "sago palms," from which sago starch is derived commercially, are species of *Metroxylon*, a Malayan genus of fan palms which are not in cultivation.
5. Miss Theresa Jaci, 2624 S.W. 29th Court, Miami, Florida.
6. Mrs. Julia F. Morton, garden column editor of the *Miami Daily News*, and Director of Morton Collectanea, University of Miami, Coral Gables, Florida.
7. The male inflorescence is malodorous, and consequently female trees are preferred in ornamental planting.

8. See Chapter Twenty-two on oldest trees. Quotation here is from Chamberlain, C.J.: *Gymnosperms, Structure and Evolution,* University of Chicago Press. (Reprinted by Johnson Reprint Corp., New York, 1934) p. 99.
9. *Carica papaya* L.
10. Singh, Majumdar, and Sharma: "Sex Reversal in Papaya." *Indian Journal of Horticulture* 18:2 (June 1961). Also see Hofmyer: "Sex Reversal as a Means of Solving Problems of *Carica papaya.*" *South African Journal of Science* 49:7 (Feb. 1953).
11. Schaffner, J.H.: "Experiments with Various Plants to Produce Change of Sex in the Individual." *Bull. Torr. Bot. Club* 52:35-47 (1925).
12. ———.: "The Fluctuation Curve of Sex Reversal in Staminate Hemp Plants Induced by Photoperiodicity." *Amer. Jour. Bot.* 18:424-430 (1931).
13. *Cannabis sativa* L.
14. Schaffner, J.H.: "Sex Reversal and the Experimental Production of Neutral Tassels in *Zea mays.*" *Bot. Gaz.* 90:279-298 (1930). Also "Control of Sex Reversal in the Tassel of Indian Corn." *Bot. Gaz.* 84:440-449 (1927).
15. ———.: "Dioeciousness in *Thalictrum dasycarpum.*" *Ohio Journ. Sci.* 20:25-34 (1919).
16. ———.: "Control of the Sexual State in *Arisaema triphyllum* Torr. and *A. dracontium* Schott." *Amer. Journ. Bot.* 9:72-78 (1922).
17. ———.: "Stability and Instability of Sexual Conditions in *Morus alba* L." *Journ. Heredity* 28:12 (1937).
18. *Taxus* sp.
19. Keen, Ray, and Chadwick, L.C.: "Warn Propagators to Watch for Sex Reversal in *Taxus.*" *American Nurseryman* 100 (6):13-14 (Sept. 15, 1954).

(2)

20. *Cinnamomum zeylanicum* Nees.
21. *Pimenta dioica* Merr. Allspice is not a mixture of spices.
22. *Eugenia caryophyllata* Thunb.
23. Nutmeg and mace both come from *Myristica fragrans* Houtt.
24. *Coumarouna odorata* Aubl.
25. *Pimenta acris* Kostel. supplies bay rum. It is not to be confused with twenty other trees called "bay."
26. *Cinnamomum camphora* T. Nees and Eberm.
27. *Abies balsamea* Mill.
28. Botting, Douglas: *Island of the Dragon's Blood.* Quoted by permission.
29. Willis: J.C.: *A Dictionary of the Flowering Plants and Ferns* and Webster's *New International Dictionary* (C. and G. Merriam) say that myrrh is a yellowish-brown to reddish-brown aromatic gum resin with a bitter, slightly pungent taste, obtained from *Commiphora abyssinica* Engl. and other species. The myrrh of the Bible may have had another resin, *labdanum,* mixed with it. The same authorities say that the frankincense tree is *Boswellia carteri* Birdw. but resins of other species are

often added. Dr. Birdwood (*Trans. Lin. Soc.* **xxvii**:11) has shown that African molibanum (another name for *Boswellia* resin) is a mixture.

30. Ibid.
31. *Plumeria* sp.
32. *Canangium odoratum* Baill.
33. *Jacaratia digitata* (Poepp. and Endl.) Solms-Laubach.
34. *Oroxylon indicum* Vent.
35. *Adansonia digitata* L.
36. *Terminalia melanocarpum* F. Muell.
37. *Sterculia foetida* L.
38. *Santalum album* L.
39. *Parinari curatellaefolia* Planch.
40. Letter from G. L. Guy, director of National Museum, Bulawayo, Rhodesia.
41. Similarly, latex of the upas tree (*Antiaris toxicaria*) is said to be extremely poisonous in Malaya, but apparently harmless in other localities.
42. Dr. F. White, Imperial Forestry Institute, Oxford, England, in correspondence.
43. *Scorodocarpus borneensis* Becc.
44. Corner, E.J.H., Cambridge University, in correspondence.
45. Burkill, I.H.: *Op. cit.*
46. *Phytolacca dioica* L. See Chapter Eight.
47. *Salvadora persica* L. Its leaves taste like mustard.
48. D. B. Fanshawe, chief forest research officer, Kitwe, Northern Rhodesia.
49. *Foetidia mauritiana* Lam.
50. *Ocotea bullata* E. Mey.
51. *Eugenia axillaris* (Sw.) Willd.
52. Buswell, Walter: *Native Trees and Palms of Florida*, pp. 34, 35. University of Miami Press, Coral Gables, 1930.
53. *Celtis cinnamomea* Lindl.
54. Philipson, W.R.: *Op. cit.*
55. One of the ant trees, *Triplaris americana*. See Chapter Sixteen.
56. Menninger, Edwin A.: *Op. cit.*
57. *Durio zibethinus* Murr.

(3)

58. *Agave americana* L.
59. *Spathelia simplex* L.
60. Hence also called maypole tree.
61. Menninger, Edwin A.: *Op. cit.*
62. *Sohnreyia excelsa* Krause [= *Spathelia excelsa* (Krause) Cowan and Brizicky.] The old name honored a Professor Heinrich Sohnrey.
63. *Diomma ulei* Engler ex Harms [= *Spathelia ulei* (Engler ex Harms) Cowan and Brizicky.]
64. Anatomy and morphology of this group are discussed by Stern and Brizicky in *Memoirs of N.Y. Bot. Garden* **10**:38-57 (1960). The taxonomic conclusions by Cowan and Brizicky are in the same *Memoirs* **10**:2, pp. 58-64.

(4)

65. Paterson, Allen: in *Gardeners Chronicle Gardening Illustrated* (Dec. 1, 1962).
66. As this cross occurred in a garden and one of its parents was not a native of New Zealand, the plant has not been mentioned in the *Flora of New Zealand*.
67. See note 65.

(5)

68. Baker, H.G.: "Apomixis and Polyembryony in *Pachira oleaginea* (Bombacaceae)." *Amer. Journ. Bot.* 47 (4):296-302 (April 1960).
69. *Garcinia mangostana* L.
70. Winters, Harold F.: "The Mangosteen." *Fruit Varieties and Horticultural Digest* 8 (4):57-58 (1953).

Chapter Eighteen: *The Two-Headed Monsters*

(pages 169-170)

1. Division of palm leaves into two kinds, fan and feather, is correct in general, though there are intermediate stages—for example, in *Johannesteijsmannia*, illustrated on the cover of the Palm Society's journal *Principes* for April 1962. Although this is classed as a fan palm, the leaf superficially is extremely similar to juvenile foliage of some of the Cocoid palms or some of the undivided *Geonoma*. Also some of the feather palms have leaves which are only feather-veined rather than pinnately divided. Of course, *Sabal* is also a good example of a genus in which there is a transition from a true fan leaf in *S. minor* to an almost half-feathered one in *S. palmetto* and others.
2. One exception is noted in this article. When more is known of some of the Cocoid palms it may be found that such genera as *Scheelea*, *Attalea*, and *Orbignya* are capable of producing more than one plant per seed or, perhaps better said, per fruit.
3. The nonpoisonous feature is not always true. The cabbage (heart) of some species of *Orania* is said to be toxic. Fruits of some palms contain an irritant juice.
4. Although palms rarely are upset by wind force, they are often broken in half by hurricanes.
5. The coconut palms are an exception, as most of them lean.
6. As shown elsewhere in this book, *Hyphaene* has branches. Single-stemmed, erect, branchless palms are the kind most commonly seen. However there are other palms that branch normally, such as *Nannorrhops* and *Nypa*, although in the latter the branching is difficult to see since the stems, like those of the saw palmetto, are usually underground. Certainly very many of the palms are multiple-stemmed (a frequent cultivated example is *Chrysalidocarpus lutescens*). There are also many vines among the palms, as witness the genus *Calamus*, which probably has the largest number of species.

7. Dr. Harold E. Moore, Jr., Director of the L. H. Bailey Hortorium at Cornell University, Ithaca, New York, and the world's foremost authority on palms. Dr. Moore is author of notes 1, 2, and 6 above.
8. *Elaeis guineensis* Jacq.
9. Unwin, A. Harold: *Op. cit.*
10. *Mangifera indica* L.
11. *Eugenia jambos* L. [= *Syzygium jambos* (L.) Alston.]

Chapter Nineteen: *The Lightest Wood*
(pages 173-175)

1. *Guaiacum officinale* L.
2. *Hardwickia binata* Roxb.
3. Ebony is the black heartwood of several kinds of persimmon trees in India, chiefly *Diospyros ebenum* Koen.
4. Only four kinds of genuine mahogany are known, most important of which are the West Indian *Swietenia mahagoni* Jacq. (the specific name is misspelled in most reference books), and the Honduras *S. macrophylla* King.
5. The heaviest timber ever examined at the Yale Forestry Research laboratory was letterwood (*Piratinera*) from British Guiana, which has specific gravity of 1.36 when dry and 1.5 when wet, half again as heavy as water. (A cubic foot of water weighs 62.4 pounds, so a cubic foot of letterwood would weigh more than 93 pounds.) In *A Manual of the Timber Trees of the World* A. L. Howard says that snakewood (*Piratinera guianensis* Aubl.) weighs 77 to 83 pounds per cubic foot.
6. Cork is the bark of an oak tree (*Quercus suber* L.)
7. *Ochroma lagopus* Swartz. There is only one species; all other names are synonyms or varieties.
8. Pierce, John H.: in *Journal of New York Botanical Garden* xliii:515 (Nov. 1942).
9. Balsa has a specific gravity of 0.12 (one-eighth the weight of water). All the following are lighter: *Aeschynomene hispida* Willd., a Cuban tree, s.g. 0.044 (one-third the weight of balsa); *Alstonia spathulata* Bl., s.g. 0.058, a Pacific Islands tree that grows in swamps and its lightest wood is found in the roots; *Cavanillesia platanifolia* H.B.K., s.g. 0.103, a big tree of the Panama Canal Zone, 16 per cent lighter than balsa; *Annona palustris* L., s.g. 0.116, slightly less than balsa. These and other trees whose wood is lighter than balsa do not occur in pure stands, or for other reasons are not available for harvesting as a crop. For more detailed descriptions of these light woods see Menninger, Edwin A.: "The Lightest Wood," in *National Horticultural Magazine* (July 1957).
10. *Aeschynomene elaphroxylon* (Guill. and Perr.) Taub. This occurs in rivers all over tropical Africa, but chiefly in the Upper Nile. According to J. M. Dalziel: *Op. cit.*, p. 243, its specific gravity varies: "A Gold Coast sample of the wood was 7 lbs. per cubic foot, as compared with 10.5 lbs. for a specimen from Uganda, and 12.35 for an Angola specimen."

11. Eggeling, William J., and Dale, Ivan R.: *The Indigenous Trees of the Uganda Protectorate*. Government Printer, Entebbe, Uganda, 2d ed. 1951.

12. Worthington, ———: *Inland Waters of Africa*. Quoted by Eggeling (*Op. cit.*, see note 12), page 296.

13. Schweinfurth, Georg August: *Op. cit.*

14. Johnston, Sir Harry: *The Uganda Protectorate*.

Chapter Twenty: *Trees That Twist*

(pages 176-190)

(1)

1. *Pinus caribaea* Morelet.

2. H. A. Lueckhoff. See note 24, Chapter Seven.

3. *Pinus sylvestris* L.

4. J. Frank McCormick, Institution of Radiation Ecology, University of Georgia, Athens, in *American Forests*, April 1964.

5. McCormick's summary of findings appeared as one of a score of letters to the editor, stemming from an article, "What Makes a Tree Trunk Spiral?" by Orville A. Lindquist in *American Forests*, June 1963.

6. Pearson, R.S.: *Commercial Guide to the Forest Economic Products of India*. Government Printer, Calcutta, 1912.

7. *Ougeinia dalbergioides* Benth.

8. Copisarow, Maurice: in *Nature* **130**:541 (Oct. 8, 1932).

9. Knorr, F.: "What Causes Twisted Trees?" *Journal of Heredity* **xxiii:2**.

10. J. Frank McCormick: *Op. cit.* (see note 4).

11. Champion, H.G., Director Forest Research Institute, Dehra Dun, India, in *Nature* **131**:133 (1933).

12. McCarthy, Edward Florence, one-time professor at New York State College of Forestry, Syracuse. See also McCarthy and Hoyle: "Knot Zones and Spiral in Adirondack Red Spruce (*Picea rubens* Sarg.)" in *Journal of Forestry* (Nov. 1918).

13. Bose, Sir Jagadis Chunder: *Growth and Tropic Movements of Plants*. Longmans, Green and Co., London, 1929.

14. Stocking, S.K.: in *American Forests* (Jan. 1964).

15. Holttum, R.E., former Director of Singapore Botanic Garden, in correspondence.

(2)

16. *Corylus avellana* L. var. *contorta* Bean.

17. *Salix madsudana* Koidz. var. *tortuosa* Reid.

18. Bowles, E.A. (1865-1954). Chapter XI, "The Lunatic Asylum" in *My Garden in Spring*, New York, 1914.

19. Knorr, F.: *Op. cit.* (see note 9).

20. *Cocos nucifera* L.

21. Photograph of the corkscrew coconut was taken by Dr. I. H. G. Derx, Director of the Treub laboratory at Buitenzorg (Bogor), and sent to

his friend Dr. David Fairchild in Florida. It appeared in the April 1949 issue of the *Bulletin of the Fairchild Tropical Garden* and is reproduced here by courtesy of Dr. John Popenoe, Director. K. Satyabalan studied foliar spiral and yield in coconut palms at Kasaragod, India, and found that the direction of leaf spiral had no effect on their yielding capacity, disproving Davis's finding that palms with a left-hand spiral would yield appreciably more than those with a right-hand twist. See *Nature* **202**: 4935, pp. 927-8 (1964).

22. *Sabal* sp.
23. *Siderocarpus flexicaulis* Small.
24. *Lannea kerstingii* Engl. and K. Krause; *L. egregia* Engl. and K. Krause; and *L. microcarpa* Engl. and K. Krause. See Hutchinson and Dalziel: *Flora of West Tropical Africa*. Crown Agents, London, 2d ed. 1963.

(3)

25. McCrum, Barrat, Hilborn, Rich: *Apple Virus Diseases*. Maine Agricultural Experiment Station Bulletin 595 (June 1960).
26. Cation, Donald, Associate Professor in Plant Pathology, Michigan State University, East Lansing, in correspondence.

(4)

27. See note 11.
28. See note 11.
29. Northcott, P.L.: "Spiral Grain in Wood." *British Columbia Lumberman* (Canadian Forest Products Laboratories) Nov. 1958.
30. *Pseudotsuga menziesii* (Mirbel) Franco [= *P. taxifolia* (Por.) Britt.]
31. Norman H. Beer, Portland, Oregon, whose specialty is burls.
32. *Pinus resinosa* Ait.
33. *Picea sitchensis* Carr.
34. See note 30.
35. Beals, Harold O., Assistant Professor, School of Forestry, Auburn University, Auburn, Alabama.
36. *Platanus occidentalis* L.
37. *Nyssa sylvatica* Marsh.
38. Brown, Panshin, and Forsaith: *Textbook of Wood Technology*. McGraw-Hill, New York, 1949.
39. Francis, W.D.: "The Development of the Corrugated Stems of Some Eastern Australian Trees." *Proc. Roy Soc. Queensland* **38**:62-76 (1927). Also Francis: *Australian Rain Forest Trees*. Francis, one-time government botanist in Queensland, lists these as the corduroy trees: *Cryptocarya corrugata* (washing-board tree) of the laurel family; *Diploglottis australia* (native tamarind), *Sarcopteryx stipitata*, *Alectryon connatus*, *Guoia semiglauca*, and *Arytera lautereriana* of the soapberry family; and *Canthium odoratum* and *C. coprosmoides* of the coffee family.
40. *Casuarina suberosa* Ott. and Dietr.
41. Charles J. J. Watson, Department of Forestry, Brisbane, Queensland, in correspondence.

42. *Pinus strobus* L.
43. *Harvard Forest Bulletin* No. 23 (1947).

Chapter Twenty-one: *Subterranean Trees*
(pages 191-192)

1. See Chapter Four.
2. See note 6 in Chapter Eighteen.
3. See Chapter Twenty-two for description of *Acacia galpini*.
4. *Populus tremula* L., commonly called European aspen.
5. The identity of this tree is disputed. The description might apply in part to *Geanthemum cadavericum* (Huber) Safford. (See *Contrib. U. S. Herb.* 18:1 pp. 66-67, 1914). Another source identified it as *Deguetia salzmannii* (which is not a valid species), or possibly a species of *Rollinia*.

Chapter Twenty-two: *The Oldest and Biggest Trees*
(pages 193-201)

1. *Acacia galpini* Burtt Davy.
2. See note 24, Chapter Seven.
3. Palmer and Pitman: *Op. cit.*
4. Palgrave, Keith C.: *Op. cit.*
5. The author had *Acacia galpini* in his Florida garden until it got so enormous and so viciously thorny, and grew so fast, that he reluctantly cut it down. Later he asked the U.S. Plant Introduction Garden at Coconut Grove, Florida, for photographs of the two trees growing there, only to elicit the response that the trees had become so enormous they had to be cut out.
6. *Sequoia sempervirens* Endl. This is the redwood monarch of the Pacific coastal ranges from southern Oregon to central California.
7. *Eucalyptus regnans* F. Muell. [= *E. amygdalina* Labill. var. *regnans* F. Muell.]
8. Baron F. von Mueller, government botanist for Victoria and a highly competent observer, was responsible for giving credence to a lot of early reports. In his book *Select Extra-Tropical Plants* he wrote: "In sheltered springy forest glens attaining exceptionally to a height of over 400 feet . . . probably the loftiest tree on the globe. Mr. G. W. Robinson, surveyor, measured a tree at the foot of Mount Baw-Baw, which was 471 feet high and 15 feet in diameter. Another tree measured 69 feet in circumference. . . ." This book continues with other excessive dimensions.
9. This is a reprint from an article by Dorothy Dixon: "These Are the Champs," in the Jan.-Feb. 1961 issue of *American Forests* magazine. In explaining how the "champion" big trees are determined she wrote: "Determination of bigness in trees listed is based on the sum of dimensions and circumference, height, and spread. To the total inches of

stem circumference (4½ feet above the ground) is added the total height in feet plus one-quarter of the crown spread footage. This gives a single figure denoting aggregate growth, with circumference as No. 1 factor, followed by the height and crown spread." Miss Dixon and Kenneth B. Pomeroy collaborated on an article in *American Forests* **72**:5 (May 1966), updating the information about these champion trees.

10. *National Geographic* **126**:1 (July 1964).
11. Fry, Walter, U.S. Commissioner, Sequoia National Park, in collaboration with John R. White, Superintendent of Sequoia National Park: *Big Trees*. Stanford University Press, rev. ed. 1938.
12. Black, J.M.: *Flora of South Australia* **III**:613. 2d ed., Adelaide. 1948.
13. *Forest Trees of Australia*. Canberra, 1960.
14. De la Ruë, E. Albert: *Op. cit.*
15. Longview, Wash., *Daily News*. March 27, 1947.
16. *Adansonia digitata* L. See Chapter Eight. The Australian baobab in northern Queensland is A. *gregorii*.
17. Lindley and Moore: *Op. Cit.*
18. Chief Scientific Officer, Forest Research Department, Kitwe, Northern Rhodesia (Zambia).
19. See note 16.
20. Willis, J.C.: *Op. cit.*
21. *Dracaena draco* L.
22. *Olea europaea* L.
23. Lindley and Moore: *Op. cit.*
24. *Taxodium mucronatum* Ten.
25. Fogg, John M., Jr.: in *Gardeners Chronicle*, August 22, 1964.
26. Macmillan, H.F.: *Op. cit.* The author undoubtedly means that this *Ficus* is the oldest tree with a known history.
27. Taylor, C.J.: *Op. cit.*
28. See Chapter Four.
29. *Pinus aristata* Engelm.
30. Cycads comprise 75 species scattered among 10 genera. All are survivors of plants that were very important 100,000,000 years ago, before the Rocky Mountains were formed. They are the lowest type of living seed-plants, and in appearance and habits are much like tree ferns, but the stem is usually short and stout, rarely treelike. *Zamia* is native to Florida; the sago (*Cycas*) is much grown in southern gardens.
31. *Lepidozamia peroffskyana* Regel [= *Macrozamia denisonii* C. Moore and F. Muell.]
32. Jackson, Sid W.: "Great Grandfather Peter." *Sydney Mail*, Sydney, N.S.W., August 19, 1936.
33. Chamberlain, C.J.: *The Living Cycads*. University of Chicago Press, 1919. Also by same author, *Gymnosperms, Structure and Evolution*. University of Chicago Press, 1935.
34. In New South Wales Department of Agriculture publication: *Contributions from the New South Wales National Herbarium*, Flora Series **1**:18 (1961).

Chapter Twenty-three: *Prehistoric Trees*
(pages 202-205)

1. *Ginkgo biloba* L.
2. Dr. Hui-Lin Li, taxonomist at the Morris Arboretum, Philadelphia, and Associate Professor of Botany at the University of Pennsylvania, in *American Horticultural Magazine* **40**:3 (July 1961).
3. *Metasequoia glyptostroboides* Hu and Cheng.
4. Dr. Francis de Vos, assistant director of U.S. National Arboretum, Washington, in *American Horticultural Magazine* **42**:3 (July 1963). Reprinted by permission.

Chapter Twenty-four: *The Man-Eating Tree*
(pages 206-208)

1. See *American Weekly* Sept. 26, 1920 and Jan. 4, 1925. These and similar yarns derived originally from Foersch.
2. *Nepenthes* species. For description of these and other bug-eaters, see *Carnivorous Plants and "The Man-Eating Tree,"* Leaflet 23, Field Museum of Natural History, Chicago, 1939. Cartoons in this chapter reproduced by courtesy of Field Museum of Natural History.
3. The word "upas" in Malay is not actually a plant name, but implies a vegetable poison acting on the blood.
4. *Antiaris toxicaria* Lesch.
5. *Strychnos tieute* Lesch., one of 200 species. The commercial drug strychnine comes from an Indian tree, *S. nux-vomica* L. The curare used by South American Indians is a mixture of poisons from *S. toxifera* Schomb. and other plants.
6. Burkill, I.H.: *Op. cit.*
7. Rumphius, Georg Eberhard: *Herbarium Amboinense* 2. Amsterdam, 1750, p. 264.
8. Kaempfer, Engelbert: *Amoenitatum Exoticarum Fasciculi* (1712), p. 575. See also Ray, John: *Historia Plantarum* 3, 1704, Appendix, p. 87.
9. For details of poison preparation see Burkhill.
10. Harry Blossfeld is a plantsman of São Paulo, Brazil, author of *Plantinagem* (Ornamental Horticulture), 1966.
11. *Monstera deliciosa* Liebm.

Chapter Twenty-five: *Trees Feared and Revered*
(pages 211-214)

1. *Antiaris toxicaria* Lesch.
2. *Anacardium occidentale* L.
3. *Mangifera indica* L.
4. *Rhus* species.
5. *Melanorrhoea usitata* Wall.
6. Corner, E.J.H.: *Op. cit.*
7. *Laportea gigas* Wedd.

8. Bailey, F. Manson: *Comprehensive Catalog of Queensland Plants*.
9. Fairchild, David: *Garden Islands of the Great East*. Charles Scribner's Sons, New York, 1943.
10. *Schrebera mazoensis* S. Moore, of the staff-tree family (Celastraceae).
11. G. L. Guy, director of National Museum, Bulawayo, Rhodesia.
12. Refreshing drinks are made from the nuts of a variety of cola trees (*Cola* species).
13. *Jacaratia digitata* (Poepp. and Endl.) Solms-Laubach.
14. Poeppig is quoted by Macbride, J. Francis: *Flora of Peru* **IV**: 143.
15. *Sapium biloculare* Pax.
16. *Pseudospondias microcarpa* (A. Rich.) Engl.
17. Irvine, F.R.: *Op. cit.*
18. *Crotalaria aschrek* Forsk.
19. Dalziel, J.M.: *Op. cit.*
20. *Loesnera kalantha* Harms. See Dalziel, p. 196.
21. *Ginkgo biloba* L. See Chapter Twenty-three.
22. *Thespesia populnea* Soland. The generic name means divine.
23. *Diospyros* species.

Chapter Twenty-six: *Trees That Tell Time and Predict the Weather*
(pages 215-216)

1. Cowen, D.V.: *Op. cit.*
2. *Samanea saman* (Jacq.) Merrill [= *Pithecellobium saman* (Jacq.) Benth.]
3. See Chapter Thirty.
4. *Tamarindus indica* L.
5. Neal, Marie C.: *In Gardens of Hawaii*. Bishop Museum, rev. ed., Honolulu, 1966.
6. Irvine, F.R.: *Op. cit.*
7. *Griffonia simplicifolia* Baill.
8. *Claoxylon hexandrum* Muell. Arg.
9. *Mitragyna ciliata* Aubr. and Pell.
10. *Trichilia heudelotii* Planch.
11. Dalziel, J.M.: *Op. cit.*
12. *Pachylobus edulis* Don.
13. *Erythrina variegata* L. var. *orientalis* (L.) Merrill.
14. Parham, J.W.: *Plants of the Fiji Islands*. Government Press, Suva, 1964.
15. *Wormia suffruticosa* Griff. [= *Dillenia burbidgei* (Hook.f.) Gilg.]
16. Corner, E.J.H.: *Op. cit.*

Chapter Twenty-seven: *Trees That Make Rain*
(pages 218-223)

1. Hutchinson, John: *Op. cit.*
2. *Oreodaphne foetens* Nees [= *Ocotea foetens* Webb and Berthel.] Gunther E. Maul, director of the Museu Municipal at Funchal, Madeira, wrote: "The species is peculiar to Madeira as well as the Canary Islands.

As to why it might be called 'rain tree' I cannot give any satisfactory answer. I have never heard it called anything but Til in Madeira."

3. Palmer and Pitman: *Op. cit.*
4. Dalziel, J.M.: *Op. cit.*
5. *Treculia africana* Decne. of the mulberry family.
6. In correspondence.
7. *Tamarindus indica* L.
8. Harry Blossfeld is a plantsman in São Paulo, Brazil.
9. *Casuarina equisetifolia* Forst.
10. *Samanea saman* Merr.
11. Macmillan, H.F.: *Op. cit.*
12. Dr. Ernst in 1875 was director of a botanical garden at Caracas, Venezuela. This quotation is from an article he wrote in *Botanische Zeitung* (1876), pp. 35-36.
13. Spruce, Richard, writing in *Kew Garden Report for 1878*, p. 46. Spruce's previous references to the rain trees were in his *Notes of a Botanist on the Amazon and Andes*. See note 3, Chapter Sixteen.
14. Cockburn, John: *Journey Overland from the Gulf of Honduras*. London, 1735, pp. 40-42.
15. Cooke, M.C.: *Op. cit.*
16. Dr. H. H. Rusby, Dean of the College of Pharmacy, Columbia University, writing in *Tropical Woods*.
17. Audas, J.W.: *Op. cit.*
18. *Glochidion ferdinandi* Muell. Arg.
19. Baron: "The Flora of Madagascar." See note 42, Chapter Four.
20. Sibree, James: *A Naturalist in Madagascar*. Seeley Service, London, 1915.
21. The Associated Press, July 22, 1957.
22. *Cercis canadensis* L.

Chapter Twenty-eight: *Trees That Make Noises*
(pages 224-229)

1. *American Horticultural Magazine*. Jan. 1962.
2. *Arbutus menziesii* Pursh.
3. *Platanus occidentalis* L.
4. Dr. George H. Hewitt, a physician who loves trees. He lives at Bellingen, New South Wales.
5. Humboldt, Alexander von, and Bonpland, Aimé: *Personal Narrative of Travels to the Equinoctial Regions of America during the Years 1799-1804*. Written in French by Alexander von Humboldt; translated and edited by Thomasina Ross, London, 1889. 3 vols. (Original title was *Voyage aux Regions Equinoxiales du Nouveau Continent*.)
6. *Couroupita guianensis* Aubl.
7. Spruce, Richard: *Op. cit.*
8. See note 8, Chapter Twenty-seven.
9. *Albizzia lebbek* Benth.
10. *Loesnera kalantha* Harms.
11. Dalziel, J.M.: *Op. cit.*

12. *Cynometra ananta* Hutch. and J.M. Dalz.
13. Dalziel, J.M.: *Op. cit.*, quotes B.I.I. 1928, pp. 285-288.
14. Burkill, I.H.: *Op. cit.*, pp. 862-867. Burkill cites 10 references to camphor language in botanical literature.
15. *Dryobalanops aromatica* Gaertn.
16. Garcia, in *Historia Aromatum* (1593) said at that time the Bornean product was worth 100 times as much as the Chinese.
17. *Cinnamomum camphora* Nees and Eberm.
18. *Harper's Weekly* 56:23 (Sept. 28, 1912).
19. Lake, H. and Kelsall: "The Camphor Tree and Camphor Language of Jahore." *Royal Asiatic Society (Straits Branch) Journal* 26:35-56 (Jan. 1894).
20. *Saurauia purgans* B.L. Burtt.
21. *Tropical Woods* 81:27.
22. *Parinari mobola* Oliv. [= *P. curatellaefolia* Planch.] See Chapter Seventeen.
23. Palgrave, Keith C.: *Op. cit.*
24. Fanshawe, D.B., chief scientific officer, Forest Research Department, Kitwe, Northern Rhodesia.
25. Dalziel, J.M.: *Op. cit.*
26. G. L. Guy, director of National Museum, Bulawayo, Rhodesia.
27. Unwin, A. Harold: *Op. cit.*
28. *Pentaclethra macrophylla* Benth.
29. Especially *Bauhinia galpinii* N.E. Br. and *B. purpurea* L.
30. Coe, Frederick W. See note 1.
31. *Hura crepitans* L.
32. Barrett, Mary F.: *Common Exotic Trees of South Florida*. University of Florida Press, Gainesville, 1956.
33. *Hevea brasiliensis* F. Muell.
34. Ridley, H.N.: *Op. cit.*
35. *Ricinus communis* L.
36. The Tree Society, 37A Havelock St., West Perth, July 1963.
37. Schaffer, H.G. "Influence of Music on Crop Yields." *Gardener's Chronicle* (Sept. 5, 1964).

Chapter Twenty-nine: *Trees That Supply Water, Milk, and Salt*
(pages 231-234)

1. *Cocos nucifera* L.
2. *Casuarina equisetifolia* Forst. and *C. glauca* Sieb.
3. Howard, Richard A.: 999 *Survived*. Survival experiences in the South Pacific. ADTIC Pub. T-100. (Feb. 1950).
4. Dalziel, J.M.: *Op. cit.*
5. *Musanga smithii* R. Br.
6. *Spathodea campanulata* P. Beauv.
7. *Ravenala madagascariensis* J. F. Gmel.
8. Story, R.: *Some Plants Used by the Bushmen in Obtaining Food and Water*. Dept. of Agriculture, Pretoria, 1958.

9. *Ricinodendron rautanenii* Schinz.
10. *Boscia albitrunca* Gilg and Benedict.
11. G. L. Guy, Director of National Museum, Bulawayo, Rhodesia.
12. *Adansonia digitata* L.
13. Luetzelburg: *Estudo Botanica do Nordeste* **III**:76, Figs. 38, 46 (1923).
14. Morton, Julia F.: *Op. cit.*
15. *Ceiba parvifolia* Rose.
16. Muller, C.H.: "Los Comotes del Pochote (*Ceiba parvifolia*) de Puebla." *Soc. Bot. Mexico Bol.* **14**:18-21 (1952).
17. Moseley, M.F., Jr.: "The Anatomy of the Water Storage Organ of *Ceiba parvifolia.*" *Tropical Woods* **104**:61-79 (1956).
18. *Brosimum utile* (HBK) Pittier, of the mulberry family.
19. Humboldt, Alexander von: *Personal Narrative of Travels to the Equinoctial Regions of America 1799-1804.* See note 5, Chapter Twenty-eight.
20. *Contributions U.S. Nat. Herb.* **20**:3:104.
21. Record and Hess: *Op. cit.*
22. Fountain, Paul: *The Great Mountains and Forests of South America.* Longmans, Green and Co., London, 1904.
23. *Sabal palmetto* Lodd.
24. *Avicennia nitida* Jacq.
25. *Musa paradisiaca* L.
26. *Salvadora persica* L.

Chapter Thirty: *Trees That Flap Their Leaves*
(pages 235-238)

1. *Trifolium repens* L. is the white Dutch clover of lawns.
2. *Samanea saman* Merr.
3. Cooke, M.C.: *Op. cit.*
4. *Mimosa pudica* L. is a weed to 18 inches, but other sensitive species of *Mimosa* are trees. The "mimosa tree" of the southern United States is not of the genus *Mimosa*.
5. *Averrhoa carambola* L.
6. Hogg, Robert: *The Vegetable Kingdom and Its Products.* London, 1858.
7. Darwin, Charles: *The Movement of Plants.*
8. *Averrhoa bilimbi* L.
9. Bruce, ———: *Philosophical Transactions for 1785*, p. 356.

Chapter Thirty-one: *Trees That Display Affection*
(pages 239-243)

1. Carroll, Lewis: *Through the Looking Glass.* Chap. 5.
2. Carroll, Lewis: *Alice in Wonderland.* Chap. 2.
3. Browning, Robert: "Rabbi Ben Ezra."
4. Barbauld, Anna Letitia: "Ode to Life."
5. Hume, H.H.: *Hollies.* The Macmillan Co., New York, 1953, p. 164.
6. See Chapter Three, section 3.
7. Described in *Album Floristico.* Serviço Florestal do Brasil, Rio de Janeiro, 1940, rev. ed. 1943.

Chapter Thirty-two: *The Tree That Gets Stark Naked*
(pages 244-247)

1. Don, G.: *Loud. Hort. Brit.*, p. 471, says, "leaves as large as those of the common cabbage."
2. Codd, L.E.W.: *Trees and Shrubs of Kruger National Park*.
3. Irvine, F.R.: *Op. cit.* Irvine gives this as translation of Ashanti name, but the significance is not explained.
4. Don, G.: *General History of Dichlamydeous Plants* 4:68 (1831). This author says the "broad opposite leaves are combined at the base by interpetiolar sheaths."
5. Codd, L.E.W.: *Op. cit.* (see note 2).
6. *Quercus suber* L.
7. Irvine, F.R.: *Op. cit.* (see note 3).
8. Deighton, F.C.: *Herbarium Kewense*. Also see Dalziel, J.M.: *Op. cit.*

Chapter Thirty-three: *The Tree That Does Arithmetic*
(pages 248-249)

1. Francis Hallé, Institute d'Enseignement et de Recherches Tropicales, Abidjan, Ivory Coast.
2. *Schumanniophyton problematicum* (A.Chev.) Aubrev. [= *Assidora problematica* A. Chev.]
3. Rubiaceae.
4. The drawing is of *Schumanniophyton magnificum* (K. Schum.) Harms.

Chapter Thirty-four: *Trees to Make Life Sweeter*
(pages 251-252)

1. *Synsepalum dulcificum* (Schum.) Daniell.
2. The same kind of sweetening effect is reported from the mucilaginous pulp surrounding the seeds of another West African plant, *Thaumatococcus daniellii* Benth., sometimes called the miraculous fruit of the Sudan. Also, chewing the roots of another plant from the same region, *Sphenocentrum jollyanum* Pierre, is reported to produce the same effect. See J.M. Dalziel: *Op. cit.*
3. Paper presented at 148th National Chemical Society meeting at Chicago, Ill., Aug. 31, 1964, by Dr. G.E. Inglett, B. Dowling, J.J. Albrecht, and Dr. F.A. Hoglan, of the International Minerals and Chemical Corporation, Skokie, Ill.
4. Fairchild, David: *Op. cit.*
5. *Stelechocarpus burahol* (Bl.) Hook.f. and Thoms.
6. Fairchild, David: *Op. cit.*
7. *Asimina triloba* Dunal.
8. *Theobroma cacao* L. See Chapter Five.
9. The Rare Fruit Council; William Whitman, President. 189 Bal Bay Drive, Bal Harbour, Florida.

Acknowledgments

So many persons helped to create this museum of trees that dare to be different, that pages would be required to recognize them all. Many are mentioned in the text, in the footnotes, and in the photographic credits. However, I would like to extend special thanks to the following:

To E. J. H. Corner of Cambridge University, England, for collaboration on the discussion of tree structure, especially roots.

To Harold O. Beals of Auburn University, Auburn, Alabama, for help on trees that twist.

To Patrick Synge, editor of the *Journal of the Royal Horticultural Society,* England, and Roger Perry for their help on gigantism.

To Richard A. Howard, director of the Arnold Arboretum in Cambridge, Mass., and his associate, Donald Wyman, for guidance over treacherous ground.

To Harold E. Moore, Jr., and John Ingram of the Bailey Hortorium, Cornell University, Ithaca, for reference work, and to Robert B. Clark for his help on research and identification.

To Douglas Elliott of New Zealand; H. M. Burkill, director of the Singapore Botanic Garden; Ernest E. Lord of Melbourne and S. L. Everist of Brisbane, Australia; Alvin K. Chock of Honolulu; T. B. Worthington of Ceylon; P. W. Richards of Trinidad; Harold Edgard Strang and Geronimo Sosa of Argentina; C. G. G. J. Van Steenis of Holland; Harry Blossfeld and Paulo B. Cavalcante of Brazil; K. M. Kochummen of the Malayan Forest Research Institute, Kepong; D. I. Nicholson of Sabah, Malaysia; and the following from Africa: J. Graham Quinn and B. J. Harris of Ghana; G. L. Guy of Southern Rhodesia; J. Anton-Smith and D. B. Fanshawe of Northern Rhodesia; G. K. Berrie of Nigeria; Francis Hallé of Ivory Coast; W. Carmichael of Tanganyika; A. G. Cabezon of the Canary Islands; Gunther E. Maul of Madeira; Emil Jensen of South-West Africa; R. J. Poynton, H. A. Lueckhoff, and L. E. Cobb of Pretoria; as well as these from the United States: H. R. Offord of the United States Forest Service; Ralph D. Cornell, Edward Gay, and Reid Moran, all of California; W. L. Cockrum of the University of Arizona; James E. Canright of Arizona State; and William F. Whitman and Mrs. Lucita H. Wait of Miami. All these people contributed substantially in ideas, suggestions, and pictures, and without them the book would have been impossible.

To my reference librarian, Mrs. Julia F. Morton of the Morton Collectanea, University of Miami, and my manuscript editor, Mrs. L. T. Hawley of the University of Alabama, I am again beholden. I am grateful too to the persons who were kind enough to read the manuscript critically and point up its many shortcomings, including my two brothers, Dr. Karl Menninger and Dr. William C. Menninger of Topeka, Kansas; Edward L. Gordy of West Palm Beach, Robert J. Godbey of Miami, Mrs. George Sollitt and Mrs. Max Zeller of Stuart, Florida; and Miss Carol H. Woodward of Roxbury, Connecticut.

Institutional help came from the Fairchild Tropical Garden, the Arnold Arboretum, the Field Museum of Natural History, the American Museum of Natural History, the American Forestry Association, the American Horticultural Society, the Smithsonian Institution, the Pan American Union, the Indian Council of Agricultural Research at New Delhi, the Indian Botanic Garden at Calcutta, the Royal Forest Service at Bangkok, Thailand, and many others.

The extensive help given on the sketch of plant life in remote St. Helena is acknowledged in the footnotes.

All these people and institutions represent a considerable company of experts, and I wish to express my appreciation of their willingness to share with others through this book some unusual, inspiring pleasures of the world of trees.

EDWIN A. MENNINGER

Index to the Trees

(Scientific names are in italics. Figures in italics denote illustrations.)

Arecastrum, 179
Argyroxiphium, 46, 264
Arisaema, 276
Arithmetic, 248, 250
Aropa, 233
Arrow Tree, 213
Artocarpus, 78, 259, 264, 265, 268
Arytera, 281
Ash, 227
Asimina, 289
Aspidosperma, 14, 15, 260
Assett, 100
Aster, 273
Astrocaryum, 2
Atkinsonia, 30, 261
Attalea, 278
Averrhoa, 230, 288
Avicennia, 261, 262, 288
Australian oak, 196
Australian pine, 184, 219, 231
Auxin, 177
Azteca, 150

B

Baikiaea, 227
Balanites, 254
Bald cypress, 29, 37
Balsa, 137, 172, 173, 279
Balsam, 158, 161
Bamboo, 70, 123, 225, 231
Bananas, 234
Banyan, 23, 26
Baobab, 8, 14, 136, 162, 199, 232, 283
Barringtonia, 14
Bastard cabbage tree, 273
Bats, 141, 143, 145
Bauhinia, 287
Bawang rutan, 163
Bay, 161, 276
Bean tree, 226
Bearberry willow, 127
Bear scratches, 189
Beaucarnea, 116, 118, 272
Beech, 14
Bellucia, 57
Belly palm, 108, 110, 271

Berlinia, 227, 230
Bertholletia, 268
Betula, 260
Big Trees, 193, 195, 197
Bilimbi, 237
Birch, 14, 16
Bird's eye, 189
Bisan, 226
Bishop pine, 228
Bixa, 74, 266
Black boys, 117, 111
Black cabbage, 129, 131, 133
Black gum, 189, 215
Black locust, 180
Black mangrove, 22
Bleeding tree, 231
Blighia, 73, 267
Blow guns, 275
Blumeodendron, 33
Boerlagiodendron, 59
Bombax, 110, 260, 271
Boogum, 268
Boojim, 268
Boojum, 89, 94, 95, 268
Boscia, 288
Boswellia, 276
Bo tree, 199, 210, 213
Bottle-tree, 106, 108, 232
Bottle gourd, 83
Brachychiton, 108, 232, 271
Brachystegia, xi, 227, 259
Bramble, 129
Bravaisia, 34
Brazilian pepper, 135
Brazil-nut, 84
Breadfruit, 78, 85, 139, 267
Breathing roots, 22, 29, 33
Bridelia, 34, 220
Bristlecone pine, 198, 200, 241
Brosimum, 288
Broussonetia, 11
Brownea, 40
Bumbo, 91, 99
Buri, 231
Burl, 186, 188
Burmese lacquer tree, 209, 211
Burrawongs, 200
Bursera, 268

El pochote, 232
Emu, 137
Entada, 82, 267
Eremophila, 63
Erica, 122, 123, 124
Erythrina, 285
Espeletia, 123, 124, 125
Eucalyptus, 8, 13, 50, 161, 163, 181, 193, 194, 196, 197, 225, 242, 244, 254, 260, 282
Eugenia, 8, 64, 157, 167, 265, 276, 277, 278
Eugeniamyrtus, 157, 167
Euphorbia, 90, 96, 269
European chestnut, 180

F

Fagara, 91, 97, 269
Fagraea, 65, 142
Fagus, 14
False nutmeg, 83
Fat-headed Lizzie, 167
Fatshedera, 167
Fatsia, 167
Fever tree, 97, 244
Ficus, 21, 23, 26, 28, 34, 35, 37, 38, 42, 45, 50, 57, 101, 138, 199, 210, 213, 261, 263, 274, 283
Fiddleback, 187, 190
Fiddle-leaf fig, 20, 138
Fig, 23, 139, 213, 223
Fig wasps, 140
Fir, 213
Firewheel tree, 165
Flask tree, 92, 99
Flooded gums, 13, 16
Florida sago palm, 156
Fluting, 8, 13, 189
Flying fox, 145
Foetidia, 277
Froghopper, 221
Forest onion, 163
Forest papaw, 17
Fountain-tree, 232
Fouquieria, 89, 268
Frangipani, 162

Frankincense, 117, 161, 162, 276
Freycinetia, 143, 144, 274

G

Gaiadendron, 30, 261
Gall flowers, 139
Garcinia, 259, 278
Geanthemum, 282
Geonoma, 278
Geranium, 124, 126, 272
Ghost men, 91, 98
Giant sequoia, 195
Giant stinging-tree, 211
Giant stringbark, 196
Gigantism, 122
Gingerbread palm, 70, 72
Ginkgo, xi, 53, 156, 163, 202, 203, 264, 284, 285
Ginkgo Forest State Park, 204
Glochidion, 286
Goldilocks, 115
Gourd, 83
Grape of Brazil, 62
Grapple plant, 96
Grass trees, 111, 271
Great Grandfather Peter, 200, 283
Grevillea, 26
Griffonia, 216, 285
Ground nuts, 38
Groundsel, 123, 124
Guaiacum, 279
Guava, 8
Guilielma, 266
Gum, 13, 15
Gumwood, 131, 132
Guoia, 281
Gustavia, 57, 159, 164, 165

H

Hackberry, 159, 164
Haha, 126
Hahalua, 126
Half men, 98
Hamamelis, 228
Hand-flower, 54
Harahara, 52

297

298

Sun-fruits, 79
Swamp gum, 196
Swartzia, 10
Sweet thorn, 219
Swietenia, 187, 279
Swiss stone pine, 228
Sycamore, 8, 189
Symphonia, 34
Symphonic flowering, 63
Synsepalum, 250, 289
Syzygium, 265, 279

T

Tacyba, 150
Tahiti chestnut, 8, 10
Talipot palm, 48
Tallest trees, 193, 194
Tamarindus, 215, 219, 285, 286
Tamia-caspi, 220
Tangarana, 151
Tapioca, 82
Tarrietia, 35
Taxodium, 29, 198, 262, 283
Taxus, 11, 14, 181, 198, 276
Terminalia, 19, 20, 162, 264, 277
Terminalia branching, 19, 20
Thalictrum, 276
Thaumatococcus, 289
Theobroma, 62, 265, 289
Thespesia, 285
Thorn trees, 95
Tococa, 151, 152
Tomato, 136, 138, 274
Tonka bean, 161
Toothbrush tree, 234
Tortoise, 136, 138, 274
Tournefortia, 264
Tovomita, 34
Travelers tree, 42, 45, 232
Treculia, 265, 268, 286
Tree fern, 17
Tree of Damocles, 81
Tree of glory, xi
Tree-of-heaven, 163
"Tree without a name," 212
Trematolobelia, 124
Trevesia, 42, 45

Trichilia, 216, 285
Tricuspidaria, 60, 265
Trifolium, 288
Triplaris, 80, 150, 277
Tropical almond, 19, 20, 51
Trumpet flower, 142
Tulip tree, 232
Tulipwood, 186
Tumbo, 41, 263
Twisted hazel, 182
Two-headed monsters, 169

U

Uapaca, 262
Ulmus, 179
Umbrella, 32, 137, 232
Umbú, 105, 232
Upas tree, 206, 209, 277, 284
Upper Nile, 175
Usnea, 123

V

Varasantha, 165
Vellozia, 119, 121
Vernonia, 79, 266
Violin music, 229
Virus diseases, 183
Voandzeia, 263

W

Walnut, 186
Washing-board tree, 190
Washingtonia, 171
Wasps, 139
Weeping tree, 221
Welwitschia, 40, 44, 191, 200, 263
West Australian Christmas tree, 30, 262
West Indies shower, 60
Western white pine, 195
Whistling thorn, 148, 151
White bark, 183
White bark pine, 13, 16, 18, 185

303

White pine, 190
White stopper, 164
Whitewood cabbage, 129, 130, 133
Wild nutmeg, 20, 29, 262
Willow, 127, 213
Witch-hazel, 227
Woman's tongue, 225
Wood-oil-nut, 137, 138, 232
Wormia, 217, 259, 285

X

Xanthorrhoea, 111, 117
Xanthoxylum, 269

Xerophyta, 101
Xylopia, 32, 262

Y

Yaccas, 111
Yaruru, 14
Yew, 11, 14, 160, 181, 198
Ylang-ylang, 158, 162
Yucca, 2, 116, 120, 259, 271, 272

Z

Zambezi almond, 137
Zamia, 283